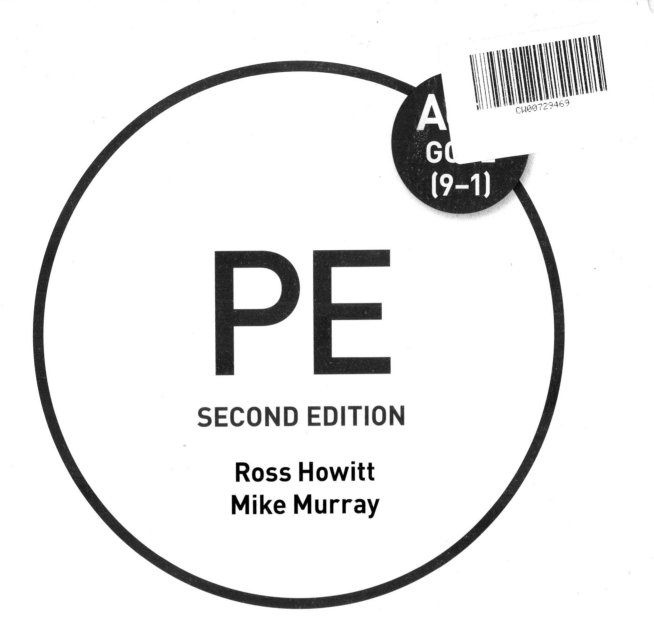

PE

SECOND EDITION

Ross Howitt
Mike Murray

AQA
GCSE
(9–1)

Approval message from AQA

This textbook has been approved by AQA for use with our qualification. This means that we have checked that it broadly covers the specification and we are satisfied with the overall quality. Full details of our approval process can be found on our website.

We approve textbooks because we know how important it is for teachers and students to have the right resources to support their teaching and learning. However, the publisher is ultimately responsible for the editorial control and quality of this book.

Please note that when teaching the *AQA PE* course, you must refer to AQA's specification as your definitive source of information. While this book has been written to match the specification, it cannot provide complete coverage of every aspect of the course.

A wide range of other useful resources can be found on the relevant subject pages of our website: www.aqa.org.uk.

HODDER
EDUCATION
AN HACHETTE UK COMPANY

Acknowledgements

Cardio-vascular endurance (aerobic power) test – multistage fitness test ratings (p.54), Co-ordination test – wall toss test ratings (p.55), Flexibility test – sit and reach test ratings (p.55), Muscular endurance test – abdominal curl conditioning test ratings (p.56), Power/explosive strength (anaerobic power) test – vertical jump test ratings (p.57), Maximal strength test – one rep max test ratings (p.58) © TopEnd Sports – www.topendsports.com/testing/norms/index.htm

Every effort has been made to trace all copyright holders, but if any have been inadvertently overlooked, the Publishers will be pleased to make the necessary arrangements at the first opportunity.

Although every effort has been made to ensure that website addresses are correct at time of going to press, Hodder Education cannot be held responsible for the content of any website mentioned in this book. It is sometimes possible to find a relocated web page by typing in the address of the home page for a website in the URL window of your browser.

Hachette UK's policy is to use papers that are natural, renewable and recyclable products and made from wood grown in well-managed forests and other controlled sources. The logging and manufacturing processes are expected to conform to the environmental regulations of the country of origin.

Orders: please contact UK Distribution, Hely Hutchinson Centre, Milton Road, Didcot, Oxfordshire, OX11 7HH. Telephone: (44) 01235 827720. Fax: (44) 01235 400454. Email: education@hachette.co.uk Lines are open from 9 a.m. to 5 p.m., Monday to Friday. You can also order through our website: www.hoddereducation.co.uk

ISBN: 978 1 3983 2652 1

© Ross Howitt and Mike Murray 2021

First published in 2016

This edition published in 2021 by

Hodder Education,

An Hachette UK Company

Carmelite House

50 Victoria Embankment

London EC4Y 0DZ

www.hoddereducation.co.uk

Impression number   10 9 8 7 6 5 4 3

Year   2026 2025 2024 2023 2022

All rights reserved. Apart from any use permitted under UK copyright law, no part of this publication may be reproduced or transmitted in any form or by any means, electronic or mechanical, including photocopying and recording, or held within any information storage and retrieval system, without permission in writing from the publisher or under licence from the Copyright Licensing Agency Limited. Further details of such licences (for reprographic reproduction) may be obtained from the Copyright Licensing Agency Limited, www.cla.co.uk

Cover image © wip-studio - stock.adobe.com

Illustrations by Aptara Inc. and Barking Dog

Typeset in MyriadPro, 11/13 pts by Aptara Inc.

Produced by DZS Grafik, Printed in Bosnia & Herzegovina

A catalogue record for this title is available from the British Library.

CONTENTS

Introduction

This book has been written and designed specifically for the AQA GCSE Physical Education specification, which began teaching in September 2016.

First examination for AQA GCSE Physical Education (8582) was in 2018.

To view the full specification and examples of assessment material for AQA GCSE Physical Education, please visit AQA's website: www.aqa.org.uk.

What's new in this edition?

- The assessment material, including Test Your Understanding and Practice Questions, has been updated to reflect past exam papers. This includes more analysis and evaluation (AO3), longer-form and higher-mark questions.
- New sport activities included on the DfE's latest GCSE PE activity list have been included as examples throughout the book and in the non-examined assessment section.
- More support has been added to topics that students often find challenging, in particular in Chapter 2 (Movement analysis) and Chapters 5a (Socio-cultural influences), 5b (Commercialisation of physical activity and sport) and 5c (Ethical issues).
- Sportspeople, sporting examples, data and statistics have all been updated to reflect current events.

How to use this book

Although the content of this new edition has been updated, we have kept many of the popular original features. Each chapter has a range of these features which have been designed to present the course content in a clear and accessible way, to give you confidence and to support you in your revision and assessment preparation.

Chapter objectives
Each chapter starts with a clear list of what is to be studied.

✔ Check your understanding
These questions have been designed specifically to help check that you have understood different topics.

Key terms
Key terms in **bold** in the text are defined in boxes nearby and in the glossary. The key terms cover all AQA subject-specific words as well as any additional words students should know for the exam.

Rapid recall
These contain hints and ideas to help you to remember things.

Activity
Activities appear throughout the book and have been designed to help you develop your understanding of various topics.

Study hint
These are suggestions to help you increase your knowledge of this subject.

Summary
These boxes contain summaries of what you have learned in each section.

PRACTICE QUESTIONS
These are to help you get used to the types of questions you may encounter in the exam.

Chapter 1a Applied anatomy and physiology

Chapter objectives

- Understand the structure and functions of the skeleton
- Understand the structure and functions of synovial joints
- Understand the movements involved at different joints

The structure and functions of the musculoskeletal system

Structure of the skeleton

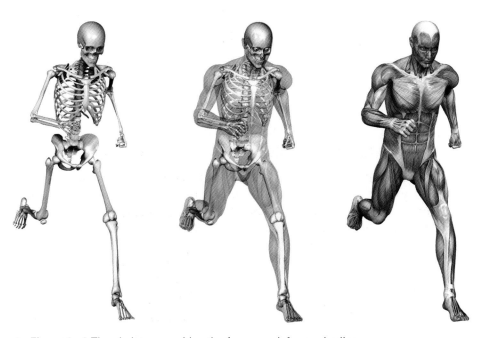

▲ **Figure 1a.1** The skeleton provides the framework for our bodies.

The skeletal system provides a framework for the muscular system to produce **movement**.

1 The skeletal system allows movement at a **joint**.
2 The shape and type of bones determine the amount of movement – short bones enable finer, controlled movements, **long bones** enable gross movement.
3 The flat bones protect vital organs.
4 The different joint types allow different types of movement.
5 The skeleton provides a point of attachment for muscles – when muscles contract, they pull the bones.

Key terms

Movement Muscles contract to pull the bones of the skeleton.

Joint Place where two or more bones meet.

Long bones The bones of the legs and arms. Long bones support the weight of the body and help with gross movements.

▲ **Figure 1a.2** The skeleton protects several vital organs from damage when playing contact sports such as rugby.

PRACTICE QUESTIONS

1 Explain, using examples, the role of flat bones in a sport such as rugby. (3 marks)

Answers are on page 170.

Key terms

Support Bones keep us upright and hold muscles and organs in place.

Protection Some bones surround and protect vital organs from damage.

Red blood cells Carry oxygen to muscles.

White blood cells Fight infections.

Rapid recall

Create a mnemonic for the functions of the skeleton:

Support	– e.g.	Super
Shape		Star
Protection		Performers
Movement		Make
Minerals		Mince
Production		Pies

The functions of the skeleton

1 **Support:** The bones are solid and rigid. They keep us upright and hold the rest of the body (the muscles and organs) in place.

2 **Protection:** Certain parts of the skeleton enclose and protect the body's organs from external forces; for example, the brain is inside the cranium, the ribs protect the heart and lungs. This function is especially important in activities that involve contact, such as rugby or boxing.

3 **Movement:** The skeleton helps the body move by providing anchor points for the muscles to pull against. The long bones in the arms and legs work as levers to allow certain movements.

4 **Structural shape and points for attachment:** The skeleton gives us our general shape, such as height and build. Tall people have long leg bones and larger vertebrae (see Figure 1a.3). People with a heavy build have larger clavicles and scapula as well as bigger pelvises. The skeleton also provides anchorage points for the muscles to attach, so when they contract we move.

5 **Mineral storage:** Bone stores several minerals, including calcium and phosphorus, which can be released into the blood when needed.

6 **Blood cell production:** The inner marrow of the long bones and ribs produces red and white blood cells. **Red blood cells** are important in activities because they carry oxygen to the working muscles. **White blood cells** are important to fight off infections in order to keep healthy.

▲ **Figure 1a.3** The skeleton gives shape for both the very tall basketball player and the very heavy sumo wrestler.

Synovial joints

Synovial joints are the most common type of joint in the body.

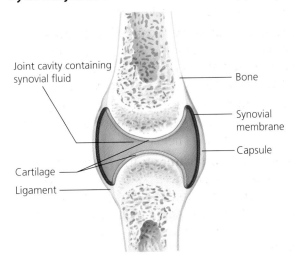

Joint cavity containing synovial fluid

Bone

Synovial membrane

Capsule

Cartilage

Ligament

▲ **Figure 1a.4** Internal structure of a synovial joint.

Synovial joints are characterised by having a fluid-filled space between smooth **cartilage** pads at the end of the bones that form the joint. Surrounding the joint is a tough joint **capsule** that is lined with a **synovial membrane**.

The outer layer of capsule often includes **ligaments** that join bones to bones and strengthen the joint to prevent unnecessary movements and possible **dislocations**. The synovial membrane lining the capsule produces an oily **synovial fluid** that lubricates the joint and reduces friction and wear.

In addition to the joint capsule and ligaments that support a synovial joint, there are several important structures surrounding the joint that help cushion and protect the joint from friction and outside forces. Small bags of synovial fluid, known as **bursae**, surround the joint to reduce friction from the movement of **tendons** across the surface of the joint.

There are many different classes of synovial joints in the body, including hinge joints and ball and socket joints.

> ✔ **Check your understanding**
>
> 4 Explain how different parts of a synovial joint provide support to stabilise the joint.
> 5 Explain how different parts of a synovial joint help it to move freely.
> 6 What is the function of tendons?
>
> Answers are on page 170.

> ✔ **Check your understanding**
>
> 1 What do we need support for?
> 2 What does the skeleton produce?
> 3 How do muscles cause movement?
>
> Answers are on page 170.

Key terms

Synovial joint Type of joint commonly found in the limbs; contains a **synovial membrane** that produces synovial fluid.

Cartilage Covers ends of bones, providing a smooth, friction-free surface.

Capsule Tough fibrous tissue – surrounds synovial joints; usually supported by ligaments.

Ligaments Join bone to bone.

Dislocation When the bones of a joint separate from their normal position.

Synovial fluid Produced by the synovial membrane to lubricate the joint.

Bursae Fluid-filled bags that help reduce friction in a joint.

Tendons Attach muscles to bones.

PRACTICE QUESTIONS

2 What are the main functions of ligaments? (1 mark)
3 What is the main function of cartilage? (1 mark)
4 What is the main function of the synovial membrane? (1 mark)

Answers are on page 170.

Activity 1

Describe the function of each of the following parts of a synovial joint:
- Cartilage
- Capsule
- Synovial membrane
- Synovial fluid
- Bursae
- Ligaments

Answers are on page 171.

Key terms

Vertebrae Bones that form the spine or backbone.

Hinge joint Joint that allows flexion and extension.

Flexion Movement where the angle between bones reduces.

Extension Movement where the angle between bones increases.

Bones that form joints

A joint is where two or more bones are attached for the purpose of motion of body parts.

The head–neck joint

There is a joint where the neck meets the head. The bones in the neck are the **vertebrae**, and the uppermost of these joins with the cranium. This joint allows a person to nod their head.

The elbow joint

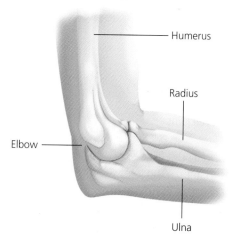

▲ **Figure 1a.5** The elbow joint is where three bones, the humerus, ulna and radius, meet.

The elbow joint is a complex **hinge joint** formed between the end of the humerus in the upper arm and the ends of the ulna and radius in the forearm.

The inner side of the end of the humerus forms a hinge joint with the ulna, while the outer side meets the end of the head of the radius. The meeting of the humerus, radius and ulna at the elbow allows the lower arm to bend and straighten in relation to the upper arm.

The correct term for bending at the elbow is **flexion**. Flexion is defined as a movement where the angle between the bone of a joint is reducing. Straightening of the lower arm in relation to the upper arm is called **extension**. Extension is defined as a movement where the angle between the bones of a joint is increasing.

Several ligaments surround the elbow joint which help the joint maintain its stability, allowing movement while resisting dislocation of the bones.

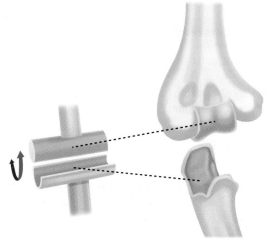

▲ **Figure 1a.6** The elbow joint is a hinge joint, moving just like the hinge on a door – forwards and backwards.

The shoulder joint

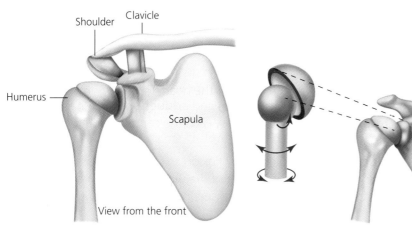

Shoulder
Clavicle
Humerus
Scapula
View from the front

▲ **Figure 1a.7** The shoulder joint is the joint between the humerus and the scapula.

▲ **Figure 1a.8** The ball at the end of the humerus fits loosely into the socket of the scapula.

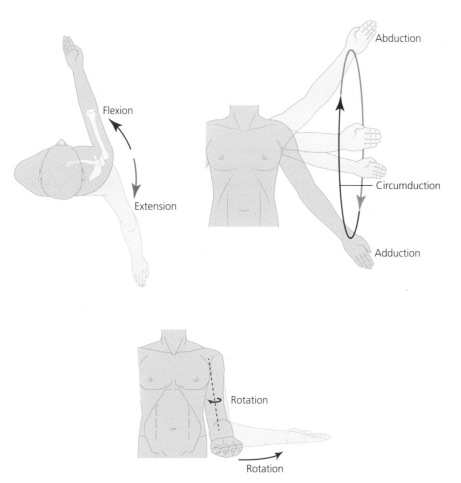

Flexion
Extension
Abduction
Circumduction
Adduction
Rotation
Rotation

▲ **Figure 1a.9** The wide range of movement of the shoulder joint allows for flexion, extension, adduction, abduction, circumduction and rotation.

Key terms

Ball and socket joint Joint that allows many movements – flexion and extension, abduction and adduction, and rotation.

Range of movement A measure of the flexibility of a joint in terms of the different movements allowed.

Abduction Movement where limbs are moved away from the body.

Adduction Movement where limbs are moved back towards the body.

Rotation Turning a limb along its long axis.

Circumduction Movement when a limb is held straight and is moved as if to draw circles with the hand/foot at arm's/leg's length; e.g. bowling in cricket.

Rapid recall

When you **add**uct the arm, you 'add' it to the side of the body.

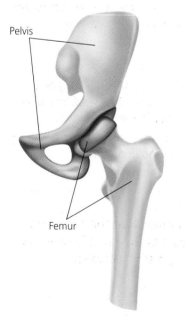

▲ **Figure 1a.10** The hip joint is formed between the femur and the pelvis.

The shoulder joint is a **ball and socket joint**. It has the greatest **range of movement** of any joint in the body – only ball and socket joints can move forwards and backwards, side to side and rotate around their axis.

Imagine standing upright with your hands by your side. The ball and socket joint at the shoulder can allow your arm to move forwards and backwards (flexion and extension), move away to the side of the body and back again (**abduction** and **adduction**), and enable the arm to **rotate** (turn your thumb in towards the centre of your body or turn it away from the centre of your body).

Circumduction is a combination of flexion, extension, adduction and abduction. It is a conical movement of the whole arm that occurs when spinning the arm; for example, when serving in tennis or bowling in cricket.

However, the big drawback of a ball and socket joint is that its extensive range of movement makes it more likely to dislocate than other, less mobile, synovial joints.

The shoulder joint is formed from two bones: the humerus and the scapula. The round head of the humerus forms a ball and socket joint with a cup-like depression of the scapula.

The joint is held together by ligaments and muscles, but the joint is vulnerable to dislocations from sudden jerks of the arm.

Chest joints

When breathing (see Chapter 1b) the chest cavity changes size because of the action of the breathing muscles. To allow that movement to happen there are joints between the ribs and the sternum, and the ribs and the vertebrae.

The hip joint

The hip joint forms where the femur meets the pelvis. The head of the femur fits into a depression in the pelvis called the acetabulum and forms a ball and socket joint (like the shoulder), which allows the leg to move in several different directions.

The main movements of the hip that occur in sport are flexion and extension. Hip flexion involves the femur moving forwards from a standing position and extension occurs when the femur returns to a standing position.

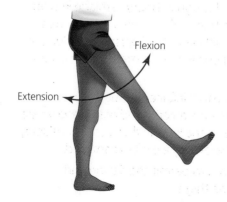

◀ **Figure 1a.11** Flexion and extension at the hip.

The knee joint

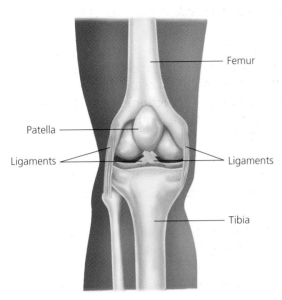

▲ **Figure 1a.12** The front of the knee joint, showing the strong ligaments that help hold the joint in place.

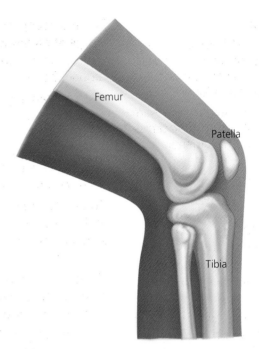

▲ **Figure 1a.13** The knee joint is formed from the femur and the tibia.

Activity 2

Describe the direction of each of the following movements that can happen at the shoulder joint:
- Flexion
- Extension
- Abduction
- Adduction
- Rotation
- Circumduction

Answers are on page 171.

The knee joint allows the lower leg to move relative to the upper leg while supporting the body's weight. Movements at the knee joint are essential to many everyday activities, including walking, running and moving into a standing position.

The knee is a hinge joint formed between two bones: the femur and tibia. The patella lies in front of the femur and is the bone we feel at the front of the knee. It is not actually part of the knee joint.

Between the femur and tibia is a layer of tough, rubbery cartilage known as the **meniscus**, which is the cartilage that is often talked about when describing knee injuries. The meniscus acts as a shock absorber inside the knee to prevent the collision of the leg bones during strenuous activities, such as running and jumping.

Many strong ligaments surround the knee to reinforce its structure and hold its bones in place. Two internal ligaments – the anterior and posterior **cruciate ligaments** – also help to keep the bones of the knee in their correct positions, and again are well known to sportspeople as they are often damaged.

As the knee is a hinge joint, its function is to permit the flexion and extension of the lower leg relative to the thigh.

Study hint
Be aware of questions that ask you to explain about joints – this means you will need to provide a reason, e.g. 'Explain the movement of the shoulder joint' means say how it moves and say why it moves in that way.

Key terms
Meniscus Cartilage acting as a shock absorber between the tibia and femur in the knee joint.

Cruciate ligaments Attach tibia to femur in the knee joint.

Study hint
Remember that the patella is not part of the knee joint – it is just a protective cover.

The ankle joint

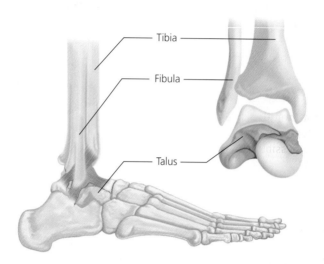

▲ **Figure 1a.14** The ankle joint is formed from the tibia and fibula of the lower leg and the talus bone in the foot.

Key terms

Plantar flexion Movement at ankle where the toes are pointed towards the ground.

Dorsiflexion Movement at ankle where the toes are pulled up towards the knee.

Rapid recall

Plantar flexion involves **p**ointing the toes.
Dorsiflexion involves **d**igging the heel.

✔ Check your understanding

7 Name the bones that form the elbow joint.
8 Which type of synovial joint allows the greatest range of movement? Give an example.
9 What movements are possible at the ankle joint?

Answers are on page 170.

The ankle joint is formed by the lower leg bones – the tibia and fibula – and the talus bone of the foot. These three bones form a synovial hinge joint.

The ankle works as a hinge joint, but the forward and backward movements have special names:

Plantar flexion is the term used for the movement that describes the pointing of the foot towards the ground, as in standing on tiptoes.

Dorsiflexion is the opposite movement, and involves the movement of the foot away from the ground, as in pulling the toes up and walking on one's heels.

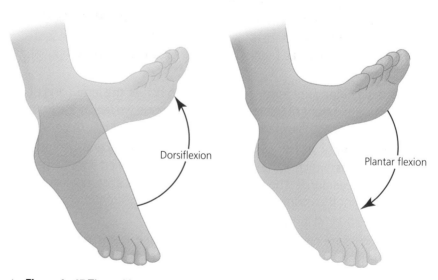

▲ **Figure 1a.15** The ankle movements of dorsiflexion and plantar flexion.

Numerous ligaments work together to limit extreme movements and dislocations of the ankle joint, while providing sufficient flexibility that helps the body walk on uneven surfaces and maintain its balance.

The shoulder, elbow, hip, knee and ankle are all examples of synovial joints.

✔ Check your understanding

10 Name the bones that form the knee joint.
11 Identify three different hinge joints.
12 What movements are possible at the shoulder joint?
Answers are on page 170.

PRACTICE QUESTIONS

5 Explain the difference between plantar flexion and dorsiflexion.

(2 marks)

6 What is the correct term for straightening the knee?

(1 mark)

7 Explain the difference between abduction and adduction.

(2 marks)

8 Evaluate the structure of the hip and shoulder joints in terms of both range of movement and stability during a team game such as netball.

(9 marks)

Answers are on page 170.

Study hint

Be aware of questions that ask for a specific number of answers – e.g. if the question is 'Name **two** bones in the elbow joint' it is possible that only your first two answers will be accepted.

Activity 3

Describe the movements that are possible at each of the following joints:
● Shoulder
● Elbow
● Hip
● Knee
● Ankle

Answers are on page 171.

Summary

- The skeleton provides a framework for movement.
- The skeleton has several different functions.
- Movements occur when bones move the synovial joints at the shoulder, elbow, hip, knee and ankle.
- The movements are caused by various muscles pulling these bones.

Chapter 1b The structure and function of the cardio-respiratory system

Chapter objectives

- Understand the pathway of air into and out of the lungs
- Understand gas exchange at the alveoli and the features that assist in gaseous exchange
- Understand the structure and function of arteries, capillaries and veins
- Understand the structure of the heart
- Understand the order of the cardiac cycle and the pathway of blood through the heart
- Understand the terms 'cardiac output', 'stroke volume' and 'heart rate', and the relationship between them
- Understand the mechanics of breathing as the interaction of the intercostal muscles, ribs and diaphragm
- Understand and interpret lung volumes through spirometer traces

The respiratory system

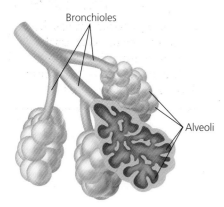

▲ **Figure 1b.1** Structure of alveoli.

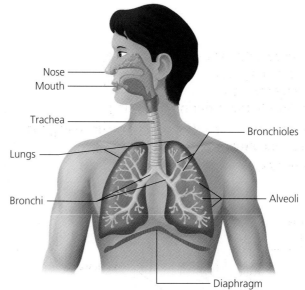

▲ **Figure 1b.2** The respiratory system.

Key terms

Trachea (or windpipe) Carries air from the mouth and nose to the lungs.

Lungs Pair of large, spongy organs optimised for gas exchange between our blood and the air.

Bronchi Carry air from the trachea into the lungs.

Bronchioles Carry air from the bronchi to the alveoli.

Alveoli Many tiny air sacs in the lungs which allow for rapid gaseous exchange.

When we breathe in, air moves through the mouth and nose and then travels into the **trachea**. The trachea carries air from the throat to the **lungs**.

The inner surface of the trachea is covered in tiny hairs called cilia, which catch particles of dust, which are then removed when coughing. The trachea is kept open by rings of stiff cartilage.

Near the lungs, the trachea divides into two tubes called **bronchi**, one entering the left and the other entering the right lung. Once inside the lung the bronchi split several ways, forming smaller and smaller bronchi.

The small bronchi further divide into **bronchioles**, which are very narrow tubes, less than 1 millimetre in diameter. There is no cartilage within the bronchioles. At the end of each bronchiole are openings to the **alveoli**. There are usually several alveoli coming from one bronchiole, forming a little clump that resembles a cluster of grapes.

The basic function of alveoli is the exchange of gases. Capillaries carrying blood surround the alveoli. The exchange of oxygen from the lungs into the blood and the exchange of carbon dioxide in the blood from these capillaries occur through the walls of the alveoli.

Gaseous exchange

Gaseous exchange at the lungs takes place by diffusion. The gases carbon dioxide and oxygen move down a concentration gradient from a high concentration to low concentration (see Figure 1b.3).

This means that the oxygen in the alveoli that is at a relatively high concentration diffuses into the blood capillaries where the oxygen concentration is lower. The oxygen that diffuses out of the alveoli is replaced by the air that we continue to breathe in.

The same thing happens in the case of carbon dioxide. Blood in the capillaries surrounding the alveoli contains a relatively high concentration of carbon dioxide and the alveoli contain a lower concentration. Thus, carbon dioxide diffuses into the alveoli from the blood and is eventually breathed out.

> **Activity 2**
>
> Copy the diagram.
>
> Label the circle as an alveolus and the tube as a blood capillary. Use arrows to show which direction oxygen and carbon dioxide move during breathing.
>
>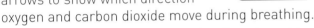
>
> Explain why the gases move in the directions they do, using the terms **diffusion** and **concentration**.
>
> Answers are on page 173.

> **Activity 1**
>
> Draw a single vertical line; then draw two lines branching off the bottom of this vertical line, rather like an upside-down Y; draw numerous branches off the ends of the λ. Label these lines as if they were the following parts of the respiratory system:
> - Trachea
> - Bronchi
> - Bronchioles
>
> Answers are on page 173.

PRACTICE QUESTIONS

1 Identify the structures that air moves through as it passes from the mouth to the alveoli. (3 marks)

Answers are on page 172.

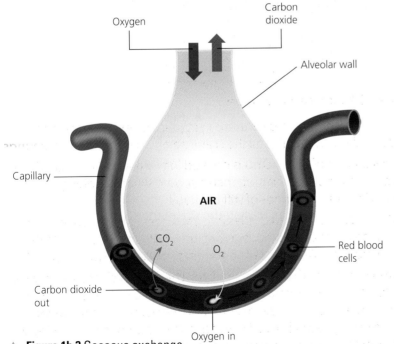

▲ **Figure 1b.3** Gaseous exchange.

> **✔ Check your understanding**
>
> 1 What is the function of cilia?
> 2 What is the difference between bronchi and bronchioles?
> 3 What is the function of the rings of cartilage in the trachea?
> 4 What is the function of the alveoli?
>
> Answers are on page 171.

PRACTICE QUESTIONS

2 Describe the process of diffusion that occurs in the lungs. (2 marks)

Answers are on page 172.

Key terms

Haemoglobin The red pigment found in red blood cells.

Oxyhaemoglobin Formed when oxygen combines with haemoglobin.

Inspiration The intake of air into the lungs.

Expiration The expulsion of air from the lungs.

Activity 3

List four factors that assist rapid diffusion, then reduce each factor to a single term. Produce and learn a mnemonic for those four factors.

Answers are on page 174.

✔ Check your understanding

5 Explain why oxygen diffuses into the blood.
6 Name four factors that assist gas exchange.
7 What is the function of haemoglobin?

Answers are on page 172.

Rapid recall

INspiration is breathing **IN**.

Rapid recall

The **IN**tercostal muscles **IN**crease the volume of the chest cavity.

The process of diffusion is a passive process and is helped by several factors:

- The alveoli are very small in size and large in number (there are millions in each lung), and so the alveoli provide a large surface area for the exchange of gases.
- The surface of alveoli and the walls of the blood capillaries are very thin (one cell thick) and moist which also helps the exchange of gases.
- The alveoli and capillaries are touching each other so there is a very short distance for diffusion to occur (short diffusion pathway).
- Each alveolus is surrounded by a network of blood capillaries, so there is a rich supply of blood for the gases to diffuse into/from.

When diffusing into the blood, the oxygen combines with **haemoglobin**, forming **oxyhaemoglobin**. Haemoglobin is a red pigment that is found in red blood cells that transports oxygen around the body. Carbon dioxide is also carried in red blood cells by haemoglobin.

Breathing

Breathing is a two-stage process. **Inspiration** (inhalation) is the intake of air into the lungs, which is brought about by increasing the volume of the chest cavity. **Expiration** (exhalation) is the expulsion of air from the lungs through reducing the volume of the chest cavity.

Both inspiration and expiration involve the use of muscles: the diaphragm and intercostal muscles. When these muscles contract, they cause the chest cavity to increase in size and, therefore, increase its volume.

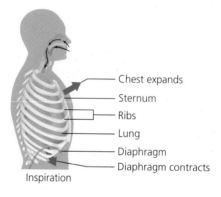

Chest expands
Sternum
Ribs
Lung
Diaphragm
Diaphragm contracts
Inspiration

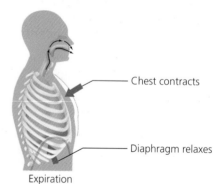

Chest contracts
Diaphragm relaxes
Expiration

▲ **Figure 1b.4** The process of inspiration.

▲ **Figure 1b.5** The process of expiration.

During inspiration, the breathing muscles contract. Contraction of the dome-shaped diaphragm causes it to flatten, thus enlarging the chest cavity. At the same time, contraction of the intercostal muscles causes the ribs to rise, thus also increasing the size of the chest cavity.

When the chest cavity expands, its volume increases. This reduces the pressure in the chest cavity and air is passively drawn into the lungs. Air passes from the higher pressure outside the lungs to the lower pressure inside the lungs.

During expiration, the breathing muscles relax. The diaphragm curves and returns to its domed shape; the weight of the ribs causes them to descend and the chest volume decreases. The reduction in the size of the chest cavity increases the pressure of the air in the lungs and causes it to be expelled. Expiration is passive; the breathing muscles simply relax. Air passes from the high pressure in the lungs to the low pressure in the bronchi and trachea.

During exercise, the active process of inspiration is assisted by the additional contraction of the **pectoral and sternocleidomastoid muscles**, which further increase the size of the chest cavity and so allow more air to enter the lungs.

Also, during exercise, the normally passive process of expiration is assisted by contraction of the **abdominal muscles**, which help force air out of the lungs and so speed up expiration.

Lung volumes

A spirometer is a piece of apparatus designed to measure lung volumes. It consists of a chamber filled with oxygen that floats on a tank of water. A person breathes from a mouthpiece attached to a tube which is connected to the chamber.

Breathing in takes oxygen away from the chamber, which then sinks down. Breathing out then pushes air into the chamber, causing it to float. During these movements, the lung volumes involved may be seen and measured.

The lung volumes are the amount of air breathed in, breathed out and found within the lungs at any given time.

Tidal volume is the amount of air that enters the lungs during normal inspiration at rest. The average tidal volume is 500 ml. The same amount leaves the lungs during expiration.

The **inspiratory reserve volume** is the amount of extra air inspired (above tidal volume) during a deep breath in. This can be as high as 3000 ml.

The **expiratory reserve volume** is the amount of extra air expired (above tidal volume) during a forceful breath out.

Residual volume is the amount of air left in the lungs following a maximal expiration. There is always some air remaining in the lungs.

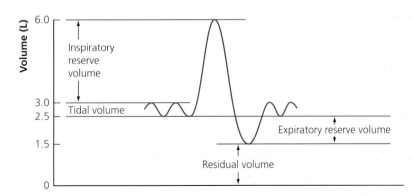

▲ **Figure 1b.6** Typical spirometer trace.

✔ Check your understanding

8 Name the breathing muscles used to inspire air during rest.
9 Name the breathing muscles used to inspire air during exercise.
10 How is air expired during rest?
11 Name the breathing muscles used to expire air during exercise.

Answers are on page 172.

PRACTICE QUESTIONS

3 Describe the mechanics of inhalation at rest. (2 marks)
4 Describe how the mechanics of breathing change when running. (2 marks)

Answers are on page 173.

Study hint
Remember to avoid using abbreviations such as TV, IRV or ERV in the exam. Write them out in full.

Key terms
Pectoral and sternocleidomastoid muscles The muscles which help increase the size of the chest cavity, allowing more air to enter during inspiration.

Abdominal muscles The muscles which help force air out of the lungs and so speed up expiration.

Tidal volume The volume of air breathed in (or out) during a normal breath at rest.

Inspiratory reserve volume The additional air that can be forcibly inhaled after the inspiration of a normal tidal volume.

Expiratory reserve volume The additional air that can be forcibly exhaled after the expiration of a normal tidal volume.

Residual volume The volume of air that remains in the lungs after a maximal expiration.

✔ Check your understanding

12 What is the tidal volume?
13 Which lung volume is used to increase the amount of air breathed in?
14 What is the name of the amount of air left in the lungs after a full expiration?

Answers are on page 172.

PRACTICE QUESTIONS

5 Analyse the changes in the mechanics of breathing during exercise that lead to greater inspiration during high-intensity interval training than at rest. (6 marks)

6 While running, a performer will experience changes in lung volumes. Complete the table below to show how the tidal volume, inspiratory reserve volume and expiratory reserve volume change during exercise. (3 marks)

▼ **Table 1b.1**

Volume name	Value at rest	Change during exercise
Breathing rate	16 breaths/min	Increases
Tidal volume	500 cm³	
Inspiratory reserve volume	3 100 cm³	
Expiratory reserve volume	1 200 cm³	
Residual volume	1 100 cm³	No change

Answers are on page 173.

Activity 4

Copy the following diagram and label the tidal volume, the inspiratory reserve volume, the expiratory reserve volume and the residual volume.

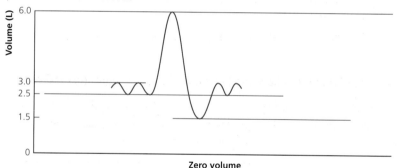

▲ **Figure 1b.7**

Answers are on page 174.

Blood vessels

Key terms

Artery Blood vessel carrying blood away from the heart.

Vasoconstriction Reducing the diameter of small arteries to reduce blood flow to tissues.

Vasodilation Increasing the diameter of small arteries to increase blood flow to tissues.

Arteries carry blood away from the heart. The blood within arteries is under the highest pressure. Arteries are elastic; they maintain the blood pressure by recoiling and narrowing when the heart is relaxing. Small arteries have muscular walls that can adjust their diameter to increase or decrease blood flow to a particular part of the body. When the rings of muscle in the small arteries contract, this makes the diameter of those arteries smaller and reduces the flow of blood through them. This is called **vasoconstriction**. The diameter of the small arteries can also increase (called **vasodilation**) to allow more blood to flow through them to the tissues. Vasodilation occurs during exercise to send more blood to the exercising muscles.

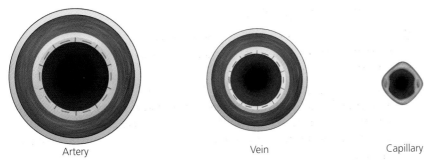

Artery   Vein   Capillary

▲ **Figure 1b.8** Blood is carried around the body in blood vessels. There are different types of blood vessel, each having a different function.

Capillaries are tiny, thin-walled blood vessels that join arteries (which carry blood away from the heart) and **veins** (which carry blood back to the heart). The thin walls of the capillaries allow gas exchange – oxygen passes from the blood into tissues and carbon dioxide passes from tissues into the blood. Nutrients also diffuse from blood in the capillaries into the surrounding tissues and waste products diffuse from the tissues into the blood.

Blood flows from the capillaries into very small veins, then into larger veins that lead back to the heart. Veins have much thinner walls than arteries because the blood pressure in veins is much lower. They also have a large internal diameter (lumen). Veins have valves to prevent blood from flowing backwards.

Table 1b.2 summarises the differences between the three types of blood vessel.

▼ **Table 1b.2** Differences between functions of arteries, capillaries and veins

ARTERIES	CAPILLARIES	VEINS
Carry blood away from the heart	Huge network of tiny vessels linking arteries and veins	Carry blood towards the heart
Most (but not all) arteries carry bright red, oxygenated blood	Very narrow – only one red blood cell at a time	Most (but not all) veins carry dark red, deoxygenated blood
Stretch as blood surges through and then return to normal shape; they have a pulse	Very thin walls (one cell thick) to allow rapid diffusion of substances into and out of the blood	No stretch; no pulse
Thick, muscular and elastic walls to withstand pressure		Thin-walled
Small lumen (internal diameter)		Large lumen (internal diameter)
		Have valves to prevent backflow of blood

Key terms

Capillaries Very thin blood vessels that allow gas exchange to happen.

Vein Blood vessel carrying blood towards the heart.

Rapid recall

Remember – **A**rteries carry blood **A**way from the heart.

✔ Check your understanding

15 What is the function of the elastic tissue in arteries?
16 Which type of blood vessel contains valves?
17 What is vasodilation?
18 Why are capillaries thin-walled?

Answers are on page 172.

Rapid recall

In diagrams of the heart, you will invariably be looking at the front of the heart, in which case the left side of the heart is on your right!

Activity 5

Draw a square and divide it into quarters. Use this as a simple diagram of the heart. Label the right and left atria and the right and left ventricles on your diagram.

Answers are on page 174.

Activity 6

Use the same diagram from the activity above. Colour the left side of the heart blue to represent deoxygenated blood. Colour the right side of the heart red to represent oxygenated blood.

Use arrows to show the direction of blood flow into and out of the different chambers of the heart.

Answers are on page 174.

Key terms

Atria Upper chambers of the heart that collect blood from veins.

Ventricles Lower chambers of the heart which pump blood out of the heart to the arteries.

Cardiac cycle Sequence of events that occur when the heart beats.

Diastole Term used to describe the relaxation phase of the cardiac cycle.

Systole Term used to describe the contraction phase of the cardiac cycle.

Structure of the heart

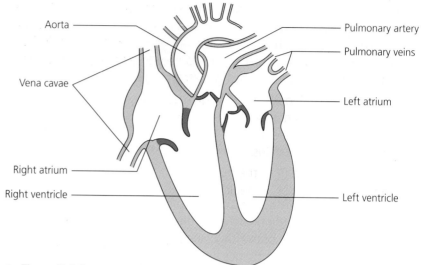

▲ **Figure 1b.9** Structure of the heart.

The heart is a muscular organ about the size of a closed fist that pumps blood around the body. It is divided into separate left and right sides, and each side has an upper and a lower chamber. The upper chambers are the **atria**, which collect blood from veins, and the lower chambers are the **ventricles**, which pump out blood through the arteries.

The right side of the heart takes in deoxygenated blood through the veins and delivers it to the lungs for oxygenation. The oxygenated blood returns from the lungs to the left side of the heart and is then pumped into various arteries that provide oxygen and nutrients to the body tissues by transporting the blood throughout the body.

Cardiac cycle

The **cardiac cycle** is the sequence of events that occur when the heart beats. There are two phases of the cardiac cycle. In **diastole**, the heart ventricles are relaxed and the heart fills with blood. In **systole**, the ventricles contract and pump blood to the arteries. One cardiac cycle is completed when the heart fills with blood and the blood is pumped out of the heart.

The events of the cardiac cycle described below trace the path of the blood as it enters the right side of the heart, is pumped to the lungs, travels back to the left side of the heart and is pumped out to the rest of the body. It should be noted that both the left and right sides of the heart go through diastole and systole at the same time as each other.

The flow of blood through the heart is controlled by pressure changes that cause different valves in the heart to open and allow blood to flow, and at other times close to prevent backflow of blood.

During diastole, the atria and ventricles are relaxed and the valves between the atria and ventricles (atrioventricular valves) are open. Deoxygenated blood from the main veins (the vena cavae) flows into the

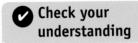

right atrium. The open atrioventricular valves allow blood to pass through to the ventricles.

Systole then occurs and the right atrium begins to contract, emptying its contents into the right ventricle. The right ventricle contracts soon after, forcing blood out of the heart along the pulmonary artery towards the lungs. The right atrioventricular valve is forced closed and prevents the blood from flowing back into the right atrium.

The deoxygenated blood flows through the pulmonary arteries to the lungs where gas exchange occurs. The blood picks up oxygen and carbon dioxide is removed before the blood returns to the left atrium of the heart through the pulmonary veins.

The oxygenated blood from the pulmonary veins fills the left atrium during diastole. Systole then begins again and the left atrium contracts and empties its contents into the left ventricle.

During systole, the left ventricle contracts, forcing the left atrioventricular valve to close, and the oxygenated blood is pumped into the aorta.

Cardiac output

Cardiac output is the volume of blood that the heart is able to pump out. It is usually measured in litres per minute.

The cardiac output represents the volume of oxygenated blood that is delivered to the body.

Two major factors form the cardiac output: the heart rate, which is the number of times the heart beats each minute, and the stroke volume, which is the volume of blood that leaves the heart during each contraction.

Increasing the heart rate increases the cardiac output, by increasing the number of volumes of blood released into the system. The heart rate increases usually before activity because of the expectation of exercise. This slight increase in heart rate before exercise is called the 'anticipatory rise'.

The stroke volume can be increased by the heart contracting with more force and so pushing more blood out with each beat.

The cardiac output, heart rate and stroke volume are related, such that:

cardiac output [Q] = heart rate [HR] × stroke volume [SV]

✔ Check your understanding

23 What is the cardiac output?
24 What is the relationship between stroke volume, heart rate and cardiac output?
25 What is the stroke volume?
26 What is the cardiac output of a performer who has a stroke volume of 70 ml and a heart rate of 70 beats per minute?

Answers are on page 172.

✔ Check your understanding

19 Distinguish between systole and diastole.
20 What is the function of the heart (atrioventricular) valves?
21 Describe the passage of blood from the right atrium to the lungs.
22 Describe the passage of blood from the lungs to the left ventricle.

Answers are on page 172.

PRACTICE QUESTIONS

7 Describe the passage of blood from leaving the right atria to eventually reaching the left ventricle.
(4 marks)

8 Analyse the changes to the cardiac cycle that occur as heart rate increases when running.
(6 marks)

Answers are on page 173.

Study hint

If you have to provide mathematical information, remember to include the units – possibly converting ml/min into L/min.

PRACTICE QUESTIONS

9 Briefly explain the terms 'cardiac output' and 'stroke volume' and the relationship between them. (3 marks)

Answers are on page 173.

Summary

- Different structures are involved in the pathway of air into and out of the lungs.
- Gas exchange in the alveoli is assisted by several features.
- Blood vessels have structures that suit their function.
- The cardiac cycle consists of systole and diastole and forces blood through the different parts of the heart.
- There is a relationship between cardiac output, stroke volume and heart rate.
- Different muscles cause changes in the volume and pressures within the chest cavity during breathing.
- A spirometer may be used to measure different lung volumes.

Chapter 1c Anaerobic and aerobic exercise

Chapter objectives

- Understand the idea of aerobic and anaerobic exercise during differing intensities
- Understand the recovery process from vigorous exercise in terms of excess post-exercise oxygen consumption (EPOC)/ oxygen debt
- Understand methods to help recover from strenuous exercise
- Understand the immediate effects of exercise (during exercise)
- Understand the short-term effects of exercise (up to 36 hours after exercise)
- Understand the long-term effects of exercise (months and years of exercising)

Exercise

When somebody exercises, they need to supply energy for muscle contractions. This energy is usually supplied by breaking down food (mainly glucose) using oxygen; because this process uses oxygen it is called **aerobic exercise**.

Aerobic exercise occurs at low to moderate levels of exertion, when energy can be produced using oxygen. Walking and jogging are good examples of exercises where the energy for muscle contractions is provided aerobically.

Anaerobic exercise is where the energy needed for exercise is provided in the absence of oxygen. Sprinting and shot putting are examples of activities where the energy is provided anaerobically (see Figure 1c.2).

The main difference between aerobic and anaerobic exercise is the intensity and the duration of the exercise involved.

Aerobic activities involve relatively gentle exercises that can be maintained for a long period of time. Aerobic activities are those where normal breathing can be used to supply the oxygen needed to the working muscles.

Anaerobic activities involve very high-intensity actions that can only be continued for a short period of time. Anaerobic exercises, if continued, will leave you breathless.

There are some activities, such as team games, that contain a mixture of aerobic and anaerobic exercise (see Figure 1c.3). During team games there will be times when the exercise is relatively gentle and the performer is walking/jogging and is aerobic. At other times, the performer may be sprinting and the exercise is strenuous and becomes anaerobic.

Rapid recall

Aerobic sounds like 'air'; air contains oxygen. If you're asked for examples of aerobic and/or anaerobic exercise, use marathon running for aerobic exercise and sprinting for anaerobic exercise.

▲ **Figure 1c.1** Jogging is an aerobic exercise.

Key terms

Aerobic exercise Exercise which uses oxygen.

Anaerobic exercise Exercise in the absence of enough/without oxygen.

▲ **Figure 1c.2** Sprinting is an anaerobic exercise.

Activity 1

Separate the following list of sports into mainly aerobic exercises, anaerobic exercises and mixed exercises:

netball, pole vault, marathon, trampolining, cricket, triathlon.

Answers are on page 176.

▲ **Figure 1c.3** Team games involve a mixture of aerobic and anaerobic exercises.

Activity 2

Identify three aerobic and three anaerobic movements/actions from a team game of your choice.

Answers are on page 176.

▲ **Figure 1c.4** Exercise may cause fatigue.

Key terms

Lactic acid Waste product from anaerobic exercise.

Oxygen debt Temporary oxygen shortage in the body due to strenuous exercise.

EPOC Increased rate of oxygen intake following strenuous activity.

Aerobic exercise involves the performer using oxygen to break down foods such as glucose. This reaction provides the energy needed for the activity and produces water and carbon dioxide as waste products. The process may be summarised as:

glucose + oxygen → energy + carbon dioxide + water

In anaerobic exercises, no oxygen is used. Because of this, the glucose is not fully broken down to carbon dioxide and water. Instead, it is converted into lactic acid while producing some energy needed for the activity. The process may be summarised as:

glucose → energy + lactic acid

Lactic acid is one of the major causes of fatigue. This is why anaerobic exercise cannot be continued for more than a minute or so. The build-up of lactic acid in muscles causes fatigue and eventually pain, and the exercise has to slow down or, if strenuous, stop.

✔ Check your understanding

1 Distinguish between aerobic and anaerobic exercise.
2 Write an equation that summarises aerobic exercise.
3 What is lactic acid?
4 Write an equation that summarises anaerobic exercise.

Answers are on page 175.

PRACTICE QUESTIONS

1 Is the marathon an aerobic or anaerobic event? Justify your answer. (3 marks)
2 Evaluate whether a team game such as netball or basketball is an aerobic or anaerobic exercise. (6 marks)

Answers are on page 175.

EPOC (oxygen debt)

During a short, intense burst of exercise such as sprinting, energy is generated anaerobically or without oxygen. When the body works anaerobically, it produces energy without oxygen and creates lactic acid as a waste product.

When the strenuous exercise stops, the performer will still be breathing heavily.

During this time, after strenuous exercise, the body takes in extra oxygen to 'repay' the **oxygen debt**. The term 'oxygen debt' is more properly known as **EPOC**: excess post-exercise oxygen consumption.

During recovery after anaerobic exercise, the body needs the extra oxygen to remove the lactic acid produced during the exercise. This is why the performer continues to breathe heavily, to repay their oxygen debt.

How long this oxygen debt lasts depends on how much lactic acid is produced, which in turn depends on how strenuous the exercise was and how long it lasted. It can take several hours to completely remove all the lactic acid produced during very intense exercise.

Activity 3

Watch a 400 m race on YouTube. Explain in your own words why the performers look so tired after the event and the processes that are occurring during their recovery.

Answers are on page 176.

Immediate effects of exercise (during exercise)

When a performer begins to exercise, the body has to supply extra oxygen to the working muscles. In order to do that, several changes take place in the body.

First, the heart begins to beat faster. Normal resting heart rate is somewhere around 70–80 beats per minute, but this can vary considerably. Exercise can easily raise the heart rate to 100–150 beats per minute or even higher, depending on how hard the exercise is.

The heart will also contract more powerfully during exercise, increasing the stroke volume. The increased heart rate and the more powerful contractions mean that more blood is being pumped around the body to supply the muscles with the glucose and oxygen they need.

The second immediate effect of exercise is that breathing rate increases. Resting breathing rate is about 15 breaths per minute. When exercise begins, not only does breathing rate increase but so does the depth of breathing, thus increasing tidal volume. The increased rate and depth of breathing allows for greater gaseous exchange at the lungs, so more oxygen enters the blood and more carbon dioxide is breathed out.

The third effect of exercise is that body temperature increases. This is because muscles are contracting more often and this generates heat, which increases body temperature. This increase in temperature is noticeable by the way the body tries to control it and keep cool. The body begins to sweat to try to lose heat by the evaporation of sweat from the skin's surface. The skin goes red as blood vessels near the skin's surface open to try to lose heat by radiation.

Short-term effects of exercise (up to 36 hours after exercise)

Exercise may also affect the body some time after the exercise has finished. Individuals may experience fatigue the day after strenuous exercise. This tiredness is simply caused by the muscles having worked especially hard and becoming swollen with fluids, which leave them feeling heavy. This effect usually passes within a day or two.

Sometimes, following an exercise session, a performer may feel dizzy and light-headed as if they might faint. This is often caused by low blood sugar or a drop in blood pressure. This is more likely to occur if the performer has sweated heavily.

Nausea is the feeling of sickness or vomiting which can occur during and after exercise. It may be caused by overexertion during exercise, or

✔ **Check your understanding**

5 What does 'EPOC' stand for?
6 Why do we get an 'oxygen debt' after strenuous exercise?
7 What is the function of EPOC?

Answers are on page 175.

PRACTICE QUESTIONS

3 What is excess post-exercise oxygen consumption? (2 marks)
4 What are the immediate effects of exercise on the body? (3 marks)
5 Analyse the use of oxygen by a performer during a game of badminton. (6 marks)

Answers are on pages 175–6.

▲ **Figure 1c.5** Sweating is normal during exercise.

Activity 4

Make a list that summarises the three immediate effects of exercise.

Answers are on page 176.

Key term

Nausea Feeling of sickness during/after exercise.

Study hint

Remember to avoid abbreviations such as DOMS or EPOC unless you have first written the term out in full.

Key terms

DOMS (delayed onset muscle soreness) The pain/stiffness felt in the days following strenuous exercise.

Cramp Involuntary contraction of a muscle.

Cool-down Undertaken after exercise to speed up recovery – e.g. walking, jogging, followed by static stretches.

▲ **Figure 1c.6** Cramp may result from strenuous exercise and a loss of fluids.

Activity 5

Make a list that summarises the five short-term effects of exercise.

Answers are on pages 176–7.

✔ Check your understanding

8 What are the immediate effects of exercise?
9 What are the short-term effects of exercise?
10 What is DOMS?
11 What causes DOMS?

Answers are on page 175.

from ending an exercise session too abruptly. Lack of water intake during exercise is a well-known cause of headaches and nausea during exercise. Exercising at a heavy rate causes blood flow to be taken away from a full stomach, another possible cause of nausea.

The pain and stiffness sometimes felt in muscles after unaccustomed or strenuous exercise is more properly called **delayed onset muscle soreness (DOMS)**. It is caused by eccentric muscle contractions performed during exercise, which cause tiny tears in muscle fibres, leading to swelling. The muscle is supposed to tear, because it repairs stronger, and this is the main benefit of training. Usually the muscle adapts rapidly to prevent muscle damage, and the soreness, if the exercise is repeated.

DOMS is different to, but often confused with, **cramp**. Cramp is a painful involuntary contraction of a muscle that is typically caused by fatigue or muscle strain, and is often linked to dehydration and loss of minerals due to excessive sweating.

PRACTICE QUESTIONS

6 People may suffer when they begin an exercise programme. Explain the causes of:

   a) fatigue

   b) DOMS.   (2 marks)

Answers are on page 176.

The recovery process from vigorous exercise

If undertaking strenuous exercise, the performer will want to avoid the problems of excessive fatigue/tiredness, nausea/light-headedness and DOMS/cramp. There are several precautions that can be taken to help recovery from exercise.

A **cool-down** should be undertaken following the exercise. A cool-down should consist of 5–10 minutes of walking or jogging to help decrease body temperature and remove waste products, such as lactic acid, from the working muscles. This should be followed by 5–10 minutes of static stretching exercises, which will help the muscles to relax.

An appropriate cool-down has the following benefits:

- aids in the clearing of waste products – including lactic acid
- reduces the potential for DOMS
- reduces the chances of dizziness or fainting caused by the pooling of blood at extremities
- allows breathing and heart rate to slowly return to their resting rates and so prevent sudden changes in heart rhythm, which could be dangerous.

Rehydration is the process of replacing the fluids that are lost during exercise, mainly through sweating.

Replacement of water on its own is not enough, because the body also loses minerals during sweating and these will need replacing as well. The performer also needs to replace the energy used during the exercise. During both aerobic and anaerobic exercise, glucose is used to produce the energy needed for muscle contractions. This glucose needs replacing. Glucose is a type of carbohydrate and the body will convert any carbohydrates it consumes into glucose. Therefore, it is advisable for the performer to take in extra carbohydrates following strenuous exercise.

These could easily be added to the fluids that are being consumed to replace the water and minerals lost during the exercise. In practical terms, drinks such as flavoured milk or meal-replacement drinks are quite suitable for manipulation of diet following strenuous exercise.

Common sense suggests that consuming large quantities of flavoured milks or meal-replacement drinks while indulging in light, rather than strenuous, exercise will cause an increase in weight rather than a beneficial effect. This is because it is very rare to exercise sufficiently hard so that the amount of energy used is equivalent to that consumed in a meal.

Another method of speeding up recovery after strenuous exercise is to use **ice baths**. The theory behind ice baths is related to the fact that intense exercise actually causes tiny tears in muscle fibres. This muscle damage stimulates the muscles to repair and strengthen themselves, but it is also linked with delayed onset muscle pain and soreness (DOMS), which occurs between 24 and 72 hours after exercise.

▲ **Figure 1c.7** Rehydration is important during and after exercise.

Key terms

Rehydration Replacing lost water, minerals and carbohydrates during and after exercise.

Ice baths Immersion in cold water to speed up recovery from exercise.

▲ **Figure 1c.8** Performers use ice baths to prevent DOMS and speed up recovery from exercise.

✓ Check your understanding

12 What should be included in a rehydration drink?

13 How do ice baths help prevent DOMS?

14 What are the benefits of a cool-down?

Answers are on page 175.

Key terms

Massage The rubbing and kneading of muscles and joints with the hands.

Hypertrophy Increase in size of muscles/heart due to long-term exercise.

Activity 6

Make a list of the three different ways that recovery from exercise can be assisted.

Answers are on page 177.

PRACTICE QUESTIONS

7 Identify two parts of an effective cool-down.
(2 marks)

8 Justify why the sport of netball has both aerobic and anaerobic needs.
(3 marks)

Answers are on page 176.

The ice bath is thought to constrict blood vessels and flush waste products, like lactic acid, out of the affected tissues. It is also supposed to reduce swelling. Both of these factors are thought to cause DOMS.

Then, once the performer is out of the ice bath and the muscles start warming up, there is an increased blood flow through the muscles, which improves the healing process.

Massage, which involves the rubbing and kneading of muscles and joints with the hands, can help reduce the pain that may be caused by too much physical activity. Massage can prevent or relieve DOMS by encouraging blood flow throughout the body, preventing muscle fatigue. It may also be used to reduce the swelling that may be causing the fatigue or stiffness in newly exercising muscles.

Long-term effects of exercise (months and years of exercising)

Many of the effects of regular training are not seen for months or even years after training has started. This is because the changes which occur are to the actual structure of the body, to allow the various systems of the body to work more efficiently during exercise.

Regular exercise will tend to reduce body weight. This is because fat stores are used to supply the glucose the body needs for energy. As well as that, if the exercise is mainly anaerobic, there will be a tendency to increase the size of the muscles involved in the exercise. This is called **hypertrophy**. The result of these two factors is that body shape may change.

▲ **Figure 1c.9** Muscles get bigger with exercise – hypertrophy.

Depending on the type of exercise undertaken, certain components of fitness may be developed. For example, if the exercise is mainly anaerobic and involves moving heavy objects around, such as weights, then there will be a build-up of muscle strength.

Similarly, regular exercises that are repeated, such as press-ups or sit-ups, will lead to an improvement in muscular endurance in those muscles involved in the movement.

Muscles, tendons and ligaments around joints get stronger and the joints become more stable. At the same time, the repeated movements involving joints means that the suppleness (flexibility) at joints increases.

Exercises that involve rapid anaerobic movements, such as sprinting, will eventually lead to an increase in speed. Similarly, exercises that involve slower, rhythmical, aerobic movements, such as running or swimming, will eventually build up the performer's cardio-vascular endurance and, hence, improve their stamina.

Less obvious is the fact that a long-term training programme will mean that the heart is beating at a higher rate than normal for long periods of time. The heart is a muscle and, like any other muscle exposed to regular intense exercise, it will increase in size. In other words, hypertrophy of the heart will occur. This increased size of the heart means that it is able to contract with greater force and pump out more blood with each beat. In other words, the stroke volume of the heart increases because of regular training.

Linked to this hypertrophy of the heart is the fact that there isn't that great a change in the overall size of the body, because the skeleton is the same shape and size, as are all the major organs. Therefore, the amount of blood that the body needs when not exercising remains essentially the same.

The amount of blood that the body receives depends on the cardiac output. Remember that:

cardiac output [Q] = stroke volume [SV] × heart rate [HR]

So, at rest, the cardiac output of a hypertrophied heart remains unchanged, but the stroke volume increases because of repeated exercise. This means that the heart rate must reduce to produce the same resting cardiac output. This reduction in resting heart rate in performers who have undertaken months or years of regular training is called **bradycardia**.

Summary

- Aerobic and anaerobic exercises involve working at different intensities.
- Recovery from exercise involves excess post-exercise oxygen consumption (EPOC)/oxygen debt.
- There are different ways to help recover from strenuous exercise.
- Exercise has immediate, short-term and long-term effects on the body.

Rapid recall

Long-term effects of exercise improve the **four Ss** – speed, stamina, suppleness, strength.

✔ Check your understanding

15 Why might body shape change following repeated exercises?
16 Explain the effects of long-term exercise on the heart.
17 In what ways does long-term exercise benefit fitness?

Answers are on page 175.

Key term

Bradycardia Lowered resting heart rate due to long-term exercise.

Activity 7

Use numbers to help you understand the idea of bradycardia.

If Q = SV × HR and Q = 12 and SV = 3, then what must HR equal?

If SV increases to 4 and Q remains the same, what must HR become?

Answers are on page 177.

PRACTICE QUESTIONS

9 The long-term effects of exercise include improvement in fitness.

a) Name four fitness components improved by long-term exercise.

(4 marks)

b) Suggest three other long-term effects of exercise.

(3 marks)

Answers are on page 176.

Chapter 2 Movement analysis

Chapter objectives

- Understand the different classes of levers found in the body
- Understand the mechanical advantages of different lever systems
- Understand how muscles work to cause movements
- Understand the planes and axes of different movements
- Understand the types of movements that occur at different joints
- Understand the names of the muscles causing movements at different joints

Levers

A lever is made up of three basic parts. These are the **fulcrum**, an **effort** (also called a force) and a **resistance** (also called the load). The fulcrum is the pivot point of a lever, the effort is the force that is applied to one part of the lever and the resistance is at the other end, working against the force of the effort. In our bodies, joints act as fulcrums, muscles act as the effort and the weight of an object and/or a limb is the resistance.

There are three classes of levers. A **first class lever** is the simplest. It has the fulcrum lying between the effort and the resistance. An example of a first class lever in the human body is the way the triceps muscle of the arm acts during extension. In this first class lever system, the elbow is the fulcrum and the hand is the load. The effort is applied by the triceps muscle to move the resistance in the hand.

Key terms

Fulcrum The part of a lever system that pivots; joints are the fulcrums in the body's lever systems.

Effort The force applied to move the resistance or weight; in the body, the effort is provided by muscles exerting a force.

Resistance The load to be moved by a lever system; usually this involves weight when the body's lever systems are involved.

First class lever Found at the elbow joint, where the triceps cause extension of the lower arm.

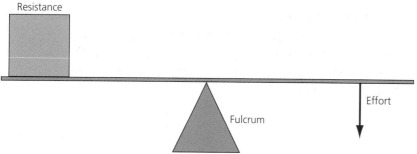

▲ **Figure 2.1** First class lever.

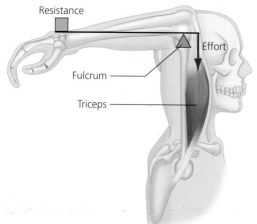

◀ **Figure 2.2** The first class lever system at the elbow joint.

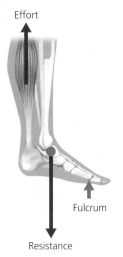

Effort

Fulcrum

Resistance

▲ **Figure 2.4** The second class lever system at the ankle joint.

Key terms

Second class lever Found at the ankle, where the gastrocnemius causes plantar flexion.

Third class lever The majority of the body's joints act as third class levers, e.g. the biceps acting at the elbow to cause flexion.

Study hint

For your exam, you need to remember that there is only one first class lever in the body – at the elbow during extension caused by the triceps. There is also only one second class lever system – at the ankle, during plantar flexion caused by the gastrocnemius. All other movements at joints involve third class lever systems.

A **second class lever** is one where the fulcrum lies at one end with the effort at the other end. The resistance then lies in the middle, between the effort and the fulcrum.

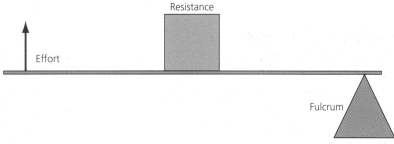

▲ **Figure 2.3** Second class lever.

In the human body, an example would be the ankle joint. The fulcrum is the ball of the foot, with the effort being the contraction of the gastrocnemius muscle. The resistance would be the weight of the person.

The final class of levers is the **third class lever**. In this kind of lever system, the fulcrum is located at one end and the resistance is at the other end of the lever. The effort is located between the fulcrum and the resistance.

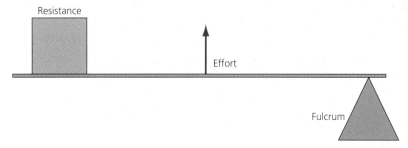

▲ **Figure 2.5** Third class lever.

An example of a third class lever in the human body is the biceps muscle in the arm acting on the elbow joint to move a resistance in the hand (see Figure 2.6 below). Other examples include the ankle and the knee joint (see Figures 2.7 and 2.8).

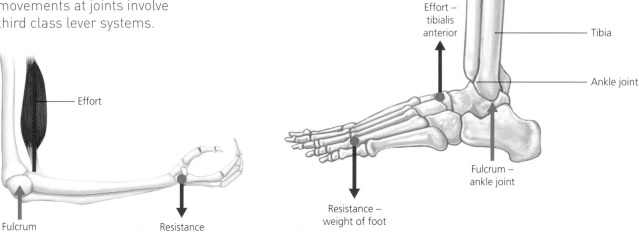

▲ **Figure 2.6** The third class lever system at the elbow joint.　▲ **Figure 2.7** The third class lever at the ankle during dorsiflexion.

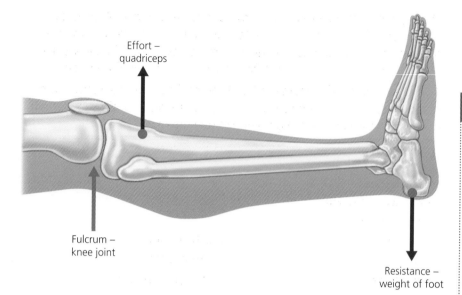

Effort –
quadriceps

Fulcrum –
knee joint

Resistance –
weight of foot

▲ **Figure 2.8** The third class lever when extending the knee joint.

Rapid recall

It might help you remember the
three classes of levers and the
corresponding positions of their
components if you remember that
in levers, the middle component
follows the acronym:

1, 2, 3 – F, R, E

In other words, in first class levers,
the fulcrum (**F**) is in the middle; in
second class levers, resistance (**R**)
is in the middle; and in third class
levers, effort (**E**) is in the middle.

Mechanical advantage

Different types of levers have different types of **mechanical advantage** in
how they work. The mechanical advantage of different levers depends on
the distance between the effort and the fulcrum when compared to the
distance of the resistance from the fulcrum. These distances are known as
the effort arm and resistance arm respectively.

mechanical advantage = effort arm ÷ resistance arm

Key term

Mechanical advantage The
benefit to a lever system of having
either a short effort arm (giving
rapid movements over a large
range of movement) or a short
resistance arm (giving the
advantage of being able to move
a heavy weight).

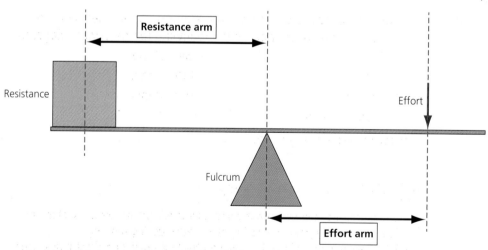

Resistance arm

Resistance

Effort

Fulcrum

Effort arm

▲ **Figure 2.9** Idea of resistance arm and effort arm.

First and third class levers have an effort arm that is much shorter than the
resistance arm, and therefore the effort arm ÷ the resistance arm is less
than one. This arrangement of short effort arm and longer resistance arm
will help speed up the movement of the resistance and produce a wide
range of movement. This occurs in the action of the biceps acting on the
elbow joint as a third class lever system.

During flexion at the elbow, the effort arm is the distance of the effort (the biceps) from the fulcrum (the elbow joint). The resistance arm is the distance of the hand from the fulcrum (the elbow joint). This allows the hand to move very quickly and through a large range of movement.

The vast majority of joints in the body are third class lever systems, with a short effort arm and long resistance arm. This means that these joints can move very quickly over a large range of movement.

> **Activity 1**
>
> Draw a diagram to show how the first class lever system operates at the elbow. Include the following terms in your diagram:
>
> - Fulcrum
> - Effort
> - Resistance
> - Triceps
> - Elbow joint
> - Effort arm
> - Resistance arm
>
> Answers are on page 179.

Second class levers, such as the ankle joint, are able to overcome a large resistance with an effort that is fairly small by comparison because the resistance arm is shorter than the effort arm. This gives a high value for mechanical advantage and, therefore, the action of the effort (gastrocnemius muscle) can easily move the resistance, which is essentially the weight of the body.

PRACTICE QUESTIONS

1 Compare plantar flexion at the ankle and flexion at the elbow joints in terms of mechanical advantage.
(9 marks)

Answers are on page 179.

> **Activity 2**
>
> Draw a diagram to show how the second class lever system operates at the ankle. Include the following terms in your diagram:
>
> - Fulcrum
> - Effort
> - Resistance
> - Gastrocnemius
> - Ball of foot
> - Effort arm
> - Resistance arm
>
> Answers are on page 179.

✔ Check your understanding

1 When running, the knee joint works as a lever system. Name, sketch and label the lever system operating at the knee during running.
2 When performing a throw-in during football or rugby, or a chest pass during netball or basketball, the arm straightens at the elbow. Name, sketch and label the lever system operating at the elbow during this type of movement.
3 Name, sketch and label the lever systems operating at the ankle during:
a) plantar flexion and
b) dorsiflexion.
4 State two mechanical advantages of the lever system that is used at the ankle joint.

Answers are on page 177.

Muscle action

Antagonistic muscle action

Muscles can only contract and pull. Therefore, joints have to have two or more muscles working opposite each other, one to pull the bones in one direction and another to pull the bones in the opposite direction.

As one muscle contracts, the second muscle relaxes. As the second muscle contracts, so the first muscle relaxes. This is known as antagonistic muscle action.

A good example of this is the upper arm, where the triceps and biceps are on opposite sides of the humerus. As the biceps contracts, the lower arm (radius and ulna) moves up towards the shoulder. The triceps relaxes to allow this movement to happen. In this action, the biceps is the prime mover or **agonist**, while the triceps is the secondary mover or **antagonist**.

Muscles are attached to bones at either side of joints by tendons. These are very strong cords of connective tissue that are embedded into the surface of the bone.

Muscle contraction for movement

There are two types of muscle contraction: **isotonic** and **isometric**.

Isotonic contractions occur when the muscle changes length as it contracts and causes movement of a body part. There are two types of isotonic contraction:

- **Concentric** contractions are those where the muscle shortens as it contracts. An example is bending the elbow from straight to fully flexed, caused by a concentric contraction of the biceps muscle. Concentric contractions are the most common type of muscle contraction and occur frequently in sporting activities.
- **Eccentric** contractions are the opposite of concentric and occur when the muscle lengthens as it contracts. This is less common than a concentric contraction and usually involves the control or slowing down of a movement started by the eccentric muscle's agonist.

In the downward phase of a press-up, the triceps contracts eccentrically to slow the movement down. Similarly, in a squat, the quadriceps contracts eccentrically to lower the body slowly towards the ground.

During isometric contractions, the muscle remains the same length. While performing a handstand, many of the body's muscles are contracting, but there is no movement as the balance is being held.

✔ Check your understanding

5 What is the difference between an isotonic and an isometric muscle contraction?
6 What is the difference between a concentric and an eccentric muscle contraction?
7 Give three examples of an isometric muscle contraction in three different physical activities.

Answers are on page 177.

Key terms

Agonist The prime mover – muscle that causes movement.

Antagonist Muscle that relaxes to allow the agonist to contract.

Isotonic Muscle action where the muscle changes length – causes movement.

Isometric Muscle action where the muscle stays the same length – used in balances.

Concentric Isotonic contraction where the muscle shortens.

Eccentric Isotonic contraction where the muscle lengthens – used to control downward movements.

Rapid recall

All **downward** movements, such as during push-ups and squats, involve **eccentric** contractions where the agonist controls the descent.

Study hint

Remember, the first answer you give for movement questions will be the one that is marked.

Study hint

In your exam, you must make it clear which part of a question you are answering. This is especially important if there is an 'and' in the question.

Planes and axes

To better understand movements, scientists use specific terms to describe the way different parts of the body are moving.

Movements are described as taking place in one of three planes. At a simple level, these three planes are:

- sagittal – forward or backward movements
- frontal – side-to-side movements
- transverse – rotational or turning movements.

To picture these three planes, imagine slicing through the body:

- First, through the centre, dividing the body into left and right parts – this is the **sagittal plane**.
- Next, through the body from the left side to the right, separating the front and back halves – this is the **frontal plane** (front side and back side).
- Finally, cutting straight through the hips to divide the top of the body from the bottom – this is the **transverse plane**.

An axis is a straight line that an object rotates or turns around. Movements of a joint are simply rotations. Bending the arm at the elbow actually involves rotating the forearm around the elbow joint. Movements at a joint take place in a certain plane about a certain axis. There are three axes of rotation:

- transverse axis
- sagittal axis
- longitudinal axis.

The **transverse axis** passes horizontally through the body from left to right. Movements in a sagittal plane (forwards and backwards) take place around a transverse axis.

The **sagittal axis** passes horizontally through the body from back to front. Movements in a frontal plane (side to side) take place around a sagittal axis.

The **longitudinal axis** passes vertically from the top of the body to the feet. Movements in a transverse plane (rotations) take place around a longitudinal axis.

Key terms

Sagittal plane and transverse axis Plane and axis for forwards and backwards movements – direction for extension and flexion.

Frontal plane and sagittal axis Plane and axis for side-to-side movements – direction for abduction and adduction.

Transverse plane and longitudinal axis Plane and axis for rotating movements – direction for rotations and spins.

Activity 3

Obtain some jelly babies and a cocktail stick. Push one cocktail stick down through the head of the jelly baby and out of its feet. The cocktail stick represents the longitudinal axis of the body. If you twist the cocktail stick, the jelly baby rotates. The plane of this rotation is the transverse plane.

Take the cocktail stick out and push it through the front belly of another jelly baby and out the back. The cocktail stick represents the sagittal axis and the jelly baby rotates around a frontal plane. Finally, push the cocktail stick through the jelly baby from one side to the other. This represents the transverse axis and the jelly baby rotates in a sagittal plane.

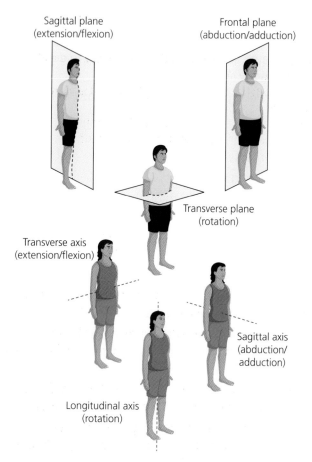

Sagittal plane
(extension/flexion)

Frontal plane
(abduction/adduction)

Transverse plane
(rotation)

Transverse axis
(extension/flexion)

Sagittal axis
(abduction/
adduction)

Longitudinal axis
(rotation)

▲ **Figure 2.10** Planes and axes of movement.

It is normal to describe a movement as taking place in the particular plane that the movement is dominated by. An example of this would be describing walking as taking place in a sagittal plane.

▼ **Table 2.1** Examples of dominant planes, actions and axes in movements.

PLANE	MOTION	AXIS	EXAMPLE
Sagittal	Flexion/extension	Transverse	Walking, running, squats, biceps curl, leg extensions, front somersault
Frontal	Abduction/ adduction	Sagittal	Star jump, cartwheel, side bend
Transverse	Rotations	Longitudinal	Discus and hammer throws, 360° twist, ice-skating spin

Activity 4

Stand in the corner of a room with your back against one wall. The walls and the ceiling (or floor) are in the same position as the planes of the body. The wall behind you that follows the line of your shoulders is the same as the frontal plane. The wall to the side of you that is going straight ahead is in the sagittal plane and the floor (or ceiling) shows the transverse plane.

PRACTICE QUESTIONS

2 Analyse the movements that take place in different planes and around different axes in a game of football. (9 marks)

Answers are on page 179.

Activity 5

Repeat the idea of standing in a corner (see Activity 4), but this time think about holding a bicycle wheel. If you position the wheel so the tyre follows the line of the walls (sagittal and frontal planes), then the spindle/axle in the wheel shows the axis of rotation of the plane (transverse and sagittal). The same process works for the transverse plane shown by the floor or ceiling and the longitudinal axis shown by the axle.

✔ **Check your understanding**

8 When a performer runs during a 100 m sprint, through which plane and in what axis do their legs move?
9 When a hammer thrower performs their throw, in which plane and in what axis does their movement occur?
10 As part of a training programme, a performer completes star jumps. In which plane and in what axis are these movements performed?

Answers are on page 178.

Key terms

Deltoid Muscle causing flexion at the shoulder.

Pectorals Muscles causing flexion at the shoulder.

Latissimus dorsi Muscle causing extension at the shoulder.

Movement analysis

Movements in the sagittal plane about the transverse axis

When movements occur in the sagittal plane and around a transverse axis, the movements are called flexion and extension (see Figure 2.11).

At the shoulder, flexion involves moving the whole arm forwards (see Figure 2.12). The main agonists causing flexion at the shoulder are the **deltoid** and the **pectorals**.

Extension at the shoulder involves moving the whole arm backwards. The main agonist causing extension at the shoulder is the **latissimus dorsi**.

Shoulder flexion occurs during backstroke swimming and when serving at badminton (see Figure 2.13). The action of the upper arm during sprinting also involves flexion (and extension) at the shoulder.

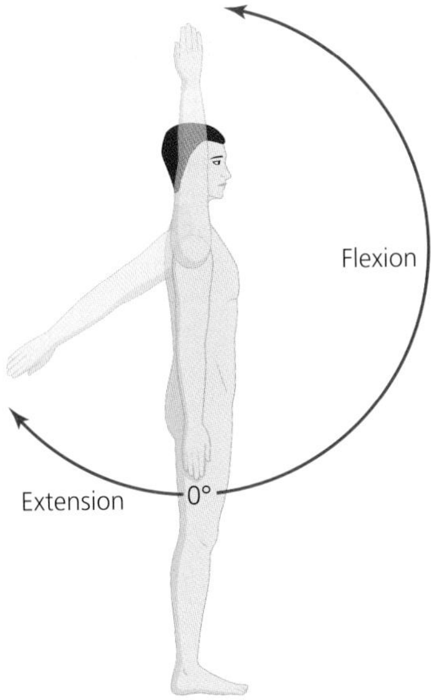

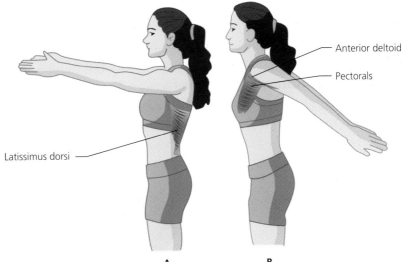

▲ **Figure 2.11** Flexion and extension at the shoulder.

▲ **Figure 2.12** Movement from A to B is extension at the shoulder caused by the latissimus dorsi. Movement from B to A is flexion at the shoulder caused by the deltoids and pectorals.

▲ **Figure 2.13** Flexion occurring at the shoulder during the badminton serving action.

Activity 6

One of the best ways of finding out which is the main agonist is to prevent the movement happening and feel which muscle is working. Have a go at this yourself!

Flexion also occurs at the elbow (see Figure 2.14). This involves the elbow bending and the hand moving towards the shoulder. The main agonist producing flexion at the elbow is the **biceps**.

Extension at the elbow is where the arm straightens. The main agonist causing extension at the elbow is the **triceps**.

These movements occur when performing a throw-in during football or rugby, and when shooting in basketball or netball.

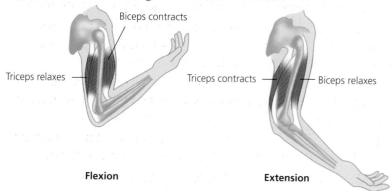

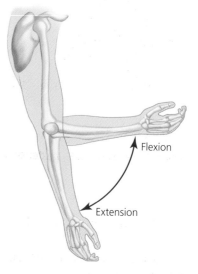

▲ **Figure 2.15a)** Biceps causes flexion at the elbow; **b)** triceps causes extension at the elbow.

▲ **Figure 2.14** Flexion and extension at the elbow.

> ✔ **Check your understanding**
>
> 11 What is the main agonist causing extension at the shoulder?
> 12 Name the movement caused by the triceps at the elbow.
> 13 What type of muscle contraction is occurring during the downward phase of a push-up? Name the main agonist.
>
> Answers are on page 179.

Answers are on page 179.

Rapid recall

The weight-training exercise is called a biceps curl because during the 'curl' or upward movement, the biceps is the agonist.

Flexion at the knee is where the joint bends and the heel moves towards the back of the upper leg (see Figure 2.16). The main agonist causing this movement is the **hamstrings** group of muscles (see Figure 2.17).

Extension at the knee is where the knee straightens. The main agonist causing this movement is the **quadriceps** group of muscles.

Flexion and extension at the knee occur when running, jumping and kicking. During the upward and downward phases of a squat there is flexion and extension at the knee.

Key terms

Biceps Muscle causing flexion at the elbow.

Triceps Muscle causing extension at the elbow.

Hamstrings Group of muscles causing flexion at the knee.

Quadriceps Group of muscles causing extension at the knee.

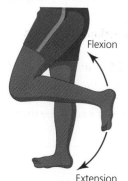

▲ **Figure 2.16** Flexion and extension at the knee.

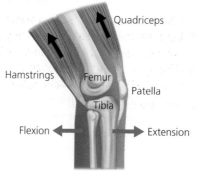

▲ **Figure 2.17** Quadriceps cause extension at the knee; hamstrings cause flexion at the knee.

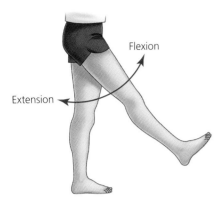

▲ **Figure 2.18** Hip flexion and extension.

Key terms

Hip flexors Main agonists at the hip during hip flexion.

Gluteals Main agonists at the hip during hip extension.

Tibialis anterior Muscle causing dorsiflexion at the ankle.

Gastrocnemius Muscle causing plantar flexion at the ankle.

Rapid recall

Plantar flexion is when you **p**oint your toes.
Dorsiflexion is when you **d**ig your heel.

Rapid recall

Flexion occurs when the angle between the bones in a joint **decreases**; extension is when the angle **increases**.

Flexion and extension also occur at the hip joint (see Figure 2.18). Flexion at the hip occurs when the straight leg moves forwards from a standing position. Flexion at the hip also occurs when you raise the leg off the floor when lying on your back. The main agonist during flexion at the hip is a group of muscles called the **hip flexors**.

Extension occurs when the leg is lowered down to the ground from a lying position and when that straight leg is returned to the standing position. The muscles causing extension at the hip, the agonists, are the **gluteals**.

Note that hip flexion and extension still occur when the knee is bent (flexed) as long as the upper leg (femur) is moving towards the upper body (flexion) or away from the upper body (extension).

Movements at the ankle are not called flexion or extension – rather, they are known as plantar flexion and dorsiflexion, even though they occur in the sagittal plane and around a transverse axis (see Figure 2.19).

Dorsiflexion is the equivalent to flexion and involves the **tibialis anterior** muscle contracting and pulling the toes up towards the shin bone.

Plantar flexion is the equivalent to extension and involves the **gastrocnemius** muscle contracting to push the foot out straight.

Plantar flexion occurs when running and jumping. Plantar flexion and dorsiflexion occur when kicking and when performing squats.

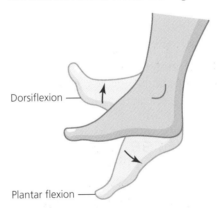

▲ **Figure 2.19** Plantar flexion and dorsiflexion.

✔ Check your understanding

14 Distinguish between plantar flexion and dorsiflexion.
15 Describe the movements occurring at the knee in the action of kicking a ball and name the agonist involved.
16 What type of muscle contraction is occurring during the downward phase of a squat? Name the main agonist.

Answers are on page 178.

Movements in the frontal plane about a sagittal axis

Abduction at the shoulder is the action of moving the arms away from the body in a frontal plane and around a sagittal axis.

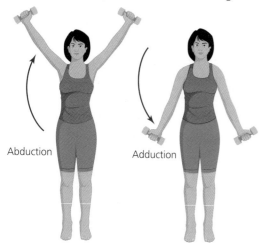

Abduction   Adduction

▲ **Figure 2.20** Abduction and adduction at the shoulder.

In abduction, the main agonist is the deltoid muscle. The downward movement is called adduction and there are two main agonists, the latissimus dorsi and the pectorals. Abduction and adduction occur in a frontal plane around a sagittal axis.

Abduction and adduction occur during swimming the butterfly stroke. Throwing the arms forward above the water is abduction; dragging the arms back through the water is adduction.

Movements in the transverse plane about a longitudinal axis

Turning the hand and forearm over while keeping the elbow straight (extended) means that the shoulder is rotating (see Figure 2.21).

The shoulder can be rotated by turning the arm towards the body (internal rotation) or away from the body (external rotation). The main agonists causing internal and external rotation are the **rotator cuff** muscles. Rotation at the shoulder occurs when bowling in cricket (see Figure 2.22).

▲ **Figure 2.22** Rotation at shoulder during the cricket bowling action (circumduction).

Study hint
Both flexion and abduction at the shoulder involve the deltoid, while both extension and adduction involve the latissimus dorsi.

Key term
Rotator cuff Group of muscles causing rotation at the shoulder.

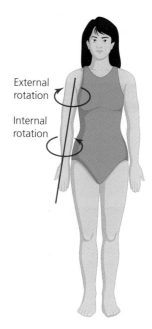

External rotation

Internal rotation

▲ **Figure 2.21** Rotation of the shoulder.

Study hint
Circumduction at both the shoulder and hip occurs in all three planes and axes.

Rapid recall

Rotation at the shoulder is caused by the **rotator** cuff muscles.

Analysis of selected movements

Push-ups

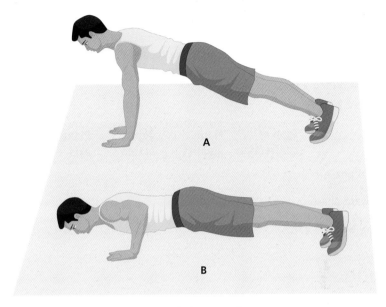

▲ **Figure 2.23** The movements during a push-up.

> ✔ **Check your understanding**
>
> 17 What two movements can the deltoids cause at the shoulder?
> 18 Which plane and what axis are involved in abduction and adduction?
> 19 What movement does the rotator cuff group of muscles cause?
>
> Answers are on page 178.

There are two parts to a push-up: the upward movement from B to A (pushing-up phase) and the downward movement from A to B (lowering-down phase).

In the pushing-up phase, there is movement at the elbow. The elbow straightens. This is extension, and the main agonist during this movement is the triceps. During this movement there is a concentric contraction of the triceps muscle.

In the lowering-down phase, the elbow bends. This is flexion. This movement has to be controlled eccentrically by the triceps muscle.

Football throw-in

Study hint

In the exam, questions often link movements to the muscles causing the movement and the plane and axis in which the movement takes place.

▲ **Figure 2.24** The movements during a throw-in.

A football (or rugby) throw-in starts with the ball behind the head (position A) and finishes with the ball leaving the hands (position B). During this movement, there is extension at the elbow. This is brought about by a concentric contraction of the triceps muscle.

> ### ✔ Check your understanding
>
> 20 Copy and complete Table 2.2 to describe the type of contraction, main agonist, the joint actions that occur, and the plane and axis involved at the elbow during a push-up movement.
>
> ▼ **Table 2.2**
>
> | | Type of contraction | Main agonist | Joint action | Plane and axis |
> |---|---|---|---|---|
> | Upward phase | | | | |
> | Downward phase | | | | |
>
> Answers are on page 178.

Running

During running, movements occur at the hip, knee and ankle joints. The movements involved in running take place in a sagittal plane and around a transverse axis.

During running, there is a short period of time when the performer's foot is in contact with the ground and the performer pushes off the floor. This is the drive phase of running.

- During this phase, the knee straightens. This is extension. This movement is brought about by a concentric contraction of the quadriceps muscle.
- Also during this phase, the hip extends. This is brought about by a concentric contraction of the gluteal muscles.
- At the same time, the performer pushes off the ground using their ankle joint. This involves plantar flexion. This is caused by a concentric contraction of the gastrocnemius muscle.

After the drive phase, there is the recovery phase, when the leg is brought forward to start another stride.

- During the recovery phase, the knee joint bends. This is flexion, which is caused by a concentric contraction of the hamstrings muscles.
- During this phase, the hip flexes because of a concentric contraction of the hip flexor muscles.
- Also during recovery, the ankle adjusts. There is dorsiflexion, caused by a concentric contraction of the tibialis anterior muscle.

A   B

▲ **Figure 2.25** Leg action during running.

> ### Activity 7
>
> To better understand the running action, watch a slow-motion sequence or search for a sequence of photographs.

Kicking

▲ **Figure 2.26** Kicking action.

Kicking is very similar to the drive phase of running.
- At the knee, the movement is from a bent knee to a straight knee. This is extension. Extension at the knee is caused by a concentric contraction of the quadriceps muscle.
- At the hip there is flexion, caused by a concentric contraction of the hip flexors.
- During the kicking action, the ankle remains plantar flexed throughout the movement. This is caused by an isometric contraction of the gastrocnemius muscle.

> ## ✔ Check your understanding
>
> 21 Copy and complete Table 2.3 to describe the type of contraction, the main agonist, the joint actions that occur, and the plane and axis involved at the hip, knee and ankle when standing up from a squat position.
>
> ▼ **Table 2.3**
>
> | | Type of contraction | Main agonist | Joint action | Plane and axis |
> |---|---|---|---|---|
> | Hip | | | | |
> | Knee | | | | |
> | Ankle | | | | |
>
> 22 Describe the joint action and name the type of contraction that occurs at the ankle during kicking.
> 23 Describe the movements occurring at the knee and ankle during the recovery phase of running.
>
> Answers are on page 178.

Standing vertical jump

The standing vertical jump starts with the performer in a crouched position (see Figure 2.27). During the movement, there is extension at the hip due to a concentric contraction of the gluteal muscles. There is also extension at the knee caused by a concentric contraction of the quadriceps muscle. There is also plantar flexion at the ankle, caused by a concentric contraction of the gastrocnemius muscle.

A   B

▲ **Figure 2.27** Standing vertical jump.

Squats

There are two distinct movements in a squat (see Figure 2.28). There is the upward phase from B to A, and there is the downward phase from A to B.

- During the upward phase, the hip extends as the gluteals contract concentrically. During the downward phase, flexion occurs at the hip. This is controlled by an eccentric contraction of the gluteal muscles.

- During the upward phase, the knee straightens. This is extension and is caused by a concentric contraction of the quadriceps muscle. During the downward phase, the action taking place at the knee is flexion. This is caused by an eccentric contraction of the quadriceps muscle as it controls the descent.

- A small amount of movement also occurs at the ankle during the upward phase of the squat. This is plantar flexion caused by a concentric contraction of the gastrocnemius muscle. During the downward phase, the movement at the ankle is dorsiflexion. This is controlled by an eccentric contraction of the gastrocnemius muscle.

A   **B**

▲ **Figure 2.28** Squats.

Shoulder action during cricket bowling

During the bowling action of a cricketer, there are two movements to note. There is rotation at the shoulder. This is caused by the action of the rotator cuff muscles. Rotation occurs in a transverse plane and around a longitudinal axis. There is also extension at the shoulder, mainly caused by the action of the deltoid muscle.

▲ **Figure 2.29** Bowling in cricket.

✔ Check your understanding

24 Name the plane and axis involved in rotation at the shoulder.

25 Copy and complete Table 2.4 to describe the type of contraction, main agonist and joint actions occurring at the knee during a squat.

▼ **Table 2.4**

	Type of contraction	Main agonist	Joint action
Upward phase			
Downward phase			

26 Copy and complete Table 2.5 to describe the type of contraction, main agonist and joint actions occurring at the ankle during a squat.

▼ **Table 2.5**

	Type of contraction	Main agonist	Joint action
Upward phase			
Downward phase			

Answers are on pages 178–9.

PRACTICE QUESTIONS

3 Figure 2.30 shows a sprinter leaving the starting blocks.

▲ **Figure 2.30**

What type of muscle contraction is occurring in this muscle in diagram A, and during sequence B–C? (2 marks)

4 Figure 2.31 shows the gymnast in a press-up position.

▲ **Figure 2.31**

a) Identify the main *agonist* and *antagonist* at the elbow joint as the gymnast moves from position A (up position) to position B (down position). (2 marks)

b) Identify the types of muscle contraction that occur:
  (i) at position A (up position) while the performer is stationary
  (ii) as the performer moves from position A (up position) to position B (down position). (2 marks)

c) Using the image, identify through what plane and about which axis the elbow action takes place. (2 marks)

5 Figure 2.32 shows phases of a tennis stroke.

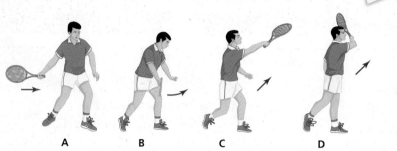

A   B   C   D

▲ **Figure 2.32**

    a) What joint actions are taking place at:

        (i) the right *shoulder* during the sequence B–C?

        (ii) the right *elbow* during the sequence C–D?   (2 marks)

    b) In the same sequence C–D, identify the *agonist* causing the movements at the elbow joint, and identify the type of muscle contraction involved.   (2 marks)

    c) In which *plane* and around what *axis* does the elbow movement C–D take place?   (2 marks)

Answers are on page 179.

Summary

- There are three classes of levers in the body.
- Different lever systems have different advantages.
- Different joints permit different types of movements.
- These movements occur in various planes and axes.
- The movements are caused by various muscles.

Chapter 3 Physical training

Chapter objectives

- The relationship between health and fitness
- The components of fitness
- How to evaluate the need for components of fitness in specific physical activities and sport
- Reasons for carrying out fitness tests
- The protocol and procedures which should be followed when carrying out fitness tests
- The limitations of carrying out fitness tests
- How qualitative and quantitative data can be gained and used when fitness testing
- The principles of training and overload and how they can be applied to training programmes
- The varying training types and the advantages and disadvantages of using them
- How training can be structured into seasons
- The reasons for warming up and cooling down

The relationship between health and fitness

The definitions of health and fitness are also covered in Chapter 6 on health, fitness and wellbeing. This chapter deals with the relationship between health and fitness, whereas Chapter 6 looks in detail at the different components of health and wellbeing.

Definitions of health and fitness

Key terms

Health A state of complete physical, mental and social wellbeing and not merely the absence of disease or infirmity.

Fitness The ability to meet/cope with the demands of the environment.

Health (as per the World Health Organization's definition: 1948) – 'A state of complete physical, mental and social wellbeing and not merely the absence of disease or infirmity.'

Be aware that 'ill health' refers to being in a state of poor physical, mental and/or social wellbeing.

Fitness – The ability to meet/cope with the demands of the environment.

▲ **Figure 3.1** To be 'healthy' is to be physically, mentally and socially well.

Looking at these terms, it is important to fully appreciate the relationship between health and fitness. It perhaps seems obvious that if you are in a good state of fitness, you are more likely to be healthy – certainly physically, but also mentally and socially. Developing a good fitness level allows you to cope better with the demands of your daily life and environment and can help to lessen your potential to be affected by illness and disease.

However, it is important to realise that, irrespective of how fit you are, there is always the potential to become unwell – that is, to suffer poor health.

The relationship between health and fitness can be summarised in the following points:

- Ill health can negatively affect fitness, as the individual may be too unwell to train – thus lowering their fitness.
- Ill health may not affect fitness if the person is still well enough to train.
- Increased fitness can positively affect health and wellbeing; for example, you may be less likely to contract certain illnesses and diseases, you may feel content and happy, and you may have enhanced your social wellbeing by taking part in activities.
- However, increased fitness cannot prevent you from contracting some illnesses and diseases and, subsequently, your health may suffer (see Figure 3.2).
- Increased fitness cannot prevent you from suffering from mental or social ill health.

N.B. Overtraining (training too much) can in fact lower your immune system and make you more susceptible to illness and disease!

PRACTICE QUESTIONS

1 Which **one** of the following is correct?
  A person who trains regularly and has a high level of fitness will:
  A definitely not catch any illness or disease ☐
  B be less likely to catch some illnesses or diseases ☐
  C definitely have good mental health and wellbeing ☐
  D definitely not have any friends or social wellbeing. ☐ (1 mark)
  Answers are on page 181.

The components of fitness, benefits for sport and how fitness is measured and improved

There are numerous components of fitness; however, for GCSE Physical Education you are required to know, define and understand the following:

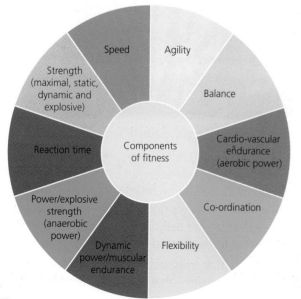

◀ **Figure 3.3** Components of fitness.

Study hint
It is a common mistake to suggest that increased fitness definitely improves health.

> ✔ **Check your understanding**
>
> 1 Define 'health' and 'fitness' and explain the relationship between the two terms.
>
> Answer is on page 180.

▲ **Figure 3.2** Elite tennis star Grigor Dimitrov tested positive for Coronavirus (COVID-19) in 2020.

Activity 1
Class debate.
'Does an increase in a person's fitness definitely mean that they will be healthier?'

▲ **Figure 3.4** Netball players need to change direction at speed, using agility to outwit opponents.

✔ Check your understanding

2 Can you evaluate why agility is needed by different sports performers?

Answers are on page 180.

Key terms

Agility The ability to move and change direction quickly (at speed) whilst maintaining control.

Balance Maintaining the centre of mass over the base of support.

▲ **Figure 3.5** Maintaining the centre of mass over the base of support in a headstand (using balance).

It is important that you can link each of these components of fitness to specific sports and skills, justifying why they are needed.

When evaluating any component of fitness, aim to state what it does and what it leads to. For example, tennis players who have well-developed agility can change direction at speed on the court so they can reach a ball before it bounces out. This prevents them from losing the point.

Agility

Agility is simply defined as 'the ability to move and change direction quickly (at speed) whilst maintaining control'. In summary, agility involves:

- changing direction quickly or at speed
- maintaining control.

Agility combines speed, co-ordination, reaction time and strength and is applicable to most sporting scenarios. However, events like the 100 metres do not require much agility as the runner does not change direction. As with all of the components of fitness, you may need to justify why agility is actually needed. It is not enough to simply state 'you need agility to change direction quickly'. Thus, a footballer who needs to change direction quickly does so to outwit another player, or to manoeuvre themselves into a suitable position to pass or shoot. Similarly, it is true that a volleyball player may need to change direction quickly so that they can react to the opposing team's use of the ball.

Activity 2

Copy and complete the table to justify why agility is required in the following sporting examples.

▼ **Table 3.1**

Sporting scenario	Justification
Rugby player	Needs to change direction to avoid a tackler or to perform a side-step so they can be free to run to the try line and score a try
Hockey player	
Badminton player	
Water polo player	

Answers are on page 186.

Balance

Balance is defined as 'the maintenance of the centre of mass over the base of support'. There are in fact two different types of balance:

- static balance (balancing whilst still), and
- dynamic balance (maintaining balance whilst moving).

An example of static balance is when performing a headstand, which is in a held position. An example of dynamic balance is simply when walking, or, more complexly, when a snowboarder aims not to fall over when making his or her downhill descent.

Balance is an essential ingredient in all sports. You get no plaudits in any sport for falling over!

Activity 3

There are lots of examples in gymnastics where balance is particularly important. Copy and complete the table below to justify why balance is needed.

▼ **Table 3.2**

Gymnastics example	Type of balance	Justification
Handstand		Position of handstand has to be held whilst maintaining control, e.g. no wobbles, which could reduce the score awarded by judges
Headstand	Static	
Cartwheel along a beam		Moving along the beam without falling off, as the score would be significantly lower Maintaining control during the jump/rotation/movement to allow a high score to be achieved
Tumble	Dynamic	

Answers are on page 186.

Cardio-vascular endurance

Cardio-vascular endurance can also be called 'aerobic power'. It is linked closely to stamina, which is being able to exercise whilst delaying the onset of fatigue. The definition of cardio-vascular endurance is 'the ability of the heart and lungs to supply oxygen to the working muscles'. It is particularly important for sports performers who:

- perform long, enduring events
- perform using the aerobic energy system (using oxygen).

Thus, you can say that it is important for long-distance runners, team-sports performers, endurance cyclists and rowers (see Chapter 1c).

Marathon runners

Marathon runners run for 26 miles and 385 yards. It is a long, gruelling event that requires the athlete to make best use of their aerobic energy system. Their ability to use oxygen is a key ingredient in whether they succeed or not.

Here is an example scenario:

- Athlete A: A marathon runner with good cardio-vascular endurance will be good at supplying oxygen to the working muscles.
- Athlete B: A marathon runner with poor cardio-vascular endurance will be poor at supplying oxygen to the working muscles.
- Summary: Athlete B will tire quickly and will not be able to maintain as fast a pace as Athlete A without making large amounts of lactic acid.

Javelin thrower

As an event, javelin lasts only a few seconds and is explosive/powerful. It does not matter if a javelin thrower can supply oxygen to the working muscles for a long period of time. Thus, cardio-vascular endurance is not required by a javelin thrower.

✓ **Check your understanding**

3 Define 'balance'. Name two different types of balance. Explain why balance is needed for certain sporting activities.

Answers are on page 180.

Key term

Cardio-vascular endurance The ability of the heart and lungs to supply oxygen to the working muscles.

Activity 4

In small groups, discuss whether cardio-vascular endurance is needed by a basketball player.

Answers are on page 186.

Study hint

It is important that you can justify why cardio-vascular endurance is/is not needed by sports performers, giving the impact that it has on performance.

▲ **Figure 3.6** Distance runners require a good level of cardio-vascular endurance.

PRACTICE QUESTIONS

2 10000m in athletics is completed by running round a 400m track 25 times. Would this require cardio-vascular endurance? Justify your answer. (2 marks)

Answers are on page 181.

Study hint

If two or more body parts are being used, co-ordination is needed.

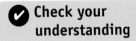

✔ Check your understanding

5 Define 'co-ordination' and suggest reasons why it is needed by performers in different sports.

Answers are on page 180.

Key terms

Co-ordination The ability to use different (two or more) parts of the body together, smoothly and efficiently.

Flexibility The range of movement possible at a joint.

✔ Check your understanding

6 Define 'flexibility' and suggest reasons why it is needed by performers in different sports.

Answers are on page 180.

✔ Check your understanding

4 Define 'cardio-vascular endurance' and suggest reasons why it is needed by performers in different sports.

Answers are on page 180.

Co-ordination

Co-ordination is defined as 'the ability to use different (two or more) parts of the body together, smoothly and efficiently'.

In simple terms, it involves effective interaction of body parts; for example, the eyes and the hands (hand–eye co-ordination). The nervous signals from the brain are timed to ensure effective use of appropriate muscles; for example, signals are sent to the shoulders, arms and hands to catch a ball.

Some examples of co-ordination being used in sport include:

- hitting a cricket ball with a bat (hand–eye co-ordination)
- kicking a ball in futsal (foot–eye co-ordination)
- arms and legs when dribbling a basketball (arms–legs co-ordination).

Flexibility

Flexibility is defined as 'the range of movement possible at a joint'. The joints of the body have maximum ranges of movement which differ in relation to the type of joint being used; for example, a ball and socket joint allows a wider range of movement than a hinge joint (see joints, Chapter 1a). Developing good flexibility is beneficial as it can prevent individuals from sustaining an injury if their body moves out of the normal range of movement.

▲ **Figure 3.7** A gymnast showing incredible flexibility.

Flexibility is required to different extents by different sports people. A gymnast usually needs a good range of movement in many of their joints to create the shapes and moves required in a floor routine to gain higher marks in their routine; for example, performing the splits.

Muscular endurance (similar to dynamic strength)

Muscular endurance is the ability of a muscle or muscle group to undergo repeated contractions, avoiding fatigue. The repeated contractions cause a limb to carry out repeated movement. The ability of a muscle/muscle group to move a limb repeatedly is needed for activities such as middle-distance running, rowing or swimming. Swimming strokes are repeated, forceful movements that need to be sustained.

▲ **Figure 3.8** Rowers perform repeated contractions, causing their limbs to carry out the strokes required. This involves muscular endurance.

Power/explosive strength (anaerobic power)

Power, also known as explosive strength or anaerobic power, is the product of strength and speed – that is, strength × speed.

The creation of 'power' is useful in many sporting skills, for example:

- to generate power whilst kicking a football – kicking with strength, moving the leg at speed
- to smash/spike a volleyball with power – hitting with strength, moving the arm at speed
- to release a discus with power – releasing with strength, moving the arm at speed
- to perform a punch with power in boxing – punching with strength, moving the arm at speed.

In all of these examples, strength is exerted at speed to create the power.

Key terms

Muscular endurance Ability of a muscle or muscle group to undergo repeated contractions, avoiding fatigue.

Power The product of strength and speed, i.e. strength × speed.

> ✔ **Check your understanding**
>
> 7 Define 'muscular endurance' and suggest reasons why it is needed by performers in different sports.
>
> Answers are on page 180.

> **Rapid recall**
>
> You can simply remember that **power = strength × speed**

> ✔ **Check your understanding**
>
> 8 Define 'power' and suggest reasons why it is needed by performers in different sports.
>
> Answers are on page 181.

▲ **Figure 3.9** The point of release when throwing a discus requires strength to be exerted at speed (power).

Reaction time

▲ **Figure 3.10** The reaction time in sprinting is the time between the gun going off and the sprinter starting to initiate a response (starting to run).

Reaction time is the time taken to initiate a response to a stimulus – the time taken from the presentation of the stimulus to starting to initiate a response (for example, from the gun sounding at the start of the 100 m to the performer starting to move out of the blocks).

(gun) ⟶ **time to start reaction** ⟶ **(reaction starts/ movement starts)**

Speed

Speed is the maximum rate at which an individual is able to perform a movement or cover a distance in a period of time. It is also defined as 'putting the body parts through actions as quickly as possible'.

Speed can be calculated as:

$$\text{speed} = \frac{\text{distance}}{\text{time}}$$

> **Activity 5**
>
> Can you calculate the following using distance ÷ time?
>
> If a sprinter runs 100 m in 10 seconds, what is the average speed in metres per second?
>
> Answers are on page 186.

Strength

Strength is the ability to overcome a resistance. It relates to the force that can be produced by a muscle or group of muscles. This can be maximal, dynamic, explosive or static.

- Maximal strength relates to the absolute maximum force that can be generated in one contraction. This is often tested using a one rep max test (see testing on page 59). It can be related to a single punch in boxing.

Key terms

Reaction time The time taken to initiate a response to a stimulus.

Speed The maximum rate at which an individual is able to perform a movement or cover a distance in a period of time, i.e. distance ÷ time.

Strength The ability to overcome a resistance.

◀ **Figure 3.11** Olympic sprinters show amazing speed.

> ✓ **Check your understanding**
>
> 9 Define 'speed' and suggest reasons why it is needed by performers in different sports.
>
> Answers are on page 181.

- Dynamic strength relates more to repeated contractions (see muscular endurance).

- Explosive strength is also known as power – the product of strength and speed. It can be expressed as strength × speed (see page 48).

- Static strength is applicable to scrummaging in rugby. When both teams push with the same force and the scrum is not moving, the muscles involved remain at the same length and the force applied is maintained. (See isometric contraction on page 30.)

▲ **Figure 3.12** Static strength being used to hold a weight in position.

PRACTICE QUESTIONS

3 Justify the importance of agility to a netball player. (2 marks)

4 Identify a sport that requires participants to have good reaction time. Justify your answer. (2 marks)

5 Which of these components of fitness is *not* required by a shot putter?

 A Power ☐

 B Flexibility ☐

 C Co-ordination ☐

 D Muscular endurance ☐ (1 mark)

6 Define balance and, using examples, justify why it is needed to play team games. (4 marks)

7 Define speed and justify why a netball player requires good speed. (2 marks)

8 Justify why strength is needed in association football. (1 mark)

9 Using a sport of your choice, explain why cardio-vascular endurance is not important to performers in that sport. (3 marks)

Answers are on page 182.

> **✔ Check your understanding**
>
> 10 Define 'strength' and suggest reasons why it is needed by performers in different sports.
>
> Answers are on page 181.

> **Activity 6**
>
> Make a list of the fitness components (see Chapter 1c) improved by repeated exercises and for each one describe the type of exercise that should be undertaken.
>
> Answers are on page 187.

Study hint

You may be required to define any of the components of fitness. You may also need to link physical activities and sports to the components of fitness, justifying why they may or may not be needed, e.g. a footballer needs agility because …

N.B. 'Justify' means to 'support a case with evidence' – that is, give a reason for your answer.

Reasons for carrying out fitness tests

It is often beneficial to test how proficient an individual is in a range of, or in specific components of, fitness. In simple terms, the main reasons for carrying out fitness tests can be summarised as:

- To identify strengths and/or weaknesses in a performance. Are there reasons for performing well or not so well? For example, perhaps your dribbling in a hockey match was poor because of a lack of speed?
- To inform your training requirements. As a result of initial tests, what components did you score poorly in and therefore may need to improve?
- To show a starting level of fitness. By testing at the start of a training programme, you can work out what level you are starting at. This links in well with the next point.
- To monitor improvement. Have the components of fitness you needed to improve actually improved over a period of time?
- To gauge the success of a training programme. If you have been training specific components of fitness, you may test how well it has gone by undertaking fitness tests.
- To compare against norms of the group/national averages. You can compare results with your peers or, for an informed appraisal, some tests have national averages (also known as normative data) that you can compare your scores to.
- To motivate/set goals. Having knowledge that they will be doing fitness tests may well motivate an individual to try harder or to train in advance of the test so as to score well. It could also be that an individual is set a specific goal to achieve in the tests, thus providing them with motivation (drive).
- To provide variety in a training programme. Training programmes can be boring and lack variety. Carrying out tests either randomly or on a planned basis may well provide the variety required to keep individuals enthusiastic and motivated.

Rapid recall

The word **TEST** can be used to remember reasons for carrying out fitness tests.

T – **T**raining programme – can inform you what needs to be trained

E – **E**valuate strengths and weaknesses

S – **S**et goals – goals can be set, e.g. to achieve a specific score in a test

T – **T**edium – to provide variety and avoid tedium/boredom in training

▲ **Figure 3.13** Fitness testing can show you your strengths and weaknesses, what you need to improve and give you a starting point from which to improve.

Fitness tests

The following fitness tests allow you to gain knowledge of:

- suitable tests for components of fitness
- what equipment is required
- what the protocol for each test is
- what the average is/national averages are for each test.

> ## Activity 7
>
> Why not try the tests out and compare your scores to the national averages/normative data provided? Please note that you should complete a thorough warm-up (see page 76) prior to attempting any of the following tests.
>
> No test should be completed without the permission and/or supervision of a teacher/responsible adult.

Agility test – Illinois agility test

The test involves the following protocol:

- Equipment: 8 cones, a measuring tape and a stop-watch.
- The cones should be arranged in a 10 m × 5 m rectangle with 4 cones down the middle – (see Figure 3.14).

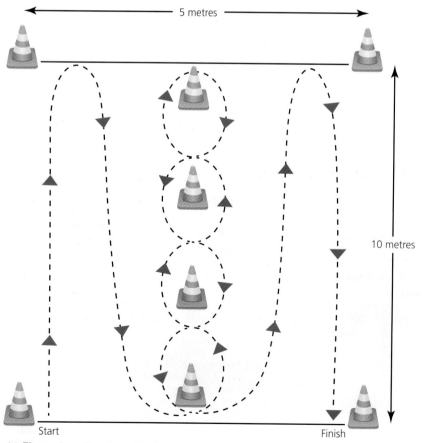

▲ **Figure 3.14** Illinois agility test.

> ## Activity 8
>
> In small groups, discuss what fitness tests you have completed. Did anyone learn anything from the results? For example:
>
> - Did you score particularly well/poorly in a specific test?
> - Is there a component of fitness that you would benefit from training to improve?
> - Has anyone completed a test more than once in the last three years? Have they improved or worsened, and why?

Study hint

'Testing protocol' refers to how each test is carried out and organised. This includes equipment needed, rules to be followed, measurements and scoring, and how comparisons and conclusions can be made, e.g. using ratings tables.

Study hint

You may need to suggest the 'protocol' to carrying out fitness tests. This means: what do you actually do to carry out the test? Remember to use the correct units when describing a test, e.g. one rep max in kilograms (kg).

- Performer starts face-down on the floor.
- The test involves running round the cones as fast as possible (it is a maximal test).
- It is timed in seconds.
- It can be compared to the ratings in Table 3.3.

▼ **Table 3.3** Illinois agility test ratings.

RATING	MALES	FEMALES
Excellent	< 15.2	< 17.0
Above average	16.1–15.2	17.9–17.0
Average	18.1–16.2	21.7–18.0
Below average	18.2–19.2	23.0–21.8
Poor	> 19.3	> 23.0

Source: Davis, B. et al. (2000) *Physical Education and the Study of Sport*

Balance test – the 'stork stand' test

This test involves the following protocol:

- Equipment: a stop-watch is required.
- The individual starts balanced on two flat feet.
- Hands are placed on the hips.
- One leg is lifted so that the toes of the lifted leg touch the inside of the knee of the planted leg.
- The timekeeper tells the individual to raise the heel on the planted leg (and the stop-watch should start).
- The individual balances on one leg for as long as possible until they lose balance or have to move the toes attached to the inside of the knee.
- The time is recorded in minutes/seconds.
- The test can be repeated and scores are compared to the ratings in Table 3.4.

▼ **Table 3.4** Stork stand test ratings.

RATING	MALES	FEMALES
Excellent	< 50	< 30
Above average	41–50	23–30
Average	31–40	16–22
Below average	20–30	10–15
Poor	> 20	> 10

Source: Johnson and Nelson (1979) *Practical Measurements for Evaluation in Physical Education*

▲ **Figure 3.15** Stork stand test.

Cardio-vascular endurance (aerobic power) test – multistage fitness test

The test involves the following protocol:

- Equipment: cones, tape measure (20 m or more), tape/CD with test, sheet to record score.
- It is run over a distance of 20 m – that is, cones/line 20 m apart.
- It is progressive – that is, it progressively gets harder.
- The individual runs 20 m in time with 'bleeps'.
- The time between bleeps gets shorter as the level increases.

20 metres

▲ **Figure 3.16** Cardio-vascular endurance (aerobic power) test.

- The individual keeps running until they cannot keep up with the bleeps (maximal test). N.B. If they do not get to the line in time, the individual is usually given one or two more attempts to 'catch up' with the timing of the bleeps.
- The score is recorded as a level and bleep (for example, level 8, bleep 4) and compared to the ratings below. The score can provide a prediction of an individual's VO$_2$ max (the maximum amount of oxygen that can be consumed per minute).

▼ **Table 3.5** Cardio-vascular endurance (aerobic power) test – multistage fitness test ratings for men.

MALES	RATING						
	VERY POOR	POOR	FAIR	AVERAGE	GOOD	VERY GOOD	EXCELLENT
12–13 yrs	< 3/3	3/4–5/1	5/2–6/4	6/5–7/5	7/6–8/8	8/9–10/9	> 10/9
14–15 yrs	< 4/7	4/7–6/1	6/2–7/4	7/5–8/9	8/10–9/8	9/9–12/2	> 12/2
16–17 yrs	< 5/1	5/1–6/8	6/9–8/2	8/3–9/9	9/10–11/3	11/4–13/7	> 13/7

▼ **Table 3.6** As above, for women.

FEMALES	RATING						
	VERY POOR	POOR	FAIR	AVERAGE	GOOD	VERY GOOD	EXCELLENT
12–13 yrs	< 2/6	2/6–3/5	3/6–5/1	5/2–6/1	6/2–7/4	7/5–9/3	> 9/3
14–15 yrs	< 3/3	3/4–5/2	5/3–6/4	6/5–7/5	7/6–8/7	8/8–10/7	> 10/7
16–17 yrs	< 4/2	4/2–5/6	5/7–7/1	7/2–8/4	8/5–9/7	9/8–11/10	> 11/11

Source: Adapted from Beep Test Ratings www.topendsports.com

▲ **Figure 3.17** Anderson ball catch test.

Co-ordination test – wall toss test (Anderson ball catch test)

The test involves the following protocol:

- Equipment: a ball (usually a tennis ball), a flat wall, a stop-watch, an observer (timekeeper and scorer).
- The tennis ball starts in one hand.
- Both feet together, 2 m from the wall.
- Upon the command of 'go' the time starts – 30 seconds.
- The individual throws the ball against the wall and catches the ball with the opposite hand.
- This is repeated as many times as possible – counting 1, 2, 3, etc.
- Two attempts are allowed. If the ball is dropped, the time continues.
- The score is compared to the ratings in Table 3.7.

▼ **Table 3.7** Co-ordination test – wall toss test ratings.

RATING	SCORE (IN 30 SECONDS)
Excellent	> 35
Good	30–35
Average	20–29
Fair	15–19
Poor	< 15

Source: Adapted from Alternate Hand Wall Toss Test www.topendsports.com

Flexibility test – sit and reach test

The test involves the following protocol:

- Equipment: sit and reach box, slider (not available on all boxes).
- The individual adopts a sitting position on the floor with their legs straight.
- Shoes should be removed and feet should be flat against the sit and reach board.
- The slider (if available) should be set to 14 cm to be in line with the toes.
- The individual reaches forward and pushes the slider as far as possible.
- The score is recorded in centimetres and compared to the ratings in Table 3.8.

▲ **Figure 3.18** Sit and reach test.

▼ **Table 3.8** Flexibility test – sit and reach test ratings.

RATING	MALES		FEMALES	
	CM	INCHES	CM	INCHES
Super	> +27	> +10.5	> +30	> +11.5
Excellent	+17 to +27	+6.5 to +10.5	+21 to +30	+8.0 to +11.5
Good	+6 to +16	+2.5 to +6.0	+11 to +20	+4.5 to +7.5
Average	0 to +5	0 to +2.0	+1 to +10	+0.5 to +4.0
Fair	−8 to −1	−3.0 to −0.5	−7 to 0	−2.5 to 0
Poor	−20 to −9	−7.5 to −3.5	−15 to −8	−6.0 to −3.0
Very poor	< −20	< −7.5	< −15	< −6.0

Source: Data supplied by Top End Sports www.topendsports.com

Muscular endurance test – abdominal curl conditioning test (sit-up bleep test)

The test involves the following protocol:

- Equipment: partners for each participant, CD of test (NCF abdominal conditioning test), gym mat.
- The individual lies on the mat in a sit-up position, while their partner supports their ankles.
- The participant sits up on the bleep and down on the bleep (staying in time).
- The test is maximal – how many sit-ups you can do in time with the bleeps.
- It is also progressive – the bleeps get faster.
- The score is how many sit-ups you complete.
- Scores are compared to national averages (see Table 3.9).

▲ **Figure 3.19** Completing the muscular endurance test.

▼ **Table 3.9** Abdominal curl conditioning test ratings.

STAGE	TOTAL SIT-UPS	MALES	FEMALES
1	20	Poor	Poor
2	42	Poor	Fair
3	64	Fair	Fair
4	89	Fair	Good
5	116	Good	Good
6	146	Good	Very good
7	180	Excellent	Excellent
8	217	Excellent	Excellent

Source: Adapted from NCF Abdominal Curl Conditioning Test www.topendsports.com

Power/explosive strength (anaerobic power) test – vertical jump test

The test involves the following protocol:

- Equipment: wall ruler, usually 2 m long.
- With feet flat, stand and push the wall ruler with the fingertips as high as possible. This provides the individual's 'zero point'.
- Apply chalk (or something to make a mark) to the fingertips.
- From a standing position, the individual jumps as high as possible, marking the ruler with the chalk.
- The observer records the height jumped in cm.
- The score is compared to the ratings in Table 3.10.

▼ **Table 3.10** Power/explosive strength (anaerobic power) test – vertical jump test ratings.

RATING	MALES		FEMALES	
	INCHES	CM	INCHES	CM
Excellent	> 28	> 70	> 24	> 60
Very good	24–28	61–70	20–24	51–60
Above average	20–24	51–60	16–20	41–50
Average	16–20	41–50	12–16	31–40
Below average	12–16	31–40	8–12	21–30
Poor	8–12	21–30	4–8	11–20
Very poor	< 8	< 21	< 4	< 11

Source: Adapted from Vertical Jump Test at Home www.topendsports.com

▲ **Figure 3.20** Performing the vertical jump test.

▲ **Figure 3.21** Performing the ruler drop test.

Reaction time test – ruler drop test

The test involves the following protocol:

- Equipment: a metre ruler.
- One person holds the metre ruler at the zero point (vertically).
- The individual being tested places their thumb and index finger of their dominant hand around the ruler (not touching it) at the 50 cm mark.
- Without warning, the ruler is released.
- The individual being tested must react to the drop and catch the ruler as fast as they can (with their thumb and index finger).
- The score to be recorded is in cm – how far from 50 cm the individual caught the ruler. The individual may have three attempts.

▼ **Table 3.11** Reaction time test – ruler drop test ratings.

RATING	MEASUREMENT
Excellent	7.5 cm
Above average	7.5–9 cm
Average	15.9–20.4 cm
Below average	20.4–28 cm
Poor	> 28 cm

Source: Norms, adapted from Davis (2000), for 16–19 year olds.

Maximal strength test – one rep max test

The test involves the following protocol:

- Equipment: appropriate weights/resistance machine – usually a bar-bell or bench press machine.
- Lift a weight once, using the correct technique.
- If completed, attempt a heavier weight until the heaviest weight the individual can possibly lift once is discovered (one correctly completed repetition).
- If a weight cannot be lifted, a lighter weight should be used to calculate the maximum weight that can be lifted.

Take your one rep max weight for the bench press or leg press and divide it by your body weight. So, for example, if you were able to lift 136 kg (300 lbs) on the leg press and you weigh 80 kg (175 lbs), that equates to a score of 1.7.

▼ **Table 3.12** Maximal strength test – one rep max test ratings.

RATING	SCORE
Excellent	> 1.60
Good	1.30–1.60
Average	1.15–1.29
Below average	1.00–1.14
Poor	0.91–0.99
Very poor	< 0.90

Source: Adapted from 1-RM Bench Press Test www.topendsports.com

Strength – handgrip dynamometer test

The test involves the following protocol:

- Equipment: handgrip dynamometer.
- The dynamometer should be held in the individual's dominant hand.
- The arm should be at 90 degrees with the elbow against the body.
- Grip may need to be adjusted to size.
- Squeeze with maximum effort and record your score.
- Repeat three times and record your best score.
- Compare your score to the ratings below.

▲ **Figure 3.22** One rep max using a bench press.

▲ **Figure 3.23** Carrying out the handgrip dynamometer test.

▲ **Figure 3.24** Carrying out the 30 m sprint test.

✓ **Check your understanding**

11 Name and describe how each test is carried out (protocol).

Answers are on page 181.

▲ **Figure 3.25** The ruler drop test involves an action that is not sport specific.

Study hint

'Validity' means that the test actually tests what it states it will test. A valid test is one which is appropriate for the sport.

'Reliability' means that if the test is repeated, similar results can be gained.

▼ **Table 3.13** Grip strength ratings for males (in kg).

AGE	WEAK	NORMAL	STRONG
12–13	< 19.4	19.4–31.2	> 31.2
14–15	< 28.5	28.5–44.3	> 44.3
16–17	< 32.6	32.6–52.4	> 52.4
18–19	< 35.7	35.7–55.5	> 55.5

▼ **Table 3.14** Grip strength ratings for females (in kg).

AGE	WEAK	NORMAL	STRONG
12–13	< 14.6	14.6–24.4	> 24.4
14–15	< 15.5	15.5–27.3	> 27.3
16–17	< 17.2	17.2–29.0	> 29.0
18–19	< 19.2	19.2–31.0	> 31.0

Source: Camry Electronic Hand Dynamometer Instruction Manual

Speed test – 30 m speed test

The test involves the following protocol:

- Equipment: 2 cones 30 m apart, tape measure, stop-watch.
- Use a flying start.
- The individual is timed running 30 m as fast as they can.
- The score in seconds is compared to ratings.

▼ **Table 3.15** Speed test – 30 m speed test ratings.

RATING	MALES	FEMALES
Excellent	< 4.0	< 4.5
Above average	4.2–4.0	4.6–4.5
Average	4.4–4.3	4.8–4.7
Below average	4.6–4.5	5.0–4.9
Poor	> 4.6	> 5.0

Source: Adapted from Davis (2000), available at www.brianmac.co.uk/flying30.htm

Limitations of fitness testing

Although there are numerous benefits from carrying out fitness tests, it is fair to say that fitness tests also have their limitations. These can be summarised as:

- Tests are often not sport-specific and can be too general. For example, the ruler drop test is not something that is carried out in any sport.
- They do not replicate movements of activities – very few sports involve direct running of 20 m up and down in a straight line like the multistage fitness test.
- They do not replicate competitive conditions required in sports – major sporting events are performed under extreme pressure. Many of the tests can be repeated/retried.

- Many of the tests have questionable reliability. As most tests are maximal, the individual must try their hardest in the test to gain an accurate score, thus motivation levels must be high. Also, as a partner sometimes measures your score – for example, vertical jump test – it is possible that they will get the scoring wrong.
- The tests must be carried out with the correct procedures and protocols, otherwise scores will not be accurate or valid.

Evaluating what tests are appropriate for different sporting performers

For GCSE Physical Education, you may be required to evaluate whether it is appropriate or relevant for certain sporting performers to carry out specific fitness tests. For example, what tests are most appropriate for a tennis player? Table 3.16 gives some examples of who each test is appropriate or less appropriate/inappropriate for.

▼ **Table 3.16** Suitability of tests for different types of performers.

TEST	REASONS WHY IT IS APPROPRIATE	REASONS WHY IT IS LESS APPROPRIATE OR INAPPROPRIATE
Illinois agility test	Tennis players need good agility to change direction at speed to follow the direction of the ball after their opponent has hit it. It is therefore worth testing to gauge how developed their agility is.	100 m runners will not need to change direction very much, so do not need to be tested on this component, as agility is not vital to their success.
Stork stand test	Gymnasts may hold balances still and so it is appropriate to work out how good their static balance is, with the aim of improving it via training.	Squash players are regularly on the move and seldom hold a still balance so will prioritise other components while training.
Multistage fitness test	Basketball players need good aerobic fitness and often run up and down the court, so they could gauge how developed their aerobic power is.	Golfers do not need to run up and down the fairway so it is less appropriate for them to test their aerobic power.
Wall toss test	Cricketers need good co-ordination and should be able to catch with both hands. The test would provide them with data on their co-ordination.	Rowers need to co-ordinate their arms and legs but do not need to catch, so the test is less specific for their needs.
Sit and reach test	Dancers need good flexibility in their legs so they can test their hamstring flexibility.	Swimmers need flexibility but do not need hamstring flexibility as much as a dancer would, so the test is less appropriate for them.
Sit-up bleep test	A goalkeeper in football may have to make regular saves involving movement of their upper and lower body so this test is appropriate for them to gauge their muscular endurance.	Marathon runners do need muscular endurance but the movement involved in the test (sitting up) does not mimic the movement of running so it is less appropriate for them.
Vertical jump test	Figure skaters need to jump using leg power so it is worth gauging their leg power score.	Kayaking does not require leg power to be applied vertically so the test score would be largely irrelevant.
Ruler drop test	Cricketers may need to react quickly using their hands to an approaching object (ball), so the test score has some relevance.	Snowboarders do need reaction time, but catching a ruler does not mimic any action they use, so it is less appropriate.
One rep max test	Boxers may need to exert maximal force in a punch so a test result would be relevant.	Middle-distance runners do not need to exert maximal force in a race so their test score would be largely irrelevant.
Handgrip dynamometer	Judo holds require maximal grip strength so the test score is worth knowing.	Sprinters have no need to use grip strength so their score would be irrelevant to their event.
30 m speed test	Basketball players may need to sprint the length of the court so their test score could prove useful for informing their sprint training.	Discus throwers have no need to use speed over a distance so their test score would be irrelevant to their event.

Study hint

If you are asked to evaluate how appropriate a test is, remember that the test provides you with a score that you could then improve. The evaluation focuses on whether that test score is relevant to the performer and their sport.

> ✔ **Check your understanding**
>
> 12 Have a look at the fitness tests. Can you think of some sports in which participants would benefit from having that component of fitness tested? Share your answers with your classmates.

Key terms

Qualitative data A measure of descriptions and opinions. More subjective than an objective appraisal, relating to quality of performance rather than quantity.

Quantitative data
A measurement which has been quantified as a number, e.g. time in seconds, or goals scored. There is no opinion expressed (qualitative). It is a fact. It is often the case that quantitative scores in fitness tests can be compared to national averages/ratings.

> **Rapid recall**
>
> Remember:
> **Quantity** – for quantitative. A quantity/number.
> **Quality** – for qualitative. A description or opinion; e.g. good or bad.

PRACTICE QUESTION

15 What do you understand by the term 'quantitative' in relation to fitness testing?
(1 mark)
Answers are on page 183.

PRACTICE QUESTIONS

10 State what equipment is needed for a multistage fitness test.
(2 marks)
11 Describe two benefits of using fitness tests. (2 marks)
12 Describe two limitations of using fitness tests. (2 marks)
13 Evaluate how appropriate an Illinois agility test score is for a netball player.
(3 marks)
14 Describe the protocol for carrying out a one rep max test. (3 marks)

Answers are on pages 182–3.

Qualitative and quantitative data

In relation to fitness testing, there are two terms that are often confused with each other – qualitative and quantitative. **Qualitative data** refers to descriptions and opinions. There does not need to be a score or number as such, it could simply be a subjective appraisal – for example, 'I did well in that test'. An individual who scores level 12, bleep 3 in the multistage fitness test may well look at the outcome qualitatively ('It was a good score but I could have done better') rather than just as a quantitative measure (level 12, bleep 3). **Quantitative data** deals with quantities. The measurement is classified as a number or a score. An individual may well look at the ruler drop test as a quantitative figure only – for example, 'I scored 15 cm'. (See Chapter 7, 'Use of data'.)

> **Activity 9**
>
> If you are able to carry out any fitness tests, compare your scores to national averages/ratings as shown on pages 53–9. Complete the table below by recording your quantitative score and insert a comment (opinion) about your score in the qualitative column; for example, 'I did really well'.
>
> ▼ **Table 3.17**
>
> | Test | Quantitative score | Qualitative appraisal |
> |---|---|---|
> | Illinois agility test | | |
> | Stork stand test | | |
> | Multistage fitness test | | |
> | Wall toss test | | |
> | Sit and reach test | | |
> | Sit-up bleep test | | |
> | Vertical jump test | | |
> | Ruler drop test | | |
> | One rep max test | | |
> | Handgrip dynamometer | | |
> | 30 m speed test | | |

The principles of training and their application to personal exercise and training programmes

The principles of training

The principles of training refer to key principles which should always be considered when designing a training programme. They act as a guide and should be considered for all prolonged periods of training. The principles are often remembered as SPORT:

- **S**pecificity
- **P**rogressive **O**verload
- **R**eversibility
- **T**edium

Specificity

Specificity refers to the fact that training should be specific to the needs of an individual and the demands of the sport that they take part in. For instance, a sprinter would be likely to do more anaerobic, speed and power work as they are all important for that activity. Any training done should be specific to the muscles used and the energy demands of the activity. Cyclists, for example, will not lift heavy arm weights as their legs are the specific body part that do most of the work.

Progressive overload

Although overload and progression are often discussed separately, they can also be grouped together. Overload is simply 'working harder than normal'. By doing this, the body will adapt and improve. However, progression refers to the fact that the overload should gradually be increased as the body adapts. The **progressive overload** on the body may mean gradually running further or lifting heavier weights. Training should sensibly overload the body as if it progresses too quickly, then an individual may suffer an injury.

Reversibility

Reversibility simply states that if an individual stops or decreases their training level, then fitness and performance are likely to drop. Muscle strength and cardio-vascular endurance can drop quite quickly if training is stopped altogether.

Tedium

Tedium refers to boredom. Training should be altered and varied to prevent an individual from suffering this.

Key term

Progressive overload Working harder than normal whilst gradually and sensibly increasing the intensity of training.

Key principles of overload

The principles of overload work on the idea that all training must overload the body's systems more than normal. Thus, overload is working harder than normal. It is a fundamental concept of training – you must work harder than normal (overload) in order for the body to adapt and improve. There are four basic principles of overload that are particularly important for exercise at a low to medium intensity:

- **F**requency
- **I**ntensity
- **T**ime
- **T**ype.

These four guidelines (FITT) should be used when designing the amount of overload to be adopted within a training programme. The details of FITT include:

- **Frequency** – refers to how often someone trains. Normally training should take place three or more times a week. As fitness increases, the ability to train more often also becomes possible.
- **Intensity** – refers to how hard you train: how fast you run/how heavy the weight is that you are lifting, etc. As fitness increases, the intensity should be suitably increased.
- **Time** – refers to how long you train for. As fitness increases, the length of time spent training may well increase.
- **Type** – refers to the type of training used; for example, continuous training. The training type must remain suitable to gain the specific fitness benefits that are required.

N.B. Further application of the principles of training are detailed in the next section on training types.

Types of training

There are many different types of training. However, they each have their benefits and specific purposes that match specific sporting needs. As with all training, it is important that safety is maintained at all times (see safety principles when training on page 73).

Circuit training

Circuit training is a flexible form of training in that it can be organised in a way to train many different components of fitness or to train a specific aspect. For example, a circuit training programme could be organised to train various components of fitness required by rugby players (speed, power, strength, etc.).

Circuit training involves different exercises being organised in different areas (or stations). Each station can be completely different from the next. Completion of all of the stations is called a 'circuit'.

Study hint

Overload does not mean to overburden the body, as that would be classed as overtraining. Overload is simply working harder than normal.

Rapid recall

When thinking about the principles of training, remember **SPORT:**
Specificity
Progressive **O**verload
Reversibility
Tedium

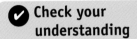 **Check your understanding**

13 Name and explain the principles of training and overload.

Answers are on page 181.

PRACTICE QUESTIONS

16 Describe what the principle of frequency is. (1 mark)

17 Explain what the term 'progressive overload' means. (2 marks)

18 Describe how the principle of specificity should be applied to a training programme. (2 marks)

Answers are on page 183.

Key term

Circuit training A series of exercises performed one after the other with a rest in between.

In order to organise circuit training, you need to consider many points:

- What is it that you hope to achieve; for example, to improve one component of fitness or several different ones?
- How much space and equipment is available?
- How much work and time should each station have and how much time should be allocated to rest between stations? This is known as the 'work to rest ratio'.

It is perhaps most common that a circuit is designed to train different components of fitness and work on different muscles/body parts. The stations could well make use of shuttles, step-ups, sit-ups, squat jumps, burpees, etc. (see Figure 3.26).

An example for rugby would incorporate the principles of training:

- Specificity – circuits would focus on specific muscles used and aspects of fitness required in rugby.
- Progressive overload – when the circuit is repeated, it should gradually be made harder.
- Reversibility – the circuit should be repeated regularly to prevent loss of fitness.
- Tedium – circuits should be varied to prevent boredom; for example, shuttle runs, press-ups, sit-ups, vertical jumps/squats, quick rugby passes, etc. (all relevant to rugby).
- Frequency – may well be completed three times a week.
- Intensity – depends on the fitness level but could start at 20 seconds of work/30 seconds of rest, with the circuit being completed 3 times. There may well be 2 minutes' rest between each circuit.
- Time – 30-minute session.
- Type – circuit training.

In the example above, it is key that the rugby player performs exercises that are appropriate and specific to rugby.

Advantages and disadvantages

Circuit training has many advantages:

- Exercises chosen can be simple to complex.
- The circuit can be manipulated to train different things; for example, repeated contraction of a muscle/muscle group to train muscular endurance.
- It can be varied to suit fitness level/age, etc.
- It is easy to monitor and alter – progressive overload can be applied by altering the work:rest ratio.

Disadvantages of circuit training include:

- An appropriate amount of space is required.
- It may require specialist equipment; for example, a medicine ball, benches, etc.
- It is difficult to gauge an appropriate work:rest ratio at the start.

Study hint

Remember that fitness tests actually *test* a component of fitness. A one-off test does *not train* the component of fitness. Training types, e.g. continuous training, actually train a component of fitness.

Activity 10

Try to design a 6–10-station circuit for a sport of your choice. Make sure the stations involve muscles/movements and energy demands which are suitable for the sport. Try to suggest an appropriate work:rest ratio for you. A starting point may be to consider:

- 20–30 seconds' work on each exercise
- 30 seconds' recovery between each exercise
- 3 sets with a 2–3-minute recovery between each set
- if you feel that your fitness level is higher, you can try more work and less rest.

Study hint

Remember that for circuit training, altering the time/rest/content of the circuit will determine what the fitness aim of the circuit is.

PRACTICE QUESTIONS

19 State three things to consider when designing a circuit training session.

(3 marks)

20 Describe what is meant by the term 'work:rest ratio'.

(1 mark)

Answers are on page 184.

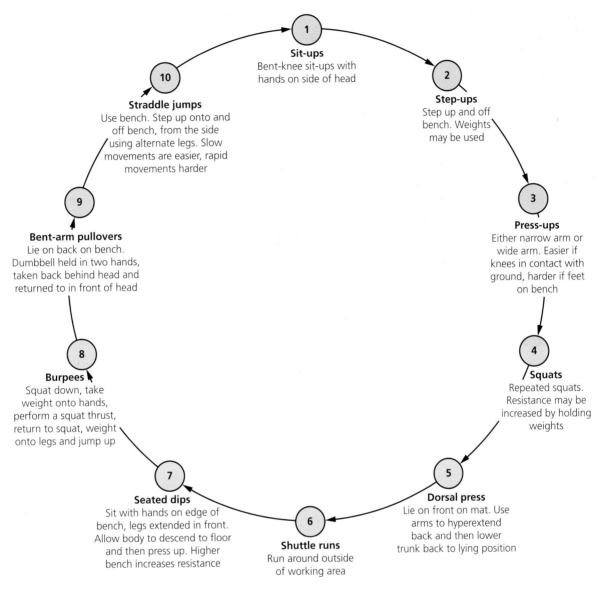

▲ **Figure 3.26** An example circuit.

Key term

Continuous training Exercising for a sustained period of time without rest. It improves cardio-vascular fitness. Sometimes referred to as 'steady state' training.

Continuous training

Continuous training involves any activity that can be sustained without rest and repeated over and over; for example, running, walking, rowing and swimming. Continuous training is used to improve cardio-vascular endurance and involves working at a constant rate or intensity. This is often referred to as 'steady state' exercise.

Continuous training is intended to work the aerobic energy system. Therefore, the difficulty or intensity should be hard enough to stress the body but with a suitable level of oxygen intake to ensure the exercise is 'aerobic'. To do this, it is most common to use your heart rate as a guide. This is known as working at your 'aerobic training zone'. In simple terms, you use your heart rate to tell you if you are working hard enough and prolonged continuous training makes your body more efficient at using oxygen.

▲ **Figure 3.27** Distance running is a form of continuous training.

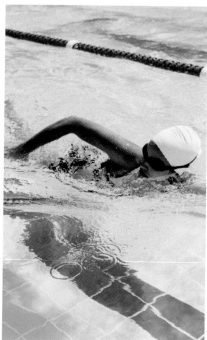

▲ **Figure 3.28** A long, steady state swim can be completed continuously.

Continuous training:

1 involves using your heart rate as a guide

2 improves your cardio-vascular endurance

3 improves your ability to work without suffering fatigue, thus your stamina improves.

N.B. Generally speaking, continuous training involves working without rests for 20 minutes or more.

Application to the principles of training:

- The activity being completed should be *specific* to the sport. For example, a marathon runner would tend not to swim in training as it is not specific to marathon running.

- The *frequency* for most continuous training programmes is a minimum of three times a week. However, a non-elite performer may only train once a week, whereas an elite performer may train on most days of the week.

- Continuous training as a *training type* should only be used for activities which are long and enduring.

Advantages and disadvantages of continuous training

Continuous training has many advantages:

- It can be done with little or no equipment; for example, simply go for a run.

- It improves aerobic fitness.

- Running can be done virtually anywhere.

- It is simple to do – keep doing the same movement over and over.

Study hint

An untrained individual will continuously work quite slowly, whereas an elite athlete will be able to continuously work at a higher intensity.

Disadvantages of continuous training:

● It can be boring/tedious.

● It can cause injury due to repetitive contractions.

● It can be time-consuming.

● It does not always match the demands of the sport; for example, in basketball, the players do not run at one speed continuously.

Calculating the correct intensity for continuous training

As previously mentioned, calculating the aerobic training zone involves using your heart rate as a guide. This involves calculating your maximum heart rate in beats per minute and working at a percentage of this:

● Calculate maximum heart rate (220 minus your age).

● Calculate aerobic training zone (60–80 per cent of maximal heart rate).

For example, a 16-year-old could calculate their aerobic training zone as follows:

● 220 − 16 (age) = 204

● 60–80 per cent of 204 = 122–163 beats per minute.

Thus, when training continuously, the heart rate should remain between 122 and 163 beats per minute.

▲ **Figure 3.29** Maximum heart rate is 220 minus age.

> ### Activity 11
>
> Can you calculate your aerobic training zone?
>
>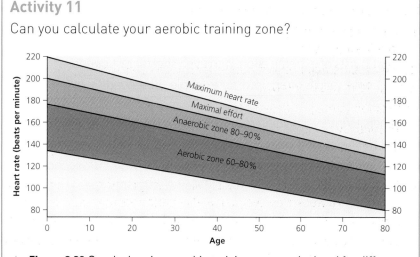
>
> ▲ **Figure 3.30** Graph showing aerobic training zones calculated for different age groups.
>
> As you can see in the image above, athletes may well decide to work at their anaerobic training zone of 80–90 per cent of maximal heart rate. This is useful for athletes whose activities are predominantly anaerobic; for example, 400 m runners. An elite 400 m runner may well complete a circuit of the track in less than 50 seconds, meaning that the aerobic system has not been utilised. Thus, such an athlete needs to prepare their body to perform at this intensity by training in their anaerobic zone.

Fartlek training

Like continuous training, fartlek training is generally used to improve cardio-vascular endurance. It is more varied than continuous training as the speed and intensity are varied. It is also known as 'speed play' and normally involves running.

Fartlek training involves:

- the speed being altered throughout; for example, sprint, jog, walk, jog, sprint
- exercises being incorporated into the activity
- running on different terrains; for example, running on the flat, on hills, etc.
- altering the intensity as this can allow the aerobic and anaerobic energy systems to be trained; for example, the more sprints involved, the more emphasis on the anaerobic system.

Interval training (high-intensity interval training)

Interval training is the name given to any type of training that involves alternating periods of work with periods of rest. It usually involves periods of intense exercise (working hard) coupled with periods of rest or low-intensity exercise. This form of interval training has become known as high-intensity interval training, or **HIIT** for short.

The intensity of interval training can be altered to suit the individual by altering the time working and the time resting.

HIIT basically means:

- short bursts of extreme effort with even shorter rest periods
- a 2:1 work ratio is often used; for example, 30 seconds' work, 15 seconds' rest.

Beginners to interval training may well start with:

- 2–3 HIIT sessions a week
- a 2:1 work ratio which may involve 20 seconds' work : 10 seconds' recovery, with the aim to increase this to 30 seconds' work : 15 seconds' recovery.

....
Study hint

The higher the intensity of the work period, the shorter the duration. For instance, 90–100 per cent effort cannot be carried out for long.

An example HIIT session for a beginner might include:

- Perform a thorough warm-up.
- Use: 30 seconds of work with 15 seconds of rest, working at 90 per cent of maximal effort.
- Perform press-ups, sit-ups, tricep dips, lunges, gluteal kicks or burpees.
- For example, 30 seconds of press-ups followed by 15 seconds of rest.
- Repeat three times.

PRACTICE QUESTIONS

21 Explain, with reference to a sport of your choice, why a performer would benefit from using continuous training. (2 marks)

22 Calculate the aerobic training zone of a 17-year-old athlete. (2 marks)

23 Evaluate how appropriate continuous training is to a 100m sprinter. (3 marks)

24 Describe how to complete fartlek training. (2 marks)

Answers are on page 184.

Key terms

Interval training Training method that incorporates periods of work followed by periods of rest, e.g. work, rest, work, rest.

HIIT (high-intensity interval training) An exercise strategy alternating periods of short intense anaerobic exercise with less intense recovery periods.

Advantages and disadvantages of HIIT

Advantages of HIIT training:

- It burns body fat and calories quickly.
- It can be altered easily to suit the individual.
- It can be completed relatively quickly.
- It can improve the anaerobic and aerobic energy systems.

Disadvantages of HIIT training:

- Extreme work can lead to injury.
- High levels of motivation are needed to complete the work.
- It can lead to dizziness and nausea.

Use of interval training

Interval training can be altered to suit the needs of a performer. HIIT involves short, high-intensity periods of work that improve the anaerobic system. However, research has shown that HIIT also has benefits for the aerobic system. Thus, it suits sports that make use of either energy system. If you're an elite performer athlete who needs energy systems to be trained for your sport, you can incorporate some sessions of sport-specific HIIT work. For example:

- sprints or high-intensity dribbling for football players
- vertical jumps for volleyball and basketball players
- heavy bag interval work for boxers.

You can also vary the length of the intervals.

- High-intensity anaerobic intervals can last anywhere from 10–60 seconds.
- Low-intensity and more aerobic intervals can last several minutes.

▲ **Figure 3.31** Burpees are common exercises used in interval training.

As with all forms of training, it is important to remember the principles of training. Intervals should involve exercises and movements which are specific to the sport, and intensity should match the intensity of the sport. For example, high-intensity sprints are fine if the sport requires some high-intensity sprinting!

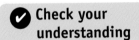

Check your understanding

14 Describe what HIIT is.

Answers are on page 181.

Activity 12

Why not try a basic HIIT training session using a 2:1 work : rest ratio? Include 30 seconds (each) of press-ups, burpees, sit-ups and lunges with 15 seconds of rest in between. Repeat the process three times.

Plyometric training

Plyometrics is a type of training that is used to increase power (strength × speed). It typically takes the form of bounding, hopping or jumping but can include medicine ball work, 'jump and clap' press-ups and box work. The aim of plyometrics is to use your body weight and gravity to stress the muscles involved. To use the example of box jumping:

1 The athlete jumps off the box.

2 As they land, their quadriceps lengthen (eccentric contraction).

3 This stores 'elastic energy' which can then be released through a further immediate jump.

4 The second jump (using the stored elastic energy) makes use of a stronger concentric contraction.

5 Thus, the eccentric contraction has caused a stronger concentric contraction.

▲ **Figure 3.32** Athlete using box jumping to increase their leg power.

Plyometrics can be used by any athlete who requires power. A basketball player or a triple jumper may well use plyometrics to increase their leg power for jumping. It is an excellent way to increase power but can result in injury due to the stress placed on the muscles and joints.

Static stretching

There are many different forms of stretching but perhaps the most common is **static stretching**. Static stretching is when a stretch is carried out and held (isometric contraction). It is an excellent way to increase flexibility – the range of movement at a joint.

Static stretches are often performed as part of a warm-up or cool-down but can be a form of training in themselves. They are used by performers who wish to improve their flexibility; for example, gymnasts and dancers.

Static stretching involves:

- stretching to the limit
- holding the stretch (isometrically) for approximately 30 seconds

PRACTICE QUESTIONS

25 Identify a component of fitness that will improve from the use of plyometric training. (1 mark)

26 Identify two benefits of using HIIT training. (2 marks)

Answers are on page 184.

Key terms

Static stretching Stretching to the limit and holding the stretch isometrically.

▲ **Figure 3.33** A static stretch being held.

> ✔ **Check your understanding**
>
> 15 Can you remember what static stretching is and some advantages and disadvantages of using it?
>
> Answers are on page 181.

PRACTICE QUESTIONS

27 Describe how static stretches are performed.
(2 marks)

28 Describe how the principle of specificity can be applied when using static stretches. (1 mark)

Answers are on page 184.

- avoiding overstretching as injury can occur
- using the correct technique; for example, avoiding dangerous stretches such as straight-legged toe touches.

Advantages and disadvantages of static stretching

Advantages of static stretching:

- It increases flexibility (the range of movement at a joint).
- It can be done by virtually everyone.
- It is relatively safe.

Disadvantages of static stretching:

- It can be time-consuming to stretch the whole body.
- Some muscles are easier to stretch than others.
- Overstretching can cause injury.

Weight training

Weight training can be used by anyone and can involve the use of free weights, resistance machines or any object which can safely be lifted. The beauty of weight training is that it allows individuals to use and, therefore, train individual muscles/muscle groups and can be designed to suit an individual's needs. A tennis player may well design a weights session to improve the muscles of the upper body and to increase power through shots, whereas a marathon runner may use weights on the lower body to improve muscular endurance in the legs.

Safety

Weight training should follow many safety guidelines:

- The exercise should be completed correctly using the correct technique; for example, the back should not be bent when picking weights up.
- If free weights are being used, a 'spotter' can be used to help in the initial lift, putting the weight down or to assist if the individual starts to struggle to lift the weight.

▲ **Figure 3.34** A spotter assisting with safety.

- Children should not lift heavy weights as they can damage growing bones.
- A thorough warm-up should be completed before lifting weights.
- A period of rest should follow every set (see below for description of sets/reps).

Calculating the correct intensity for weight training

As previously mentioned, weight training can be altered to suit the needs of an individual. In order to calculate the correct intensity, it is important that the person training knows what muscles they aim to train and how they wish to train them.

- **One repetition (or rep)** is completing one lift of the weight (up and down).
- **One set** is the completion of a number of reps.

In its simplest form, if an individual wishes to improve strength/power, they tend to lift heavy weights and complete few reps, but how do you calculate just how heavy the 'heavy' weights are?

One rep max

You may remember the one rep max test from earlier in the chapter. Calculating your one rep max is the first part of working out a suitable intensity of weight to lift. Once you know your one rep max, you can adopt the following principles:

- Strength/power training involves lifting heavy weights with a low number of reps:
  - This involves lifting over 70 per cent of your one rep max with approximately 3 sets of 4–8 reps.
  - For example, if a one rep max for bench press is 100 kg then the individual may well lift a 70 kg bar-bell, completing 3 sets of 6 reps (to improve strength).
- Muscular endurance involves lifting lighter weights with a high number of reps:
  - This involves lifting below 70 per cent of your one rep max with approximately 3 sets of 12–15 reps.
  - For example, if a one rep max for bench press is 100 kg then the individual may well lift a 50 kg bar-bell, completing 3 sets of 15 reps.

N.B. Using your one rep max to help you calculate intensity also ensures that overload is occurring. Remember that the principles of training should always be applied, so muscles being worked should be the ones usually used in the sport. Also, the choice of whether to calculate intensities for strength or muscular endurance will depend on the demand of the sport; for example, marathon runners would tend to use muscular endurance whereas discus throwers would tend to need strength.

Advantages and disadvantages of weight training

Advantages of weight training:

- It can easily be adapted for different fitness aims; for example, muscular strength or muscular endurance.
- It is relevant to all sports.

Key terms

One repetition (or rep)
Completing one lift of a weight (up and down).

One set The completion of a number of reps.

Rapid recall

Remember:
Strength/power – high weight/low reps
Muscular endurance – low weight/high reps

Activity 13

If you had a one rep max of 50 kg, how could you calculate intensity to improve muscular endurance?

Answers are on page 187.

✓ Check your understanding

16 Calculate suitable sets and reps for strength and/or muscular endurance using one rep max.

Answers are on page 181.

PRACTICE QUESTIONS

29 Describe how an appropriate intensity for improving muscular endurance using weight training can be calculated. (2 marks)

30 Using a sport of your choice, explain why a performer may use weight training to improve their strength. (2 marks)

31 Discuss the use of the principles of training by a weight-lifter who decides to train using weight training. (9 marks)

Answers are on pages 184–5.

Activity 14

In twos, without using your books, see how many training safety considerations you can remember.

Rapid recall

The word SAFER can be used to remember aspects of safety when training:
S – **S**tretches should be completed as part of a thorough warm-up.
A – **A**ppropriate intensity should be used.
F – **F**ootwear and clothing should be appropriate to allow support/ movement.
ER – **E**xercise and **R**est; allow appropriate rest in between exercise sessions.

- It is relatively straightforward to carry out – you simply need something to lift.
- Strength gains can occur.

Disadvantages of weight training:
- Heavy weights can increase blood pressure.
- Injury can occur if weights are too heavy or incorrect technique is used.
- Calculating one rep max requires high levels of motivation.

Safety principles when training

All training types must be completed with safety in mind. As a result, many factors must be considered to prevent injury. These are summarised below:

▲ **Figure 3.35** Considering safety when training can help to prevent injury.

- The training type and the intensity used should match the training purpose; for example, training for aerobic sports may well use continuous training at 60–80 per cent of maximal heart rate.
- A warm-up and cool-down should be completed prior to and after training.
- Overtraining should be avoided; for example, appropriate weights should be lifted.
- Appropriate clothing and footwear should be worn which protect/ support and allow movement.
- Taping/bracing should be used as necessary to protect and support areas of weakness.
- Hydration should be maintained with fluid intake.
- Stretches should not be overstretched or bounced.
- The technique used should be correct; for example, lifting technique.
- Appropriate rest should be given in between sessions to allow for recovery.
- Spotters should be used when weight training if heavy weights are being attempted.

Specific training technique (high-altitude training)

One specific training type used by elite athletes is high-altitude training. High-altitude training involves carrying out training at high altitude; that is, high above sea-level. Many athletes need to travel to different parts of the world in order to gain access to appropriate training areas at appropriate heights. High-altitude training is a form of aerobic training; that is, it trains the aerobic energy system and can improve a person's cardio-vascular endurance.

How high-altitude training is carried out:

- The individual trains at a high altitude – usually 2000 m or more above sea-level.
- There is less oxygen in the air at high altitude. This makes training very difficult as the body finds it harder to carry oxygen to the working muscles.
- As a result, the body compensates by making more red blood cells to carry what oxygen there is in the air.

Therefore, in simple terms:

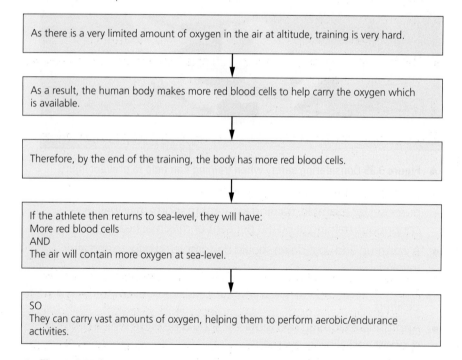

▲ **Figure 3.36** Summary of high-altitude training.

In summary, altitude training benefits:

- endurance athletes – for example, marathon runners
- athletes who work aerobically – that is, athletes who sustain exercise over a long period of time.

N.B. Altitude training has virtually no benefit for anaerobic athletes.

Study hint
Altitude training does not have any benefit for athletes who perform anaerobic exercise, e.g. sprinters, discus throwers.

✓ **Check your understanding**

17 Describe the positives and negatives of training at altitude.
Answers are on page 181.

Study hint
You may be required to explain the basics of altitude training – less oxygen at altitude, body compensates by making more red blood cells, etc. However, you do not need to know how to calculate intensities for training at altitude.

PRACTICE QUESTIONS

32 Evaluate whether altitude training is useful to a sprinter. (2 marks)
33 State three negative effects that altitude training can have. (3 marks)
34 Evaluate how appropriate altitude training would be for a sprinter and for a marathon runner. (9 marks)

Answers are on page 185.

Study hint
It is a common mistake for students to confuse the word 'seasons' with spring, summer, autumn, winter. Remember that seasons refer to pre-season, competition season and post-season.

▲ **Figure 3.37** Altitude training increases red blood cell count.

High-altitude training is a specific form of training and is complex in that many athletes need to travel to train in a foreign country. It has many limitations/negative effects:

- It can be very difficult to complete training. Some people find it too hard and actually train less than if they were at sea-level.
- This means that fitness can actually be lost.
- Some athletes can experience altitude sickness – a feeling of nausea.
- The benefits are lost quite quickly – that is, when returning to sea-level, red blood cell count starts to decrease again.

The three training seasons

Although not all sports follow distinctive seasonal patterns, there are three 'traditional' parts to the training season which are still followed by many performers:

- pre-season (also known as preparation)
- competition season (also known as peak/playing season)
- post-season (also known as transition).

Each of the traditional training seasons has common aims and objectives:

- Pre-season/preparation – the aim is to improve general and aerobic fitness. This is often done via aerobic training; for example, long runs. It is also an aim to improve specific fitness needs so that the performer is ready for the competitive season; for example, agility for tennis. A swimmer may well undertake long duration swims, before working on specific aspects of their technique. Similarly, a cyclist may attempt to increase their general and aerobic fitness on a bike, whilst also working on specific skill aspects like climbing.

- Competition/peak/playing season – the aim is to maintain fitness levels. The performer should be at peak fitness and will aim to maintain this. They may well also work on specific skills used in their sport.

- Post-season/transition – the aim is to rest and recover from the season. Many performers also continue some light aerobic training so that fitness levels do not drop too low.

▲ **Figure 3.38** Long, enduring runs may be included as part of pre-season training to improve aerobic fitness levels for activities that require running. The method of building up general aerobic fitness should be specific to the sport, e.g. cycling for a cyclist.

Effective use of warm-up and cool-down

Warming up and cooling down are two very important aspects that a performer must consider to help prevent injury or ill effects of exercising.

Warming up

There are several parts that a good warm-up should include in order to be fully effective:

- a gradual pulse-raising activity – for example, fast walk/jog/light swim to increase the amount of oxygen to the working muscles
- stretching – of all relevant muscles
- skill-based practices/familiarisation activities; for example, ball work in football
- mental preparation – starting to get focused, using techniques to control arousal; for example, deep breathing.

By completing these parts of a warm-up, the individual will benefit in the following ways:

- Body temperature will increase, ready for exercise.
- Stretching will increase the range of movement possible.
- There will be a gradual (not overdemanding) increase in effort towards 'competition pace' – that is, you gradually work up to the intensity required for the game/event.
- You will be focused and psychologically prepared.
- Movement skills that will be used have been practised before starting the game/match/event.
- There will be less chance of suffering injury.
- There will be an increase in the amount of oxygen being carried to the working muscles – helping with the production of energy.

Rapid recall

For the training seasons, remember **PA CMA TRA**:
PA – **P**re-season, build **A**erobic fitness
CMA – **C**ompetition, **M**aintain **A**erobic fitness
TRA – **T**ransition, **R**est, small amounts of **A**erobic work

PRACTICE QUESTIONS

35 Describe the main aim of the post-season/transition section of training. (1 mark)

Answers are on page 185.

▲ **Figure 3.39** Warming up.

Rapid recall

The sections of a warm-up can be remembered by using **GRASS M**:
GRAdual pulse raiser
Stretches
Skill-based activity
Mental preparation

▲ **Figure 3.40** A pulse raiser is vital as part of a warm-up.

Cooling down

Performing a cool-down is often overlooked and undervalued by sports performers. However, it holds a high level of importance and should not be ignored. An effective cool-down should include:

- an activity to maintain an elevated breathing and heart rate; for example, walk, jog
- a gradual reduction in intensity; for example, jog to light jog to walk
- stretching of all main muscles used in the activity.

The benefits of cooling down can be summarised as follows:

- It allows the body to start to recover after exercising.
- It helps with the removal of lactic acid, carbon dioxide and waste products.
- It can help to prevent the delayed onset of muscle soreness, sometimes referred to as DOMS.

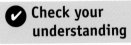

Check your understanding

18 Describe the parts of an effective warm-up and cool-down.

Answers are on page 181.

▲ **Figure 3.41** Cooling down should include some stretches.

Activity 15

In twos, design a suitable warm-up and cool-down for a sport of your choice.

Study hint
Remember: It is important that a cool-down should allow the body to gradually slow down. Intensity of exercise should be gradually reduced.

PRACTICE QUESTIONS

36 State the main components of a good warm-up.　　(3 marks)
37 Identify two benefits of cooling down.　　(2 marks)

Answers are on page 185.

Rapid recall

The benefits of warming up can be remembered by using **TIMO**:
T – **T**emperature increases
I – **I**njury chances reduce
M – **M**ental preparation
O – **O**xygen to the working muscles (more)

Similarly, the benefits of cooling down can be remembered using **R COMS**:
R – (Start to) **R**ecover gradually
C – **C**arbon dioxide removed
OMS – **O**nset of **M**uscle **S**oreness reduced

Summary

- There is some relationship between health and fitness but fitness does not guarantee being healthy (and vice versa).
- Performers in sporting activities need various components of fitness, but these vary in importance from sport to sport.
- Fitness testing can help you to develop a training programme, evaluate strengths and weaknesses, assist in the setting of goals and prevent tedium.
- When carrying out fitness tests, the correct procedures and safety considerations must be followed.
- Quantitative data refers to quantities or numbers/facts.
- Qualitative data refers to the quality of something. It is an opinion.
- The principles of training should be applied when undertaking any training programme: specificity, progressive overload, reversibility, tedium.
- The principles of overload should be applied when undertaking any training programme: frequency, intensity, time and type.
- Suitable training types should be chosen to develop the desired components of fitness relevant to the sport.
- Warming up and cooling down should be part of any training session.

Chapter 4 Sports psychology

Chapter objectives

- What is a skill and what is an ability?
- Classification of skills
- Justification of classification
- Definitions of types of goals
- The use and evaluation of setting performance and outcome goals in sporting examples
- The use of SMART targets to improve and/or optimise performance
- Basic information processing model
- Examples and evaluation of the effectiveness of the use of types of guidance with reference to beginners and elite level performers
- Examples and evaluation of the effectiveness of the use of types of feedback with reference to beginners and elite level performers

- Arousal and the inverted U theory
- How optimal arousal levels vary according to the skill being performed in a physical activity or sport
- How arousal can be controlled using stress management techniques before or during a sporting performance
- Understand the difference between direct and indirect aggression with application to specific sporting examples
- Understand the characteristics of introvert and extrovert personality types, including examples of sports which suit these particular personality types
- Intrinsic and extrinsic motivation as used in sporting examples

Key terms

Skill A learned action/behaviour with the intention of bringing about predetermined results with maximum certainty and minimum outlay of time and energy.

Abilities Inherited from your parents, abilities are stable traits that determine an individual's potential to learn or acquire skills.

Rapid recall

The word skill has two 'L's. The word ability only has one. The one with the most 'L's is the one that has to be **Learned**.

✔ Check your understanding

1 What is a skill and what is an ability?

Answers are on page 187.

What is a skill and what is an ability?

As part of GCSE Physical Education, you need to understand the difference in meaning of the words 'skill' and 'ability'. Although these terms are sometimes used in the same way by sports commentators on television, they do in fact mean different things.

Skills are learned and, when mastered, are consistently done in a way that looks easy and uses the correct technique. Although skills can be mental (thinking skills), we tend to think of sporting skills as physical; for example, passing a netball or shooting in basketball.

Abilities are inherited. They are known as 'traits' which remain fairly stable during your life. Balance, agility and co-ordination are examples of abilities you are born with. Abilities can help performers to learn skills; for example, greater inherited balance will help a gymnast learn the skills required on a balance beam.

▲ **Figure 4.1** A gymnast showing incredible balance (ability).

▲ **Figure 4.2** A rugby player performing the skill of passing.

Classification of skills

You are not able to perform sporting skills immediately when you are born; they must be learned. In learning how to perform skills in sport (such as a pass or a dribble in hockey), performers tend to learn the basic skill first followed by more advanced versions.

For example, you may learn how to simply kick a ball first. Then you may learn how to strike a ball with some power using the laces, before learning how to bend a ball with the inside or outside of the foot.

Skill classification

To understand skilled actions in sport, it can help to classify skills into categories or groups. This is called skill classification and allows us to better understand basic, commonly performed skills. In doing so, skills can be positioned or placed onto continua (lines). These skill classification lines are called:

- the **basic** to **complex** continuum
- the **open** to **closed** continuum
- the **self-paced** to **externally paced** continuum
- the **gross** to **fine** continuum.

The basic to complex continuum

Basic —————————————————————————— Complex

In deciding where a sporting skill falls on the basic to complex continuum, certain factors must be considered:

- Who is the skill being taught to; for example, a beginner or a more experienced performer?
- How much decision-making is involved – do you have to use high level thinking?
- Are the movements easy to carry out without much experience?

▼ **Table 4.1** Comparison of basic and complex skills.

BASIC SKILL	COMPLEX SKILL
Few decisions to be made.	Complex decision-making.
Few decisions actually affect the success of the movement.	Lots of decisions to be made in order to be successful.
Tend to be taught as a beginner.	Tend to be taught after experiencing success in basic skills.
Learned fairly quickly.	Can take considerable time to master.
Walking is a basic skill. Jumping is a basic skill.	High jump is a complex skill requiring co-ordinated running in an accurate bend, followed by a correctly timed jump and effective body position to clear the bar.

▲ **Figure 4.3** The skill of free-throw shooting in basketball. Skills are actions which have been learned.

Study hint

You should be able to choose and justify the appropriate classifications in relation to sporting examples.

✓ **Check your understanding**

2 Can you remember how to determine whether a skill is basic or complex?

Answers are on page 187.

▲ **Figure 4.4** A forward roll is basic.

Figure 4.5 A double somersault is more complex.

Key terms

Open skill A skill which is performed in a certain way to deal with a changing or unstable environment, e.g. to outwit an opponent.

Closed skill A skill which is not affected by the environment or performers within it. It tends to be done the same way each time.

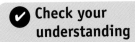
Check your understanding

3 What makes a skill open or closed?

Answers are on page 187.

Study hint

The environment does NOT refer to the weather. It refers to the situation in which the skill is being performed, e.g. who is there, what they are doing, etc.

Activity 1

Look at the illustration of a forward roll and the picture of the double somersault. In pairs, classify both these skills and justify your choice of answers.

Answers are on page 191.

The open to closed continuum

Open _____ Closed

In deciding where a sporting skill falls on the open to closed continuum, certain factors must be considered:

● What is going on in the environment when performing the skill?
● Is the environment stable – is it changing or not?
● Do other people affect how the skill might be done; for example, opposition players?
● Do decisions need to be made as to how to do the skill because of things going on within the environment? For example, an opponent may try to tackle you in rugby so you change direction to avoid them.

▼ **Table 4.2** Comparison of open and closed skills.

OPEN SKILL	CLOSED SKILL
Unstable environment.	Stable environment.
The way you do the skill is affected by people around you.	The way you do the skill is not affected by people around you.
You may decide to do the skill differently to 'normal' because of the environment, e.g. what your opponents are doing.	You will not change how you do the skill. It is done the same way every time because there are no factors/people within the environment to affect how you do it.
The skill is often externally paced.	The skill is typically self-paced.
Examples: A football pass may be carried out in a certain way to avoid oncoming opponents, e.g. passed round them or chipped over them. A rugby tackle may need to be performed in a certain way to catch and stop a moving opponent, e.g. if they get past you, the tackle becomes a rear tackle rather than a front tackle. Both skills have been performed in a certain way because of opposition players. They may be performed differently next time.	Examples: A somersault in gymnastics. You would try to replicate/repeat the skill in the same way, as you do not need to change how you do it. A javelin throw is replicated each time. There is nothing to affect the direction of throw. The way you carry out these skills is not affected by factors or people around you (in the environment). You aim to carry these out the same way each time.

Figure 4.6 shows an athlete throwing the javelin. She aims to repeat the action of the throw each time. Nothing in the environment changes how it is done. She does not have to react to opponents when throwing. It is repeatable and self-paced. It is therefore a closed skill.

PRACTICE QUESTIONS

1 Describe a difference between a skill and an ability. (1 mark)
2 Classify the following skills as either open or closed. Justify your answers.
- A shot in football during open play.
- A pass/setting in volleyball.
- A forward roll in gymnastics.
- A high jump.
- A goalkeeper trying to save a penalty flick in hockey.
(5 marks)

Answers are on page 188.

▲ **Figure 4.6** An athlete throwing the javelin.

The self-paced to externally paced continuum

Self-paced _____ **Externally paced**

In deciding where a sporting skill falls on the self-paced to externally paced continuum, certain factors must be considered:
- Who or what controls when the movement/skill should start?
- Who or what controls the speed, rate or pace at which the movement/ skill is performed?

▼ **Table 4.3** Comparison of self-paced and externally paced skills.

SELF-PACED SKILL	EXTERNALLY PACED SKILL
The start of the movement is controlled by the performer. For example, when performing a long jump, you choose when to start the run up.	The start of the movement is controlled by external factors. For example, when receiving a badminton serve, you only start your returning shot after your opponent has performed their serve.
The speed, pace or rate of the movement is controlled by you. For example, when running a long-distance race, you decide how fast to run.	The speed, pace or rate of the movement is controlled by external factors. For example, when marking an opponent in netball, your movement is affected by the movement of your opponent.

✔ Check your understanding

4 What makes a skill self-paced or externally paced?

Answers are on page 187.

Study hint
A skill is self-paced if you decide when to start the skill without a significant influence from an external source.

Key terms
Self-paced skill The skill is started when the performer decides to start it. The speed, rate or pace of the skill is controlled by the performer.

Externally paced skill The skill is started because of an external factor. The speed, rate or pace of the skill is controlled by external factors, e.g. an opponent.

▲ **Figure 4.7** Match sprint velodrome cycling.

▲ **Figure 4.8** Pole vault.

Activity 2

In pairs, try to classify the following as either self-paced or externally paced skills. In doing so, make sure you can explain your choice.

- A javelin throw.
- A sprint start.
- A conversion (kick) in rugby.

Answers are on page 191.

In match sprint velodrome cycling, two cyclists cycle head to head over three laps of the track. They usually go slowly for most of the race but have to respond if their opponent starts to sprint. Responding to your opponent's speed would make the skill externally paced.

In pole vault, you control how fast you run up. This is self-paced.

The gross to fine continuum

Gross _____Fine

In deciding where a sporting skill falls on the gross to fine continuum, certain factors must be considered:

- How much of the body is being used to perform the skill?
- Are large muscle groups being used or small muscle groups?

▼ **Table 4.4** Comparison of gross and fine skills.

GROSS SKILL	FINE SKILL
Involves big movements of the body.	Involves small, precise movements.
Involves the use of large muscle groups.	Involves the use of small muscle groups.
Movements tend not to rely on accuracy and precision, e.g. kicking a ball, running, throwing a javelin.	Movements tend to involve precision and accuracy, e.g. dart throw, archery, snooker, table tennis block shot.

Study hint

Large movements of the body tend to be gross skills whereas small, precise movements tend to be fine skills.

Check your understanding

5 What makes a skill gross or fine?

Answers are on page 187.

PRACTICE QUESTIONS

3 Discus is an athletic event involving a rotation and a throw. Classify a discus throw as either gross or fine. Justify your choice.
(2 marks)

4 Analyse how the skill of swimming may change from being a self-paced skill to an externally paced skill in a race. (6 marks)

Answers are on page 189.

▲ **Figure 4.9** A rugby tackle involves large muscle groups and is a gross skill.

▲ **Figure 4.10** A net shot in badminton requires precision and only a small movement of the wrist. It is a fine skill.

Goal setting

In order to improve or to provide motivation, sports performers often set themselves goals or have goals set by their coaches. Goal setting gives performers a target to aspire to and helps to prepare performers both physically and mentally.

Although goals generally follow the principles of SMART goals (see below), for GCSE there are generally two types of goal which can be considered by performers/coaches:

- performance goals
- outcome goals.

Performance goals

A **performance goal** does not involve the performer comparing themselves to other performers. They simply compare themselves against what they have already done or suggest what they are going to do.

A 100 m runner could set the following performance goals:

- to make a better start than they achieved in the last race
- to aim to time their dip at the line better than they did in the last race.

An ice skater may set the following performance goals:

- to make their footwork smoother and more controlled than it was in their last routine
- to control a spin better than they controlled it in their last routine.

Outcome goals

Outcome goals are simply used to judge the end result. They usually involve comparison with other competitors. The performance standards may not be that important. It is the outcome that matters.

For example, a football player:

- may wish to win the match
- may wish to score two goals to increase their team's goal difference.

The use of performance and outcome goals

Performers should really set themselves short-term and long-term goals. In doing so, they have short-term targets to achieve and can then remain motivated to achieve their next goal.

However, it is important to realise that performance and outcome goals (used together) might not always be beneficial for all performers. Although they can be combined, it is generally accepted that beginners may be better avoiding outcome goals as they rely on factors that cannot be controlled; for example, other performers.

Beginners (usually) prefer to avoid outcome goals as failure could demotivate them. It might be that winning may be an unrealistic goal for some performers. Beginners may be better concentrating on performance

▲ **Figure 4.11** A sprinter may have a performance goal of getting a good start or beating a personal best.

Key terms

Performance goals Personal standards to be achieved. The performer compares their performance against what they have already done or suggests what they are going to do. There is no comparison with other performers.

Outcome goals Focus on the end result, e.g. winning.

▲ **Figure 4.12** Greg Rutherford, Olympic long jump champion in 2012.

> ✔ **Check your understanding**
>
> 6 What is the difference between a performance goal and an outcome goal?
>
> Answers are on page 187.

Study hint

Performance goals are more appropriate than outcome goals for beginners.

▲ **Figure 4.13** Performers who have a SMART goal to achieve tend to be motivated to achieve it and persist in their attempts to accomplish it.

goals and trying to better themselves without worrying about their result compared to others.

On the other hand, elite athletes are often driven by one thing and one thing only – winning! The use of performance goals can help to motivate them to work on individual aspects of performance, but the outcome goal of winning, or gaining a medal, may increase their desire to succeed even more. The best performers persist, even when they fail, and become even more determined to succeed next time.

As Olympic champion, long jumper Greg Rutherford was under extreme pressure to perform well at the Glasgow 2014 Commonwealth Games. In terms of an outcome goal, it was simple for Greg – he wanted to win, stating 'That's what it's all about for me'. He achieved this outcome goal by winning a gold medal.

However, in the lead up to the event, Rutherford was also known to have set himself performance goals to drive hard in the sprint and stay tall at take-off.

PRACTICE QUESTIONS

5 Complete the table below. What performance and outcome goals could be set for the badminton beginner and elite javelin thrower? (4 marks)

▼ **Table 4.5**

	Performance goal	Outcome goal
A complete beginner playing badminton against a more experienced player		
An elite level javelin thrower performing at the Olympic Games		

Answers are on page 189.

SMART target setting

It is generally accepted that whatever goals are set, they should follow the SMART principles. The goal should be:

S – Specific – specific to the demands of the sport/muscles used/movements involved

M – Measurable – it must be possible to measure whether it has been achieved

A – Accepted – it must be accepted/agreed by the performer and the performer's coach, if they have one

R – Realistic – it must actually be possible to complete the goal; the person is physically capable

T – Time-bound – it must be set over a fixed period of time

> **Activity 3**
>
> With a partner or in small groups, try to explain what each part of SMART stands for. You could take a letter each to start with and do this as a 'Mexican wave' around the table.
>
> Answers are on page 191.

Basic model of information processing

Having looked at what a skill is earlier in this chapter, it is now important to understand how skills are chosen and how decisions are made.

Information processing is using available information in order to make a decision; this is choosing a suitable skill or movement.

In choosing an appropriate skill to use in sport, you also have to decide how to use it.

Beginners tend to attempt to perform a skill the same way every time, whereas elite sportspeople are able to vary how they use skills.

For example, a beginner serving a tennis ball may simply try to serve it. They have one serve that they can use, so attempt it and hope that it goes in. Elite players can serve a tennis ball in many ways. They can serve with speed, with spin, etc.

▲ **Figure 4.14** In a penalty kick, the performer will choose *how* to kick the ball, e.g. with power, placement, etc.

▲ **Figure 4.15** Elite tennis players have a vast array of serves that they use when performing.

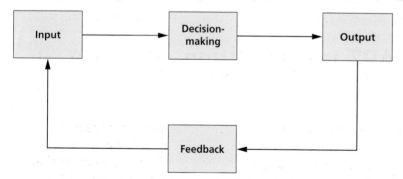

▲ **Figure 4.16** Basic model of information processing.

Input

- The performer takes in information from the environment/display (for example, what they can see, hear and feel).
- They choose what is the most relevant signal/cue/stimulus/piece of information to them at that time.
- For example, the performer uses sight when watching a cricket ball flying through the air. This is called selective attention. It is a filtering process whereby they pick out the most important parts of the display that are relevant and discard those that are not.

Key terms

Basic model of information processing This shows the simple processes that a performer carries out in order to decide what skill to use.

Information processing This is making decisions. It involves gathering data from the display (senses) and prioritising the most important stimuli to make a suitable decision, e.g. choosing a suitable skill.

Study hint

You need to be able to draw the information processing model (Figure 4.16). You may also have to say what happens at each stage of the model.

As you can see from the model, there are four parts – input, decision-making, output and feedback.

Activity 4

Try to draw the various stages of a basic information processing model and fill in the names of each stage.

Answers are on page 192.

Decision-making

- This is where the performer selects an appropriate response (movement/skill) from memory; perhaps one they have used in this situation before.
- The short-term memory (STM) is the 'working memory'. Information from the display that has been attended to is held in the short-term memory for a short time (approximately 30 seconds). If your attention is directed to something else, the information is lost.
- The long-term memory (LTM) holds information that has been rehearsed and stored. Thus, if a memory or past experience is relevant to what is required at that time, it is compared to information in the short-term memory so that a suitable decision can be made.
- The cricketer may have attended to the sight of a ball in the air. He/she recalls the memory of a previous catch (from LTM) and compares it to what he/she is currently seeing (STM) so that the decision to catch can take place.

Output

- The decision chosen is sent to the appropriate muscles to carry out the response.
- For example, impulses are sent to arms and hands to start the appropriate muscular movements for the catch to take place.

Feedback

- Information is received from within themselves (intrinsic) and/or from others (extrinsic) regarding the success (or not) of the action.
- Feedback is received while doing the skill as well as after the skill.
- Note, the feedback received may affect how you complete this skill in the future.
- For example, you can feel the ball in your hands (intrinsic) and your teammates cheer when you catch it (extrinsic).

Activity 5

Describe how each stage of a basic information processing model is used when performing a sporting *skill* of your choice. The example below shows the stages of information processing when making the decision to play a smash shot in badminton.

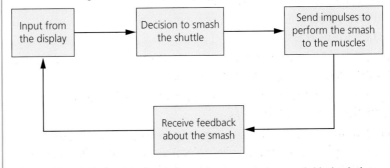

▲ **Figure 4.17** Example of an information processing model in badminton.

PRACTICE QUESTIONS

6 Describe the process of 'selective attention'. (1 mark)

7 Explain how the input stage and the decision-making stage are used when hitting a tennis ball. (4 marks)

8 Evaluate the importance of each stage of a basic information processing model in making the decision to perform a sports skill of your choice. (9 marks)

Answers are on page 189.

✔ **Check your understanding**

7 What are the four stages of a basic information processing model?

Answers are on page 187.

Guidance

Having already performed or whilst learning how to perform a skill, performers need help from their coach or teacher in order to improve. Such help may come in the form of **guidance**.

There are four types of guidance:

- visual (being shown something)
- verbal (being told something/given instructions)
- manual (physical assistance with the movement)
- mechanical (use of objects/aids).

In order to choose what type of guidance to use, the biggest factor to consider is the experience level of the performer. A beginner is obviously in need of a lot of guidance to allow them to learn and progress. However, an elite, experienced performer may also require guidance to fine-tune performance or stop minor errors.

Visual guidance

Visual guidance is simply when the performer can see something. For example, a coach, teacher or fellow performer may well show them something.

Visual guidance includes:

- demonstration of technique or skill by another person; for example, the coach
- footage of performance via DVD, analysis software, slow motion, different angles
- still images; for example, posters or photographs.

For a beginner, visual guidance is very important so that they can see and start to understand what they are expected to do. If a coach explains a new skill to a performer for the first time, the performer will benefit from seeing it first. Verbal guidance may not be enough for a beginner without also getting to see the skill.

Demonstrations for beginners will work only if they are:

- clear
- relatively concise
- quick
- easy to understand
- of a realistic standard for the beginner to copy or aim towards
- backed up with simplistic verbal guidance (allowing the performer to concentrate on the main points).

Study hint

Make sure you are able to identify appropriate examples of guidance for beginners and elite level performers.

Key terms

Guidance Methods to help a learner understand movement patterns.

Visual guidance Guidance that you can see, e.g. a demonstration.

▲ **Figure 4.18** A coach uses visual guidance to show performers how the skill should be done.

▲ **Figure 4.19** The golf coach manually guides the beginner golfer to help them use the correct technique.

For elite performers, visual guidance is not used as much. However, it can be used to highlight minor errors in technique via analysis software or slow motion. It is combined with verbal guidance as the performer is able to understand complex terminology.

Verbal guidance

Verbal guidance is commonly used with visual guidance. It involves another person (usually a coach or teacher) telling the learner what they are doing right or wrong. It can also be used as a key word trigger; for example, 'point your toes'.

Verbal guidance may involve:

- a coach/teacher talking to a performer, highlighting technique
- a coach/teacher highlighting a key 'trigger point'; for example, 'and push' when a performer hits the trampoline.

Verbal guidance will only work for beginners if:

- it actually relates to the visual guidance being given
- it is not too long or complex, so that the beginner understands what is being said.

Verbal guidance can work with elite performers. It might:

- be longer and more complex than it is for beginners
- not need to be supplemented with visual guidance as elite performers are likely to know what the skill should look like.

Manual/mechanical guidance

Manual and **mechanical guidance** are very similar and can be roughly grouped together. They involve either physically moving the performer, such as the coach supporting the movement through physical touch, or using mechanical aids, such as arm bands. The physical support or use of mechanical aids allows the performer to produce the required movement when they may not have been able to do it by themselves.

Manual/mechanical guidance may involve:

- physically guiding the performer; for example, the coach moving the learner's arm through the correct motion of a forehand drive in golf

Key terms

Verbal guidance Guidance that is provided by another person speaking to you.

Manual guidance Physically moving the performer, e.g. the coach supporting the movement through physical touch.

Mechanical guidance Using mechanical aids to assist a performer, e.g. using a float in swimming or a harness in trampolining.

- supporting the performer for safety, so that the required movement takes place; for example, supporting a gymnast whilst they try to do a vault.

Sporting examples include:

- the use of arm bands (mechanical)
- the use of a trampoline harness (mechanical)
- holding a performer's wrist in tennis to guide them through the movement of a forehand shot (manual)
- standing behind a golfer at the driving range and holding their hands through a golf swing (manual).

Manual/mechanical guidance can be useful for beginners because:

- it can help the beginner feel safe/supported
- it can help the beginner complete the required movement for a skill
- it can help the performer start to understand how a movement should feel (intrinsic feedback).

However, manual/mechanical guidance must be used to develop the correct movement as mistakes in technique (as a result of using manual/mechanical guidance) might start to become the normal learned response. Manual/mechanical guidance should not be used for too long as performers can become reliant upon it. Elite performers do not usually require manual or mechanical guidance unless unexpected flaws in technique start to occur.

Table 4.6 summarises the differences between beginners and elite performers.

▼ **Table 4.6** Comparison of beginners and elite performers.

BEGINNERS	ELITE PERFORMERS
Definitely need visual guidance to understand what a skill looks like.	Are unlikely to need visual guidance other than to highlight minor faults, e.g. use of slow motion.
Also need verbal guidance but it should not be too long or complex.	Will need verbal guidance. It is likely to be longer and more complex than that given to a beginner. It allows fine-tuning of technique.
Are also likely to need manual/mechanical guidance to support them through the correct technique.	Elite performers are unlikely to need manual/mechanical guidance unless there is an unexpected flaw in technique.

- Visual guidance is used more for beginners.
- Verbal guidance is used more for elite performers.
- Mechanical guidance is used more for beginners.

Beginners are likely to need visual guidance first with simple verbal instructions. They may also need manual/mechanical guidance.

Feedback

Feedback is simply information that a performer receives. It can be received before, during or after performance and can come from a variety of sources:

- from within (intrinsic)
- from others (extrinsic)
- from results/scores (extrinsic).

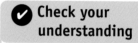

PRACTICE QUESTIONS

9 State how manual and mechanical guidance can differ. (2 marks)

10 For a beginner in the sport of basketball, describe how visual, verbal and manual/mechanical guidance might be provided. (3 marks)

11 Evaluate how appropriate visual and verbal guidance are for a beginner in a sport of your choice. (6 marks)

Answers are on pages 189–90.

✔ Check your understanding

8 What types of guidance suit beginners and/or elite performers?

Answers are on page 187.

▲ **Figure 4.20** A coach gives simple verbal instructions to a group of beginners.

The varying types of feedback are:

- positive/negative
- knowledge of results/knowledge of performance
- extrinsic/intrinsic.

In choosing the correct type of feedback to use, it is important that the experience of the performer is taken into account. Unlike experienced performers, beginners are unable to fully understand the intrinsic feedback received.

Positive and negative feedback

Positive and negative feedback are, of course, opposites. Both are given by other people (extrinsically); for example, coach, teacher or a fellow performer.

Positive feedback is used to inform the athlete what was correct about the movement. Performers need to know if a movement is correct as this provides the reference point for future attempts at the movement. Positive feedback is essential in motivating athletes.

Negative feedback is used to inform the athlete what was incorrect about the movement. Negative feedback must include information on the action(s) required by the performer to achieve the correct movement.

Knowledge of results/knowledge of performance

Knowledge of results is sometimes known as 'KR'. It focuses on how successful you have been in achieving what you set out to do (the outcome). It is generally factual and given to you by a coach or teacher, although you may be able to see it yourself; for example, the distance you jumped in long jump.

Examples include:

- whether you scored or not with a free throw in basketball
- what score you recorded in golf
- whether your shot in football went in the goal or not
- how quickly you ran the 100 metres.

Knowledge of results may be obvious to an elite athlete, but a beginner may need this type of feedback to understand whether what they did was a success or not.

Knowledge of performance (KP), on the other hand, provides more detail about how well you did, irrespective of the result. It may relate to technique used, or specific aspects of the movement you produced. It deals with the quality of the performance, not the result.

▲ **Figure 4.21** Positive feedback is important for beginners to keep them motivated.

Study hint

Positive feedback is more important for beginners. Negative feedback tends to be used more with elite performers.

Key terms

Knowledge of results (KR)
Feedback about the outcome.

Knowledge of performance (KP)
Feedback about the quality of performance, e.g. technique.

Examples include:

- the technique used when performing a free throw – 'excellent elbow extension'
- 'your swing was excellent in that golf shot' – 'great balance'
- 'excellent power through the laces' when shooting at the goal in football
- quick out of the blocks in the 100 metres with high knee lift
- 'excellent rotation' when performing an ice-skating spin
- 'great control' when playing futsal.

Extrinsic/intrinsic feedback

Extrinsic feedback is information received about performance which comes from outside of the performer; for example, from a coach or teacher. Extrinsic feedback may also come from fellow performers or the spectators and is generally given verbally, or it could be given on a score card; for example, a score out of 10 in ice-skating. As beginners often struggle to understand or interpret the success of their movement, they rely heavily on feedback from others.

Key terms

Extrinsic feedback   Feedback from an external source.

Intrinsic feedback   Feedback from within, e.g. kinaesthetic feel.

▲ **Figure 4.22** An elite performer like Rory McIlroy is able to give himself feedback. He will know from intrinsic 'feel' if his golf shot has been struck well or not.

Intrinsic feedback is information which is received from within the performer; for example, how something feels, information from the senses or muscles. As performers progress and become elite, they develop the ability to interpret such sensory information. In effect, they can 'feel' if a skill has been performed well. This 'feeling' or sense that the movement of the muscles and joints has gone well (or not) is often called kinaesthesis.

For example:

- An elite golfer will know from the 'feel' of their swing if it was a good shot.
- An elite hockey player will know from the 'feel' of their shot at the goal if they have struck it well or not.
- An elite tennis player will know from the 'feel' of their serve whether they have generated enough spin on the ball.

Study hint

Beginners tend to need positive feedback, knowledge of results and extrinsic feedback.

Elite performers tend to accept negative feedback, have knowledge of performance and can provide themselves with informed, intrinsic feedback.

▼ Table 4.7 Summary of the effect of different types of feedback on beginners and elite performers.

BEGINNER	ELITE PERFORMER
May be demotivated by negative feedback.	More accepting of negative feedback.
Cannot interpret complex feedback on performance.	Can interpret complex feedback on performance.
Receive intrinsic feedback but find it hard to interpret.	Can interpret the intrinsic feedback they receive.

PRACTICE QUESTIONS

12 State whether visual guidance or verbal guidance tends to be more important for beginners. (1 mark)

13 Explain why negative feedback should not be used excessively with beginners. (1 mark)

14 A beginner new to tennis requires feedback on their first attempt at serving. Identify whether knowledge of results (KR) or knowledge of performance (KP) should be given. Justify your answer. (2 marks)

15 Evaluate how useful intrinsic feedback and extrinsic feedback are for a beginner learning to ski for the first time. (6 marks)

Answers are on page 190.

Rapid recall

Use the following acronyms to help you remember the facts:

Beginner **REP** – Beginners are more suited to **R**esults (knowledge of), **E**xtrinsic and **P**ositive feedback.

Elite **PIN** – Elite performers are more suited to **P**erformance (knowledge of), **I**ntrinsic and **N**egative feedback.

The types of feedback can be remembered with '**REPPIN**':

R – **R**esults (knowledge of)	**P** – **P**erformance (knowledge of)
E – **E**xtrinsic	**I** – **I**ntrinsic
P – **P**ositive	**N** – **N**egative

Activity 6

Copy and complete Table 4.8 to link the types of guidance and feedback to beginners and/or elite performers.

▼ **Table 4.8**

Beginner	Who requires the following and why?	Elite performer
	Visual guidance	
	Verbal guidance	
	Manual/mechanical guidance	
	Positive or negative feedback	
	Knowledge of results/performance	
	Extrinsic or intrinsic feedback	

Answers are on page 192.

Arousal

Arousal is a physical and mental (physiological and psychological) state of alertness/excitement varying from deep sleep to intense excitement, as shown by the continua below.

Deep sleep ———————————— **Intense excitement**

Low level of arousal ——————— **High level of arousal**

Arousal affects both the physical and mental state of a performer. Physically, increases in arousal may cause a rise in heart rate or cause a performer to sweat more. As arousal increases, performers must use specific strategies to control the level of arousal because if arousal is not at the correct level, performance may suffer.

The inverted U theory of arousal

Yerkes and Dobson (1908) developed a theory called the inverted U theory, which visually shows how a performer can be under or over aroused, or at the correct (optimal) level.

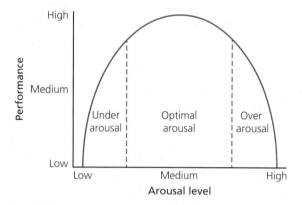

▲ **Figure 4.23** The inverted U theory.

The inverted U theory can be explained in the following way:

- As arousal increases, so does performance.
- Up to the optimal/perfect level.
- If arousal increases further, performance will decrease.

In order to understand this theory, you must understand that the optimal/perfect level of arousal varies for different sporting skills. For example:

- Fine/precise movements involving accuracy require a low optimal level of arousal.
- Gross skills requiring power, strength and/or large muscle movements require a high level of arousal.

Low optimal level of arousal ————— **High optimal level of arousal**

Fine/precise ——————— **Gross/large muscle movements**

Archery ————————————— **Rugby tackle**

Snooker ————————————— **Sprinting**

Darts ————————————— **Weight-lifting**

> ✔ **Check your understanding**
>
> 9 What do you understand by the term 'arousal'?
>
> Answers are on page 187.

Study hint

It is not a sporting example, but threading a needle requires a low optimal level of arousal as it is a precise movement which uses small muscle groups and requires accuracy. These are the main criteria for requiring a low level of arousal.

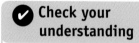

PRACTICE QUESTIONS

16 Explain how arousal affects performance according to the inverted U theory. (3 marks)

Answers are on page 190.

Study hint

Remember that as part of your GCSE Physical Education course you may need to draw an inverted U graph showing the correct level of arousal on the x-axis and performance on the y-axis.

▲ **Figure 4.24** Athlete Tom Daley mentally preparing himself for a dive.

✔ **Check your understanding**

10 Explain how optimal arousal level differs for different skills when playing a team game of your choice.

Answers are on page 187.

▲ **Figure 4.26** Cristiano Ronaldo has used deep breathing in preparation for taking free kicks. The exaggerated breathing has allowed him to focus on the skill being performed throughout his long career.

Key term

Deep breathing A physical/somatic technique which involves the performer exaggerating their breaths in and out.

As different skills require different optimal levels of arousal, the inverted U can be placed on different points of the graph according to the skill being performed. This is shown below:

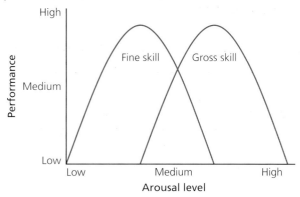

▲ **Figure 4.25** Differing optimal levels of arousal for different skills.

Controlling arousal levels

Sports performers, such as platform divers, need to control their arousal on a diving platform in order to ensure their performance is the best it can be. An incorrect level of arousal may result in mistakes being made as a result of under or over arousal.

▲ **Figure 4.27** An archer who requires a low level of arousal could easily experience over arousal due to nerves or anxiety (worry).

▲ **Figure 4.28** A weight-lifter who does not get aroused enough may experience under arousal and be unable to lift the weight.

Methods to control arousal can be in the mind (mental/cognitive) or through use of the body (physical/somatic). The main methods that sports performers use are:

- deep breathing (physical/somatic)
- mental rehearsal/visualisation/imagery (mental/cognitive)
- positive self-talk (mental/cognitive).

Deep breathing

Deep breathing is a physical/somatic technique which involves the performer exaggerating their breaths in and out. The top half of the body should be relaxed, and slow, deep breaths should be used to allow the performer to control arousal and focus their thoughts on the task in hand. This can be used before performance to calm nerves and control arousal. It can also be used during performance to focus the mind.

Mental rehearsal/visualisation/imagery

Mental rehearsal, visualisation and imagery are very similar techniques used by performers to control their arousal levels. These techniques are done in the performer's mind (mental/cognitive). Mental rehearsal involves the performer picturing themselves performing the skill perfectly before attempting it. This can also be classed as imagery, although imagery can also involve the performer imagining themselves in a calm, relaxing place. Both methods relax and focus the mind on the task at hand and can be used before and during performance to control arousal levels. Visualisation involves you imagining a relaxing scene or place.

Examples of when mental rehearsal could be used during performance include:

- controlling arousal prior to kicking a rugby conversion
- controlling arousal before playing a cricket shot
- controlling arousal prior to throwing a javelin.

Jonny Wilkinson famously adopted a 'pose' before converting a rugby ball. This pose was copied by many other rugby players. However, the background to Jonny's pose is that he was using deep breathing and mentally rehearsing his kick. He visualised the ball going between the posts. Jonny subsequently controlled his arousal levels and focused his mind on the task at hand.

Positive self-talk

Self-talk is a mental/cognitive technique whereby the performer talks to themselves in their head. This technique is usually positive and can reassure performers that they are doing well or are well-prepared and can relax their body and mind, controlling their arousal level.

Examples of sports performers using positive self-talk could include:

- a golfer reassuring themselves that they can hole a putt
- an athlete in the blocks confirming to themselves that they are good enough to win
- a netballer quietly encouraging themselves to score; for example, 'Come on, you can do this'.

Activity 7

Performers may use a mixture of techniques at different times, but the key is to realise that the arousal level must be optimal for the skill being done.

Analyse the information below and copy and complete the table.

▼ **Table 4.9**

Sporting situation	Arousal level	Do they need to control/adjust their arousal level?	If yes, suggest an appropriate technique
Archery	Medium		
Weight-lifting	High		
Snooker game	High		

Answers are on page 192.

✔ Check your understanding

11 What do you understand by the terms 'somatic technique' and 'mental/cognitive technique'?

Answers are on page 188.

▲ **Figure 4.29** Jonny Wilkinson in his famous 'pose'.

Study hint

Remember that players can be under aroused or over aroused. If under aroused, performers may need some form of motivation to increase their arousal level.

Key terms

Mental rehearsal A mental technique involving the performer picturing themselves performing the skill perfectly before attempting it. This mental/cognitive relaxation technique involves control of mental thoughts and imagining positive outcomes.

Self-talk A mental/cognitive technique whereby the performer talks to him/herself in their head to reassure themselves.

PRACTICE QUESTIONS

17 Identify a mental/cognitive technique that could be used to control arousal. (1 mark)

18 Identify and describe a somatic relaxation technique that could be used to control the arousal level of a performer suffering from over arousal. (2 marks)

19 Evaluate the use of mental rehearsal, deep breathing and self-talk as a means to control arousal for a performer in a sporting activity of your choice. (9 marks)

Answers are on page 190.

Answers are on page 190.

Study hint

Remember that acts of aggression can be classified as direct aggression or indirect aggression. It is important that you understand the difference between the two.

Aggression

For the vast majority of sports, an element of aggression may be required in order to succeed or win.

It is first important to understand what aggression is. Acts of aggression can be classified as direct aggression or indirect aggression.

Direct aggression

Direct aggression is when there is actual physical contact between performers. The 'aggressor' uses physical contact to directly and deliberately inflict harm upon their opponent. Examples of direct aggression include:

- a futsal player kicking their opponents' shins rather than tackling the ball
- a judo performer throwing their opponent illegally and with excessive force
- a boxer punching their opponent below the belt.

Indirect aggression

Indirect aggression does not involve physical contact. The aggressive act is taken out on an object to gain an advantage over an opponent. It does not physically harm or injure and the act may be within the rules of the sport. The 'harm' as such is usually mental harm; that is, it makes the opponent(s) feel less confident or more worried. Examples include:

- smashing a badminton shuttle very hard to win a point but also harming the confidence of the opponent
- in tennis, hitting a volley with power to win the point (but also to lower the opponent's confidence).

Study hint

Direct aggression involves physical contact. Indirect aggression does not.

> ✔ **Check your understanding**
>
> 12 Describe the difference between direct and indirect aggression.
>
> Answers are on page 188.

Activity 8

Look at the following examples and see if you can work out whether they are examples of direct or indirect aggression. Share your answers with a partner.

▼ **Table 4.10**

Activity	Direct or indirect?
A tennis player smashes a return.	
A sailor cuts across an opponent's sailing line.	
A netball player deliberately sticks their elbows out to catch an opponent's face.	
A hockey player tackles an opponent, swiping their legs with their stick.	

Answers are on page 193.

Introvert and extrovert personality types

Sports psychologists try to understand the personality of performers. The unique 'parts' of a person's personality distinguish them from other people. Everyone is different, but certain 'types' of personality can be grouped into categories. Two commonly used personality types are **introvert** and **extrovert**. The main things that classify a person as introvert or extrovert are:

- how much arousal they need for optimal performance
- whether they need others around them to stimulate them.

Introvert

A person with an introvert personality does not need a high level of arousal. They can become over aroused when overstimulated. They get their energy from being quiet, thoughtful and solitary.

N.B. Introverts tend to play individual sports as they are self-motivated and don't need others to motivate them.

Introverts tend to play individual sports when:

- concentration/precision (fine skill) is required
- low arousal is required.

Extrovert

A person with an extrovert personality needs a high level of arousal. They can lack concentration and often seek exciting situations. They tend to get their energy from interaction with others, are sociable, are aroused by others, are often enthusiastic, talkative and prone to boredom when isolated.

Study hint
Remember to work on linking acts of aggression in sport to the terms 'direct aggression' or 'indirect aggression'.

PRACTICE QUESTIONS

20 When defending between an opposing player and a netball post, the defender deliberately pushes the player in the back to clear the space to catch the ball. Is this act of aggression direct or indirect? Explain your answer. (2 marks)

Answers are on page 191.

Key terms

Introvert Personality type characterised by being quiet, passive, reserved and shy – usually associated with individual sports performance.

Extrovert Personality type characterised by being sociable, active, talkative and outgoing – usually associated with team sports players.

▲ **Figure 4.30** Open-water swimming is a sport often performed by introverts.

Figure 4.31 Team sports performers tend to be extroverted. They seek out excitement with others and often make good leaders.

> ✔ **Check your understanding**
>
> 13 Describe the difference between an introvert and an extrovert.
>
> Answers are on page 188.

Extroverts tend to play team sports when there is a fast pace, concentration may need to be low and gross skills are used.

N.B. Extroverts are often leaders within a team.

> **Activity 9**
>
> Look at the list of the following activities and descriptive words. Group them into the categories of stereotypical introvert or extrovert personality types.
>
> ▼ **Table 4.11**
>
> | Introvert | | Extrovert |
> |---|---|---|
> | | Pistol shooting | |
> | | Shy | |
> | | Seek excitement | |
> | | Rugby player | |
> | | Snooker player | |
> | | Calm | |
> | | Sociable | |
>
> Answers are on page 193.

PRACTICE QUESTIONS

21 Multiple choice (choose one).

Which one of the following tends to describe an introvert personality?

A Easily excited ☐

B Enjoys sociable occasions ☐

C Usually shy ☐

D Very talkative ☐ (1 mark)

Answers are on page 191.

Motivation

Key terms

Motivation The drive to succeed or the desire (want) to achieve something.

Intrinsic motivation The drive that comes from within the performer. •

Extrinsic motivation The drive experienced by a performer when striving to achieve a reward (tangible or intangible).

Motivation is simply defined as the drive to succeed or the desire (want) to achieve something. What actually motivates you can be divided into two main categories:

Intrinsic motivation and **extrinsic motivation**.

Intrinsic motivation

Intrinsic motivation is the drive that comes from within the performer. The need to achieve something may well have the reward of a feeling of pride, self-satisfaction or general achievement. The performer is driven to achieve something for the feeling it brings them.

Extrinsic motivation

Extrinsic motivation is the drive experienced by a performer when striving to achieve a reward. The external reward is provided by an outside source or person. Such reward can be divided into:

- tangible rewards – such as certificates, trophies, medals, etc.
- intangible rewards – such as praise or feedback from others or applause from the crowd.

Evaluation of the merits of intrinsic and extrinsic motivation in sport

It would be wrong to think that intrinsic and extrinsic motivation are used in isolation from each other. They are usually used together, and although a trophy may act as an extrinsic motivator, the pride or satisfaction from winning may also be a major intrinsic motivator.

The majority of educational and sporting research has concluded that intrinsic motivation is more powerful than extrinsic motivation. Intrinsic motivation is generally deemed more effective for a variety of reasons:

- Performers can become too reliant on extrinsic motivation. They only play for the reward/prize/money.
- Intrinsic motivation is more likely to lead to continued effort and participation – that is, a performer who is playing for pride is more likely to persist and continue participating over a period of time.
- The overuse of extrinsic can undermine the strength of intrinsic. In other words, if too many rewards are on offer, it may cause performers to forget why they were playing in the first place – for the love of the game.

However, the value of extrinsic rewards should not be underestimated. Winning a prize, trophy or certificate may well spur a performer on and actually cause feelings of pride and self-satisfaction.

The value of intrinsic and extrinsic motivation is individual and personal to a performer. Although the research stresses the importance of intrinsic motivation, there is no doubt that many performers are motivated by the extrinsic rewards available.

PRACTICE QUESTIONS

22 Describe what is meant by the term motivation. (1 mark)

23 Explain the difference between intrinsic and extrinsic motivation. (2 marks)

24 Evaluate whether winning the Premier League trophy is likely to be the main motivator for a Premiership football player. (6 marks)

Answers are on page 191.

Study hint

You may need to explain appropriate examples of intrinsic and extrinsic motivation linked to sporting activities.

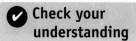

✔ Check your understanding

14 Explain the term 'motivation'.

Answers are on page 188.

Rapid recall

The value of intrinsic motivation can be remembered with the acronym **SUPER**:

Stronger – Intrinsic generally believed to be stronger/better

Undermine – Overuse of extrinsic can undermine intrinsic value

Persist – More likely to persist if motivated intrinsically

Effort – More likely to be sustained if intrinsically motivated

Reliance – Performers can become too reliant on extrinsic motivation.

▲ **Figure 4.32** The potential to win a trophy can provide extrinsic motivation. Winning it may provide intrinsic motivation, e.g. feelings of pride and self-satisfaction.

Summary

- Skills are learned and abilities are inherited.
- Skills can be classified on continua depending on their characteristics.
- Outcome goals involve the outcome whereas performance goals involve technique or mastery.
- Outcome goals tend to be more effective with elite performers than with beginners.
- SMART targets are specific, measurable, accepted, realistic and time-bound.
- Information processing is using information to make decisions. It involves input, decision-making, output and feedback.
- Decisions come from the working memory (short-term memory) but may need to be recalled from the long-term memory.
- Feedback received can be positive, negative, intrinsic and/ or extrinsic, as knowledge of results or as knowledge of performance.
- Feedback can be given in a variety of ways.
- Guidance involves visual, verbal and manual/mechanical.
- Some guidance types are better suited to beginners; for example, visual, manual/mechanical.
- Some guidance types are better suited to experts; for example, verbal.
- Arousal is an excitement level. The correct (optimal) level of arousal varies from skill to skill.
- Arousal can be controlled using stress management techniques.
- Direct aggression involves physical contact with an opponent with the intent to harm.
- Indirect aggression is taken out on an object to gain an advantage.
- Introverts are usually shy, can arouse themselves and prefer individual sports. Extroverts need others to arouse them and prefer team sports.

Chapter 5a Socio-cultural influences

Chapter objectives
- Understand the engagement patterns of different social groups
- Understand the factors affecting participation

Participation

It has been government policy for the last 50 years to try to make sure that every individual in the country has the opportunity to participate in sport and other forms of physical activity.

▲ **Figure 5a.1** There are many forms of physical activity.

▲ **Figure 5a.2** There are many forms of physical activity.

We have seen the building of sports halls, the provision of outdoor recreation and sports facilities, the opening up of the countryside, an ongoing information campaign and a focus within school physical education programmes on increasing participation. All of these efforts have been part of an attempt to get more people involved in physical activity and sport. Has it worked?

According to Sport England in 2017/18, 62 per cent of people aged 16 years and over in England were classed as 'physically active' – that is, they did 150 minutes or more of moderate-intensity physical activity a week.

The research also showed some differences in levels of participation between **social groups**:

- The percentage of physically active people in Asian, Black, Chinese and other ethnic groups was lower than the national average of 63 per cent, ranging from 55–60 per cent.
- More men (65 per cent) were classed as physically active than women (60 per cent).
- People became less physically active the older they were – 76 per cent of people aged 16–24 years were physically active, compared with 57 per cent of those aged 65–74 years.

Key term

Social groups People who interact with one another, share similar characteristics and have a sense of unity/togetherness.

- Rates of physical activity were highest among people in managerial and professional occupations (71 per cent), followed by full-time students (70 per cent). Rates were lowest among the long-term unemployed (49 per cent).
- Only 17 per cent of people with a disability participate regularly in physical activity and sport.

The term used to describe how levels of participation vary across different social groups is **engagement patterns**.

Social groups have a huge influence on people and will affect whether or not people become involved in sport and physical activity and which activities they become involved in. One of the biggest factors that determines a person's engagement in physical activity is a person's gender.

▲ **Figure 5a.3** There are many forms of physical activity.

Participation by women

During the growth in sport and physical activity over the last 100 years, women's participation has been adversely affected by a range of stereotypical views. For example:

- Women lack the strength or endurance to do the same range of sports or physical activities as men.
- Women who are competitive are not being feminine.
- Too much physical activity limits a woman's ability to give birth.
- Women who train hard and develop muscles become more 'male-like' and have their sexuality questioned.
- A woman's role is to be the carer, mother and manager of the home and this prevents involvement in sport.

The majority of these **stereotypes** tend to be held by men about women, and although society is becoming more accepting of female sporting participation, there are some who still think along these lines.

Because of these stereotypical views, other **barriers to participation** have been put in place which discourage women from participating in as wide a range of sports as men. For example:

- Sport is a male-dominated activity.
- Elite female sport performers receive less media coverage than men.
- Women may receive less support from their peers and family.
- Facilities for women have developed more slowly than those for male performers.

PRACTICE QUESTIONS

1 Discuss whether the opportunities for women to take part in sport and physical activity are the same as for men. (4 marks)

Answers are on page 194.

Key terms

Engagement patterns Trends/tendencies in involvement.

Stereotype Widely held but fixed and oversimplified idea of a particular type of person or group.

Barrier to participation An obstacle that prevents a group within society from participating in sport or physical activity and therefore reduces overall levels of participation.

- Media coverage of elite female performers is more likely to include details that are not relevant to their performance – their appearance, whether they are married or have children, etc.

Participation by ethnicity

Another barrier to participation in physical activity and sport is a person's race, religion or culture. An **ethnic group** is defined as a group of people who share common origins – be they racial, religious or cultural.

Key term

Ethnic group A community made up of people who share a common cultural background.

> ✓ **Check your understanding**
>
> 1 What are engagement patterns?
> 2 What do you understand by the term 'stereotypes'?
> 3 Identify five ethnic groupings.
> 4 List four barriers to women's participation in sport.
>
> Answers are on page 193.

In the UK, there is a wide variety of minority ethnic groups. These groups have different levels of participation in sport and physical activity.

▼ **Table 5a.1** Levels of participation in sport and physical activity in the UK.

ETHNIC GROUP	AVERAGE LEVEL	ASIAN	BLACK	CHINESE	MIXED	WHITE BRITISH	WHITE OTHER
Participation level % (men) in sport or physical activity	65	59	60	62	73	65	67
Participation level % (women) in sport or physical activity	60	50	54	59	70	61	64

The reasons for these differing levels of participation are linked to the different priorities and expectations of the groups.

There is also an unevenness of representation of different ethnic groups at elite levels of sport. For example, in the England football and the UK athletics squads, about 30 per cent of players are from minority ethnic groups. This compares to the general population, in which about 13 per cent are from minority ethnic groups.

A response that is sometimes given to these numbers is to perpetuate the stereotype that people specifically from Black Caribbean and African groups have better physiological or anatomical attributes due to their genetic make-up. Some people say they have an innate advantage in some sports.

Athletics and football require speed, power and strength, and it is sometimes suggested that these ethnic groups have a higher proportion of fast-twitch muscle fibres or have a longer Achilles tendon, allowing for greater power transfer, or have a higher ratio of muscle to fat. The idea of a lower proportion of fat is sometimes also used to explain why there is a low representation of black people in competitive swimming.

There are many other sports that require similar physiological characteristics to athletics and football – for example, tennis, sprint cycling and rugby union – yet we do not see the same high representation of black people there.

▲ **Figure 5a.4** International rugby player Maggie Alphonsi has been an inspirational role model for many people.

The imbalances that minority ethnic groups have, both in levels of participation in sport and at an elite level, are due to a range of factors and are caused by several influences; there is no one single reason.

Other factors affecting participation

Surveys have shown that individuals from lower **socio-economic groups** are less likely to participate in physical activity. Many people from minority ethnic groups are also in lower socio-economic groups and, therefore, have lower **disposable incomes**.

This may explain the high proportion of elite footballers and athletes from certain minority ethnic groups. These activities are relatively inexpensive to participate in, especially when compared to activities such as tennis or golf.

Socio-economics has an effect on participation in that participation invariably involves a cost to the participant. In the UK, you usually 'pay to play', and some physical activities may cost a lot of money.

Another factor affecting participation in sport and physical activity is age. All students at school participate in physical activity, because PE is a compulsory subject in schools. It is after students leave school that participation levels drop. There is a '**post-school drop-out**' in sport, especially among females.

Not surprisingly, sports participation tends to be lower in older people than younger people, because many activities are restricted by physical fitness and as this declines with age, so participation levels drop. The type of activity undertaken also varies by age, with younger people more involved with team sports and older people more likely to be involved in individual activities.

PRACTICE QUESTIONS

2 Give three reasons for the lower participation rates among some minority ethnic groups.   (3 marks)

Answers are on page 194.

Key terms

Socio-economic group A group's place within society; depends on a number of factors, including occupation, education, income, wealth and where they live.

Disposable income Income available to be spent or saved as one wishes.

Post-school drop-out The reduction in participation levels in young adults after they leave full-time education.

✔ Check your understanding

5 Suggest reasons for the high percentage of minority ethnic England footballers.
6 How might age affect participation?

Answers are on page 193.

A person's family and friends are a huge influence on their participation in sport and physical activity. These influences can be both positive and negative. A family can have positive effects on participation through their support of a performer. This support can be financial, through paying for kit or fees for coaching. They may also provide transport for training and/ or matches. The support can be simply emotional, when they watch the young performer and cheer them on.

Many parents also act as **role models** for their children. Occasionally, a lack of family support can be a negative influence on participation.

Peer groups are a big influence on individuals and, therefore, their possible participation in sport. Peers exert pressure on their friendship groups. There is a tendency to conform to the rest of the peer group. If your friends/peer group play football, you are quite likely to play football as well. Members of your peer group may go to an aerobics class and you may be encouraged to participate in that type of activity. We often choose to do certain activities because our friends do them too.

▲ **Figure 5a.5** Friends play sport together.

Key terms

Role model A person looked up to by others as an example to be copied.

Peer group A group of people of approximately the same age, status and interests.

Disability A physical or mental impairment that has a substantial and long-term negative effect on a person's ability to do normal daily activities, such as sport.

Participation by people with disabilities

A person is disabled under the Equality Act 2010 if they have a physical or mental impairment that has a 'substantial' and 'long-term' negative effect on their ability to do normal daily activities. This may include physical activities such as sport.

▲ **Figure 5a.6** Disability is not a barrier to sports participation.

A wide range of conditions come under the term '**disability**', and it is easy to make general assumptions about a person with a disability, without paying attention to their specific needs to allow disabled people equality of opportunity.

There are three main categories of disability:

- mobility impairments
- sensory impairments
- mental impairments.

Key terms

Integration Involving the full participation of all people in community life, but usually referring to people with a disability.

Adapted sports Competitive sports for individuals with disabilities. While they often parallel existing sports played by athletes without a disability, there may be some modifications in the equipment and rules to meet the needs of the participants.

Discrimination The unjust or prejudicial treatment of different groups of people, especially on the grounds of race, disability, age or sex.

PRACTICE QUESTIONS

3 Women's participation in physical activities is often dependent upon the opportunities available to them. Explain the term 'discrimination'. (2 marks)
4 What is meant by the terms 'stereotyping' and 'inclusiveness'? (2 marks)

Answers are on pages 194–5.

Activity 1

Use the internet to research the events at the 2016 Paralympics. From that list identify six adapted sports.

Answers are on page 195.

There is disagreement over the best way to provide opportunities for those with a disability. Is it best for performers with a disability to participate with performers without a disability? This is called **integration**. Or is it better to develop **adapted sports**, such as wheelchair basketball, specifically for performers with a particular disability?

The benefits of integration include:

- reduced possibilities of **discrimination**
- less stereotyping
- fewer barriers to participation.

The benefits of adapted sports providing separate opportunities include:

- a greater range of opportunities through specifically designed programmes.

One way that people with a disability are able to participate in sport is by either adapting an existing sport or by designing a new sport. Changing a sport for people with disabilities is known as adapted sport. For example, visually impaired footballers can play with a ball that has a bell inside and use their hearing rather than vision as a stimulus.

It is now generally thought that integration rather than separateness is better for mental and social health and, therefore, physical education and sport continue to seek ways of integrating sport and physical recreation opportunities for those with a disability.

Some sports have been designed to enable people with a disability to take part. They include the following:

- boccia – a bowls-type game, played at the Paralympics and suitable for players of all abilities
- goalball – an active court game for visually impaired or sighted players.

✔ Check your understanding

7 What do you understand by the term 'integration'?
8 What is discrimination?
9 What are the three types of disability?
10 Suggest why integration is thought to be better than separation.

Answers are on page 193.

▲ **Figure 5a.7** Boccia at the 2012 Paralympics.

▲ **Figure 5a.8** Goalball at the 2016 Paralympics.

Barriers to participation

A barrier to participation is an obstacle that prevents a group within society from participating in sport or physical recreation and, therefore, reduces overall levels of participation.

A range of barriers to participation has been identified:

- attitudes
- role models
- accessibility – to facilities/clubs/activities
- media coverage
- sexism/stereotyping
- culture/religion/religious festivals
- family commitments
- available leisure time
- familiarity
- education
- socio-economic factors/disposable income
- adaptability/inclusiveness.

An **attitude** is an opinion about something and means that people have a tendency to respond in a certain way towards something. These attitudes are generally learned from family and friends. Attitudes can be positive or negative. A person may have a negative attitude about exercise and therefore does not participate, whereas another person may have a positive attitude about exercise and does take part.

Attitudes are long-lasting, but they can be changed. If we want more people to participate in sport and physical activity, we may need to change their negative attitude to a positive one. Attitudes can be changed by convincing the performer of all the good things about an activity, such as explaining the health benefits of exercise. They may also be changed by getting the performer to take part in the activity and finding out that they actually enjoy it, rather than hating it as they expected.

Attitudes to participation do change. The idea of women playing rugby or cricket attracted negative attitudes from most people 30 years ago, but now that general idea has changed; similarly with women's football. After the England women's success in winning the bronze medal at the 2015 World Cup, attitudes towards women's football have become much more positive.

Role models have a great influence on attitudes and participation in general. Role models can be from a sport, from family, or from a peer group. Role models tend to encourage participation in sport. They may also encourage people to play in a certain way and even influence fashion choices both on and off the field.

Knowledge of the possibility of being a role model can also influence the behaviour of the role model.

A very important factor in terms of whether a person participates in a physical activity is accessibility. Many physical activities require a certain type of facility in order to participate. For example, skiing needs snow or an artificial surface; disabled swimmers may need a hoist to enter and

Key term

Attitude An opinion about something that tends to make people respond in a certain way.

leave the water. If that facility is not easily available, then participation becomes difficult.

Some activities are only available in certain locations. Clubs, and therefore opportunities to participate, are quite difficult to locate in some parts of the country. White-water canoeing needs access to the type of water found in fast-flowing rivers usually found in rural areas; it is much less accessible in cities.

Some activities are not accessible because of the cost or difficulty of transport. There are very few Olympic-size swimming pools in this country, making it difficult if you live a long distance from one of them. Many elite sportspeople have to go and live near a facility to make access to the facility easier.

Media coverage usually has a positive effect on participation in that it often generates role models or simply general interest that encourages participation. A lack of media coverage, or bad media coverage, however, can have a negative effect on participation.

Table 5a.2 compares the potential positive and negative effects of media coverage.

▲ **Figure 5a.9** Different forms of media.

Key terms

Media coverage The content included in the media (television, radio, internet, print, etc.).

Sexism The belief that one sex is naturally superior to the other. It involves and leads to prejudice, stereotyping and discrimination.

▼ **Table 5a.2** Potential effects of media coverage.

POSITIVE	NEGATIVE
Attendances may rise as people want to see the best players/role models	Attendances may fall as more people watch from home
Supporters become better informed	Only few sports on TV; minor sports not shown
Easier to attract sponsorship	Sports personalities lose privacy
Encourages participation	Events can be sensationalised to promote the media rather than the sport
Develops personalities and role models	Changes to playing season, e.g. summer rugby league
Multiple cameras give viewers a close-up view of the action	Changes to event timings, e.g. Premier League matches on Friday and Monday nights
	Changes to the rules, e.g. new scoring system for badminton

✔ Check your understanding

11 What are attitudes?

12 Identify four different forms of media.

13 Describe four negative effects that the media may have on sport.

Answers are on pages 193–4.

Sexism is the belief that one sex (usually the male) is naturally superior to the other. It involves and leads to prejudice, stereotyping or discrimination, typically against women, on the basis of gender.

Elite sport is sexist in that it separates men and women. The men's decathlon has been an Olympic event since 1912 but there is no place for the women's event. While men play five sets at tennis Grand Slam events, women can only compete over three sets.

In terms of participation, 1.9 million fewer women than men participate in sport at least once a month. Women make up only 18 per cent of qualified coaches and 9 per cent of senior coaches. Less than 1 per cent of sports sponsorship in the UK goes to women's sport and men generally get more prize money than women. Finally, only 7 per cent of all sports media coverage in the UK is dedicated to women's events.

Activity 2

Use the internet to find the eventual final position of the England teams in these events and copy and complete Table 5a.3 to show the comparative success of women's sports:

▼ **Table 5a.3**

Event	Women	Men
Football World Cup	2015 –	2014 –
Rugby World Cup	2014 –	2015 –
Cricket World Cup	2013 –	2015 –

Answers are on page 195.

But sport is not isolated from society. The feminist movement has made great advances towards equality for women and most of these inequalities are being challenged.

There are certain groups of women affected by these issues more than others; for example, teenage girls (aged 15–19) participate less as they grow older. The major reasons for the decline in participation by teenage girls are based on the lack of interest in physical activity from their friends and family, concerns over their weight and appearance and associated feelings of lack of confidence.

Muslim women participate less than women from other social or cultural groups. Not only does this **cultural group** face the same inequalities as other women, but they also need to follow a strict dress code and the need to only mix with other women.

This is just an example of how culture and/or religion may affect participation. Other influences on the participation of minority ethnic groups include the effects of discrimination as a result of **prejudice**, which may lead to reduced opportunities either through limited access or by individuals choosing not to participate.

Another reason for lower participation rates is that a higher percentage of minority ethnic communities are in economically deprived areas and have lower disposable incomes, and therefore cannot afford to participate. Certain cultural groups may not see sports participation as a worthwhile use of time, and may place greater emphasis on academic success. There may be a need for a cultural group to observe their religious festivals, which may limit participation at certain times of the year.

Another factor is **family commitments**. Individuals may need to look after other members of their family and this may limit opportunities to participate in sport and physical activities.

Key terms

Cultural group A group of people who share a common race, religion, language or other characteristic.

Prejudice Preconceived opinion that is not based on reason or actual experience.

Family commitments Having to invest a certain amount of time to fulfil obligations that assist parents, siblings, partners and other family members.

▲ **Figure 5a.10** Family participation in sport.

Leisure time is the time people have when they are not working, taking care of themselves or completing their family and home duties. In general, the amount of leisure time has increased in recent years for most people because they tend to now have shorter working days and shorter working careers. Linked to this is the fact that people now tend to live longer.

People also have better/easier working conditions; work tends to be less arduous and the number of paid holidays has increased. More and more people are job-sharing and involved in part-time rather than full-time work. There are also many inventions that make life easier, which means that housework takes less time.

More leisure time should mean more time for sport and physical activity, but there are still many people who, through choice or through necessity, still have limited leisure time due to work or other commitments.

One of the main factors that influence a person's choice of physical activity is their familiarity with that activity. Most people would rather be involved with something they already know about and understand. One of the more common ways to have familiarity with an activity is through parental influence, where children become involved in the same activity as their parents. Participating in the same activity as a role model is another example of the use of familiarity as a deciding factor.

Activities for participation are not always a person's own choice; quite often the choice is made for you. This is certainly the case in terms of the influence of **education** on participation. Compulsory physical education lessons give every child an introduction to activities that they may continue to participate in after leaving school.

▲ **Figure 5a.11** School sport.

Key term

Leisure time The time we have when we are not working, taking care of ourselves or completing our family and home duties. It has increased as a result of shorter working careers and increased life expectancy.

Education The process of learning, especially in a school or college, and the knowledge that you get from this.

Many factors affect a school's PE programme. Some schools simply have better and/or newer facilities than others. Many schools have PE teachers who have interests in certain sports that they emphasise in their PE lessons, but this in turn may actually limit a child's experience to certain activities. In much the same way, a school may have a tradition in a certain area – a 'rugby-playing school', for example.

In many schools the timetable can be a problem, as there may be a greater emphasis, and more lessons, given to academic subjects, and so there is insufficient time allocated to PE. Facilities and/or finance can also affect PE provision. For example, without a pool, a school may find it very expensive to provide swimming lessons for its pupils. A similar restriction occurs with outdoor and adventure activities, which are expensive to organise, especially when travel and accommodation become part of the cost.

As previously mentioned, socio-economic factors have a big influence on participation in physical activity. Surveys have shown that individuals from lower socio-economic groups are less likely to participate in physical activity.

The main reason for this lower level of participation by certain socio-economic groups is because of the lower disposable income available to spend on leisure activities. In much the same way, people from lower socio-economic groups may have limited leisure time because of the need to work long hours. But also, some activities are associated with certain social groups, leading to possible rejection or discrimination, and some activities still have membership that is restricted to certain socio-economic groups. For example, there is a need to own a pony, which is expensive, in order to participate in polo.

Finally, one way that people with limited access to an activity, such as those with a disability or with limited disposable income, are able to participate in sport is by either adapting the sport or by designing a new sport. This makes many activities inclusive to all. For example, the sport of basketball can be adapted to wheelchair basketball for wheelchair users. The sport of polo can be adapted to bicycle polo for people with limited disposable income. Adapting an activity to enable more people to participate is making an activity **inclusive**.

✔ Check your understanding

14 Suggest four factors that affect participation of people with disabilities.
15 Suggest four different factors that affect participation of women.
16 Suggest four reasons why women's participation numbers are increasing.
Answers are on page 194.

Summary

- Engagement patterns differ between different social groups.
- There is a variety of factors that affect engagement patterns of different social groups.

PRACTICE QUESTIONS

5 Suggest reasons for the lower participation rates for people with a disability.
(4 marks)

6 Analyse the factors that may influence an individual's participation in sporting activity. (9 marks)

Answers are on page 195.

Study hint
The majority of the factors affecting participation affect most social groups. Learn the groups and how each factor could affect participation.

Rapid recall

Use the acronym **TIME** to help remember factors affecting participation.

T – **T**ime (lack of)
I – **I**ncome (lack of)
M – **M**obility (no transport)
E – **E**ducation (awareness of benefits)

Activity 3
Make a list of the factors that could affect the participation of women in physical activity and sport.

Answers are on page 195.

Key term
Inclusive Including everybody.

Chapter 5b Commercialisation of physical activity and sport

Chapter objectives

- Understand the idea of commercialisation and the relationship between sport, sponsorship and the media
- Understand the positive and negative impacts of sponsorship and the media
- Understand the positive and negative impacts of technology

Key terms

Commercialisation The process by which a new product or service is introduced into the general market.

Media The main ways that people communicate (television, radio and newspapers) collectively.

Sponsorship Where a company pays money to a team or individual in return for advertising their goods.

Golden triangle The financial relationship between sport, sponsorship and media.

Spectators People who watch sport; can be at the event or watching/listening/reading – 'armchair spectating'.

Activity 1

Watch the YouTube clip on the golden triangle at: www.youtube.com/watch?v=tLJf0caobrE

Commercialisation

Commercialisation is the process of introducing a new product into commerce – the activity of buying and selling, especially on a large scale. Sports and sports performers are products that can be bought or sold. Teams can buy and sell players, sports can sell competitions, **media** can buy and sell sports, businesses can buy and sell sports. Businesses can buy and sell competitions, grounds, teams and players. Sports, grounds, competitions, teams and players can advertise businesses.

Every aspect of sport has now become a commodity that can be bought and sold. Virtually all professional sports teams and sports organisations employ a marketing manager whose job is to sell the sport/team to anybody willing to buy part of that sport/team.

In today's society, sport is inextricably linked to the media and to **sponsorship** in what is known as the **golden triangle**.

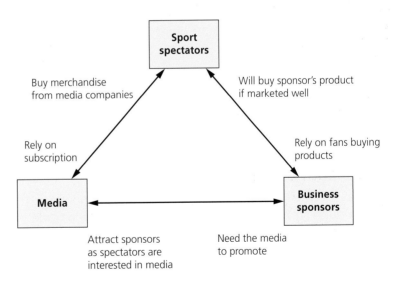

▲ **Figure 5b.1** The golden triangle.

The media includes radio, newspapers, magazines, books and the internet, but the major impact is through television.

Sports are watched by **spectators**, either live at the event or at home on TV.

Sponsorship is the idea of a company providing resources in return for some business-related favour/advantage. Sponsorship is simply a form of advertising to increase sales of a product and/or make the company's name more well-known.

In this relationship, the sport is sold to businesses as a means of advertising the business' product. The business sponsors the sport to obtain advertising space and publicise its product. The sport is shown on the media, which promotes the product, and the sport spectators see the advertising and buy the business' product.

Commercialised sport is driven by the need to make a profit for the people involved, and the need for success. This may lead to a change in attitude by the people involved because of the need to win to make money. Performers are forced to promote the sport to sell the sponsor's product being advertised.

Sport has become much more professionally managed. Teams and sports are now run and organised by people with a background in business. This is because in order to make money, a sport (or team) must attract sponsors, but sponsors are only interested if the sport gets good media coverage that will advertise the sponsor's product.

Sponsorship

Sponsorship appears to be a great benefit to sport. In fact, without sponsorship, sport as we know it would have to change, because of all the money involved. Businesses sponsor sport mainly as a means of advertising their product. If the sponsored sport is regularly in the media then spectators will see the sponsor's name and this publicity may increase sales of the product.

Many businesses sponsor a sport in order to associate the name of the product with a successful or popular team or individual. The thought they are hoping to get into the spectator's head is that if this team is quality then the sponsor's product must be quality. The sponsor wants the spectator to buy its product.

There are sponsors whose main aim is not so much to gain increased sales of its product, but rather to support the local community. Local businesses will often support local sports teams simply with the intention of helping others. This is almost a form of charity and is said to be **philanthropic**.

What does the sponsor get out of this? Money used by a business for sponsorship is tax deductible; in other words, part of what is spent by a sponsor is regained by getting a lower tax bill.

The sponsor is not always providing money; other forms of support such as company products are more usually provided. Sponsors may provide items such as equipment, clothing or footwear. Similarly, the sponsorship is not always to a sport; businesses can sponsor an individual, a team, a competition, a stadium or a stand.

There are negatives to sponsoring a sport. The sponsor's name becomes linked to the activity, which is good provided that the activity is seen in a positive light by the spectators. But being linked to an activity that is performing badly reflects badly on the sponsor. Similarly, any negative aspects to a sport, such as cheating, violence or bad results, reflect negatively on the sponsor's product.

▲ **Figure 5b.2** An example of sponsorship in sport.

PRACTICE QUESTIONS

1 In commercialised sport, how does the 'golden triangle' work? (4 marks)
2 What are the benefits and disadvantages of this golden triangle? (4 marks)
3 Analyse the relationship between sport and commercialisation.
(6 marks)

Answers are on pages 196–7.

Activity 2

Watch the following video about the different types of sponsorship and the benefits and disadvantages of sponsorship for sport and the sponsor. Note down any new points you find especially interesting.

www.youtube.com/watch?v=96i-u0YzyVc

Key term

Philanthropic Trying to benefit others; generous.

Rapid recall

Reasons for sponsoring form the acronym **PAST**.
Publicity
Association
Support
Tax

PRACTICE QUESTIONS

4 Evaluate the effects of media on sporting events.
(6 marks)

Answers are on page 197.

Key terms

Television Modern TV includes local and national terrestrial, Freeview, subscription or pay-per-view, interactive, on-demand, Red Button services, satellite and cable.

Radio An easily accessible form of media that provides detailed information about sport. Radio programmes can include commentaries from sports events and in-depth interviews, with performers or sports experts giving information and opinions.

The press News media, traditionally with reference to printed newspapers and magazines, but can now also include news reports via the internet.

Internet A global system of interconnected computer networks. It carries a huge range of information and services, such as documents that link to other resources, World Wide Web (WWW), email, communication systems and file sharing.

Social media Websites and applications that allow users to create and share content.

▲ **Figure 5b.3** Sponsorship advertises the sponsor's name.

Activity 3

Choose a sport and research it on the internet. Make a list of various sponsors linked to that sport. For each sponsor, try to suggest the main reason for their sponsorship.

✔ Check your understanding

1 What is commercialised sport?
2 What are the three parts of the golden triangle?
3 What is sponsorship?
4 State three benefits of sponsorship to the sponsor.

Answers are on page 195.

Sport and the media

Media can be defined as 'the main means of mass communication (broadcasting, publishing and the internet) regarded collectively'. The media includes **television**, **radio**, **the press**, **the internet** and **social media**.

The media has four main functions: to inform, educate, entertain and advertise. Sport uses the media to promote itself and, in turn, the media uses sport to promote and maintain people's interest in its products. In other words, the media uses sport to sell itself.

Sport is a fairly cheap form of entertainment for TV companies; it costs less to show a sporting event than a drama production or a soap. It also has most of the requirements of a 'good' programme – lots of excitement and only a few periods when the action slows.

In order to publicise itself, a sport must be attractive to the media. This has led to some sports changing to make themselves more attractive to the spectator. In 'good to watch' sports, there are short bursts of maximum excitement; for example, 100 m sprint or a goal in football.

There have even been examples of new forms of a sport being created simply because they were more attractive to a TV audience; for example, Twenty20 (T20) cricket.

Many aspects of popular sports have been changed for TV. Kick-off times at the World Cup (and other competitions) are scheduled to attract a maximum viewing audience. Football has its biggest TV audience in Europe, so wherever the finals are held, the European teams involved will kick off at a time that presents them playing at about 8 p.m. in Europe, when maximum viewing figures can be guaranteed.

In terms of media, television is viewed as the 'best' form of media for sport, because it provides images that can be transmitted live. Television, radio and newspapers are all easy to access, but television, because it is live, may sometimes be unable to provide as much in-depth information as radio and newspapers.

Satellite and cable television (Sky and BT Sport) exist as competition to the traditional terrestrial channels (BBC and ITV). This competition is essentially based on sport, with football having the highest viewing figures for all satellite programmes.

Sport can also be easily left for a few minutes without the viewer losing the plot. Sports coverage has also benefited from developments in technology, with 'action replays' leading the way.

The media requires sport to fit its needs. Sport that is good for television has the following characteristics:

- It demonstrates skill, strength and physical fitness.
- It is competitive and spectacular with detail available.
- It has simple rule structures.
- It fits into a reasonable timescale.
- Personalities are easily identified.
- It is easy to televise; for example, cameras able to keep up with play, reasonable-sized playing area.

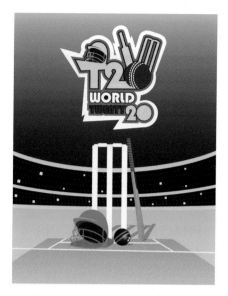

▲ **Figure 5b.4** New forms of sport have been invented for TV.

> **Activity 4**
>
> Choose one individual sport and one team sport and list examples of how they fit into the idea of what is required for 'good' television.

Radio readily provides information about sport and can do so in great detail. Radio programmes can provide commentaries from sports events. These are intended to 'paint a picture' for the listener. Similarly, radio often offers in-depth interviews, with performers or experts in sports providing information.

Both radio and television can be 'live', whereas newspapers and social media are delayed to a certain extent. The internet can be both live and delayed.

News, including sports news and updates, is reported by the press. This was traditionally printed in daily newspapers and in weekly or monthly magazines, but these days most people prefer to access news and sport online, on newspapers' and broadcasters' websites. Sales of newspapers have declined significantly since news became easily accessible via the internet; however, sports pages of newspapers remain a big selling point.

▲ **Figure 5b.5** There are different types of newspapers.

Activity 5

Obtain a broadsheet and a tabloid newspaper (this could be done as a classroom activity). Calculate how many 'column inches' are used for each sport in each newspaper. Draw a graph to show your results.

Broadsheet newspapers tend to emphasise themselves as an information service; they have less of the total paper devoted to sport, but a more varied coverage in terms of a wider range of sports. The broadsheets also tend to provide critical analysis of events and issues affecting sport.

The tabloid newspapers tend to sensationalise events and personalities. They tend to focus on a narrow range of popular sports – for example, football, horse racing – and have little coverage of minority sports. Most tabloids have a larger proportion of the total newspaper (up to a quarter) devoted to sport.

The internet and social media are fast becoming the major forms of media in sport. The internet is now regularly used for sports coverage, allowing people to obtain the latest news about their favourite team, sport or event. The methods that are available for delivering sport to different sections of society continue to grow rapidly.

It has been said that the new media explosion makes 'any sport, any event, any time, any device' a reality for the fan. The list of possible outlets for sport is ever-increasing: high-definition and 3-D television, Internet Protocol TV, mobile phones, YouTube, web streaming, digital radio, iPlayer, games consoles and social networking sites.

Originally, the internet was mostly a one-way experience. People visited a website to read the content but had limited ways to interact. Access was by a computer. More recently, the internet has become more social. People can interact, generate and share multimedia content across the web. Websites have become interactive in terms of content and are accessible from multiple devices – computers, tablets, mobile phones, interactive TV, media players and games consoles.

Social media is media for social interaction. Social media uses web-based technologies to turn communication into interactive discussions. Social media is all about sharing rather than discovering information.

Spectators are using social media channels not only to take in information, but also to create information and interact with other users. Facebook, Twitter, Instagram, Reddit, TikTok and Snapchat are examples of social media platforms that sports fans and performers can use to interact with teams and other performers, to keep up with the latest news and results, and to share opinions.

▲ **Figure 5b.6** Social media allows performers to share their experiences with fans.

> ✔ **Check your understanding**
>
> 5 State five forms of media.
> 6 How do radio and newspapers try to compete with TV?
> 7 What are the two main types of newspaper?
>
> Answers are on page 196.

Commercialised activity and the performer

The media often focus on individual personalities rather than the event. Therefore, performers have to be aware of the need to entertain in order to increase their **marketability**.

The high income of many elite performers and the lifestyle it offers restricts the performer's ability to move in 'normal' society, especially with the amount of media intrusion into their social background.

Sponsorship usually means that the team or individual performances improve because the additional income gives them more time to train, better venues to train in and better equipment to use – all of which should mean that skills and fitness develop.

The performer may get free equipment, clothing or footwear. They may even be paid for wearing that clothing and using that equipment. The performer will be under less stress to win because of the reduced worry about finances.

However, there are some negative aspects. The contract between the sponsors and the performer may demand that the performer has to submit to various commitments, such as meeting corporate hosts and talking to the media, which may mean a loss of free time or privacy.

The sponsor's product may not be entirely suitable in terms of the performer's values, such as being thought of as unhealthy. A run of poor results may lead to a loss of sponsorship and, therefore, income. Such a trend could lead to a performer looking to cheat to prevent such a run and maintain their sponsorship.

Commercialised activity and the sport

Sponsorship has increased the income for many sports, so they do not have to rely on income from spectators. Sponsorship has provided the finances for the development of new competitions and has provided increased media interest.

But not all sponsorship is good. Sponsorship relies on the media. The media concentrate on the 'best', often to the detriment of the 'not quite the best'. So the big sports (for example, football in the UK) get the big money and minor sports get very little.

Key term

Marketability Ability to be sold.

Activity 6

Survey at least five of your friends, family and classmates to find out how they use social media to keep up with their favourite sports.

- What do they have in common?
- What is different?
- Does it vary according to the sport or the person?
- Why do you think this is?

PRACTICE QUESTIONS

5 Suggest disadvantages to a sport of increased media control. (4 marks)

Answers are on page 197.

Activity 7

Amazon Prime achieved the rights to show Premier League football for the three years from 2019 to 2022. Find out how much it paid to show its package of matches.

Answers are on page 198.

Activity 8

Research and make a list of how many different sports are on television (all channels) in any three-day period. What are the five main televised sports?

▲ **Figure 5b.8** Mark Clattenburg, football referee.

For example, the broadcasting rights to Premier League football, bought by Sky and BT Sport for the three years from the 2016/17 season to the end of the 2019/20 season, were worth over £5 billion. That means an average price of £10 million for the teams when their game is shown live. This is the same amount as the annual sponsorship being given to UK Athletics by Sainsbury's.

Sponsors, because they are putting so much money into sport, are gaining more and more control over sport in terms of what is shown on TV, when it's shown and who is shown. For example, the images that are shown on TV are invariably arranged to show the sponsor's name. The sponsor decides where to place the sponsor's name and logo, and where to place the cameras in order to get the sponsor's name maximum exposure and maximum publicity.

![On-pitch advertising showing CORAL and BLACK LIVES MATTER signage]

▲ **Figure 5b.7** On-pitch advertising.

The timings of events are now determined by the sponsors to maximise the potential for publicity. Premiership football, again, is the best example. Matches are staged at different times over different days of the weekend to maximise the number of spectators.

Teams change their strips to suit their sponsors. Most sponsorship deals last two or three years and each new deal will involve several new kits.

Effects of commercialisation on officials

Commercialisation of sport is all about money. The money brings its own benefits and problems for officials.

Officials can get paid to officiate, and their income has increased in recent years. People who officiate elite sport are invariably full-time; officiating is their job (see Figure 5b.8). In most elite sports, if matches are being played more frequently, then more matches can be officiated by the relatively few high-calibre officials.

A top football or rugby union referee can earn £50 000–100 000 per year. Matches are held around the world, so there is the opportunity to travel. Many officials can become nearly as famous as the players they control.

But there are downsides, mainly because of the media coverage involved. Officials are regularly placed in the media spotlight over decisions they have made. Making a bad decision can lead to being dropped from the elite panel of officials and, with social media, severe criticism from the general public.

The modern-day official has to be prepared to take the rough with the smooth in much the same way as the professional sportsperson in terms of accusations of not performing well, being biased, cheating, etc.

> ### ✔ Check your understanding
>
> 8   List four ways that sponsors can support an individual other than supplying money.
> 9   State three possible disadvantages of sponsorship to an individual.
> 10 Suggest three ways that sponsors can influence a sport.
> 11 Suggest two benefits and two disadvantages of commercialisation for officials.
>
> Answers are on page 196.

Effects of commercialisation on spectators

In general, commercialisation has been beneficial for spectators. There is more money available for better players to be brought in and matches are played at a higher standard. Facilities have improved for spectating at the match, with many teams updating existing facilities or moving to new, improved facilities.

▲ **Figure 5b.9** The Tottenham Hotspur Stadium opened in 2019.

The spectators can be more involved through the use of huge TV screens to show replays, statistics and other information, which also makes them more informed and knowledgeable about the activity. The spectators can associate themselves more clearly with the activity through buying merchandise.

PRACTICE QUESTIONS

6   Describe how commercialisation has had an impact on officials.
(4 marks)

Answers are on page 197.

▲ **Figure 5b.10** TV screens provide information and replays for spectators.

Changing the format of a sport, together with longer seasons, means that there are more opportunities for spectators to watch their favourite sport.

The armchair spectator can see many more games using a wide range of different camera angles. There are more sports available to watch than ever before, with dedicated sports channels on TV, radio and websites. There are also sport-specific newspapers.

The main problem for the armchair spectator is the isolation from the live match, but TV tends to compensate for that through the use of crowd noise, specialist camera positions, the use of the red button to offer a preferred view and informed opinions from 'experts'.

Effects of commercialisation on sponsors

Commercialisation provides sponsors with the publicity they require for their product. The advertising through sport attracts a very large audience and many people will want to be associated with sporting success. The status of the product is linked to that success. There could be increased sales of the product and, therefore, increased income for the business.

On the negative side, anything that occurs in a sport that is harmful to that sport, team or individual will also affect the sponsor and, potentially, the sales of the product. So things such as crowd trouble, a run of poor results, cheating or drug-taking may affect the reputation of the sponsor.

PRACTICE QUESTIONS

7 In what ways has an increase in the commercialisation of sport been beneficial for performers and the sport?
(4 marks)

Answers are on page 197.

✔ Check your understanding

12 List three benefits to spectators of commercialisation.
13 List two disadvantages of commercialisation for spectators.
14 Describe a sporting situation that would be perfect for a sponsor.

Answers are on page 196.

Technological developments in sport

Sport has changed over the years, and the use of more and more **technology** has made an impact on many modern-day sports. If it wasn't for technology there would be no instant replays, third umpires or even microphones for referees to communicate with their assistants.

In other words, technology is used by performers, coaches and officials to try to improve performance, it is used to improve the experience of spectators and it can be used to improve a sport.

One criticism of the use of technology is that it can slow down the speed of the game, but on the other hand, for many people, it makes watching sport more enjoyable as they can see the correct decisions being made. For example, technology such as **Hawk-Eye** in cricket and tennis or the **Television Match Official (TMO)** in cricket and rugby is used by the officials to make sure their decisions are correct, and such technology has now become part of the sports' spectator appeal.

▲ **Figure 5b.11** Hawk-Eye is used in tennis for line calls.

Positive and negative impacts of technology on the performer

For the performer, recent developments in sporting technologies have created a variety of products aimed at improving performance. The health and wellbeing of performers can be maintained and observed, and injuries treated, through the production of technologies such as heart-rate monitors, pedometers and body-fat monitors.

Nutrition and fitness are probably the most important factors which can affect an athlete's performance in sport. Technology such as software programs are being used to monitor and analyse an athlete's nutrition and fitness levels in much more accurate ways than previously.

Technology in the form of computer software and 'calorie counters' means that diets are now manipulated so that athletes reach peak nutrition for their event.

This type of technology has given individuals greater knowledge of the body's ability to absorb repeated exercise, which in turn has allowed performers to train and become much fitter, resulting in better performances.

The safety of those involved has also been increased through the development of certain sporting equipment, such as the helmets and body protection used in cricket and hockey to help prevent injuries.

Activity 9

Read this article about how technology is affecting sport: www.topendsports.com/resources/technology.htm

Discuss with a partner how technology has affected a sport of your choice and how you think technology could improve this sport.

Key terms

Technology A method that is developed to try to improve performance.

Hawk-Eye An optical ball-tracking device used as an aid to officiating in tennis and cricket.

Television Match Official (TMO) Used in rugby union and rugby league to make decisions using replays of incidents.

Activity 10

Choose a sport. Write down all the methods of technology being used in that sport.

Identify which of the methods in your list assist the performer, the sport, the officials, the spectators or the sponsors.

Key terms

Oxygen (hypoxic) tents Tents that contain high oxygen concentrations to speed up recovery after injury.

Hyperbaric chambers High pressure chambers that force oxygen into an injury to speed up recovery.

Prosthetics Artificial aid; often replacing a limb.

Match analysis Computer software that provides detailed statistical data about individual and/or team performances.

PED Performance-enhancing drug.

▲ **Figure 5b.12** Prosthetic limbs are used by many performers who have a specific disability.

Rehabilitation from injuries is now much quicker because of advances in technology through the use of ice baths, **oxygen (hypoxic) tents** and **hyperbaric chambers**.

Sports equipment such as clothing and footwear needs to be user-friendly and includes valuable properties such as strength, flexibility, toughness, resistance to moisture and, more importantly, has cost advantages.

Clothing such as the full-body suits used in cycling, where winning or losing is measured in hundredths of a second, has become increasingly important. Sporting equipment, such as the composite tennis racket, has been created in order to provide increased ball speed and reduce the potential for overuse injuries on the elbow.

Prosthetics have also been made for athletes with a specific disability. Examples include those worn by those athletes without a lower limb, which act with a 'springboard' effect, to help the performer run.

All performances are now studied in detail through DVD recordings, and developing computer software leads to detailed **match analysis**. The analysis can tell a coach when a player is beginning to lose fitness so they may be substituted. It can also be used to analyse opponents' weaknesses and enable tactical adjustments to be made.

The negatives to the use of technology for the performer are generally based around cost. As technology develops, so the performer needs to keep up to date, and buy and use the latest technology in order to gain that slight advantage that separates the winner from the loser.

Technology also means that the performer is never alone. In much the same way as a performance can be analysed for weaknesses so that it can be improved, it can also be analysed by the opposition to highlight those weaknesses, or to copy all the good aspects.

Increased use of technology to improve performance could lead to the increased chance of injury and the possibility of shorter careers for the performers. Developments in technology could also lead to more cheating; for example, new performance-enhancing drugs (**PED**s) being developed and used by performers. Similarly, the attempt to improve though the use of technology could lead to cheating; for example, through the use of electric motors being fitted inside racing bikes to improve performance.

> ### ✔ Check your understanding
>
> 15 State one benefit and one disadvantage of using Hawk-Eye.
> 16 List four benefits of technology to performers.
> 17 List two disadvantages to the spectator of technology.
>
> Answers are on page 196.

Positive and negative impacts of technology on sport

Technology has changed sport. For example, judgements are made not based on the human eye or an official's instinct, but rather through electronic timing, photo-finish cameras, instant replays, third umpires and technologies such as Hawk-Eye.

Sports must appeal to the technology and, if necessary, change to accommodate technology. Advances in technology have had a deep impact on sport, including:

- analysis of sports performance has allowed coaches to greatly improve the quality of feedback given to performers
- increased accuracy in time and distance measurements of performance
- referees, umpires and other officials are enabled to make better decisions on rule infringements
- improved design of sports equipment, clothing and footwear
- providing spectators with better viewing of sport.

But technology has also had its disadvantages in that sports are now not often undertaken on an equal basis. Those with access to the best technology are often the winners. Also, the time taken waiting for off-field decisions is sometimes frustrating for spectators.

Positive and negative impacts of technology on officials

Technology is available for officials to use to make correct decisions. In most team sports, the various officials are able to communicate with each other through microphones and headsets.

In sports such as tennis and cricket, technology such as Hawk-Eye, which is essentially a ball-tracking software, is used to ensure officials' decisions are accurate.

A similar situation occurs in rugby union and rugby league, where another, off-field official is able to make decisions based on multiple camera angles.

These delays in making decisions are thought by some to slow the game down, but for many the waiting creates excitement. Such technology also provides coaches and/or players with the benefit of appealing a decision, which was not available in the past.

The technology available to officials means that some of the pressure or criticism levelled at them is reduced because decisions are made with the benefit of the technology, rather than instantaneously.

Unfortunately, the technology can never be perfect and decisions are still made that some feel are wrong. There is also the danger that officials become over-reliant on technology and slow the game down too much while making a decision. In doing so, it changes the nature of the sport, which is probably why football has yet to make full use of technology in deciding things such as offside or penalties – the wait for a decision would change the game too much.

Another problem with technology is the cost. Not all sports/teams/individuals can afford the latest technology.

> **Activity 11**
>
> Focus on the part of this article about assisting the umpires and referees: https://bit.ly/2HnpgA6
>
> Discuss with a partner – is technology making officiating easier?

▲ **Figure 5b.13** The crowd waiting for a decision from a Television Match Official.

PRACTICE QUESTIONS

8 Suggest how the increased use of technology has helped officials to make the correct decision. (3 marks)

Answers are on page 197.

▲ **Figure 5b.14** An all-weather surface pitch.

Positive and negative impacts of technology on spectators

Technological developments mean that spectators have an increased experience at home through the use of more cameras. There is a wider range of sports accessible through technology; for example, using glass walls and a reflective ball in squash.

The use of all-weather surfaces has led to improved skills from the performer because of the truer bounce. These surfaces have also meant that more matches can be played without damaging the surface.

Spectators now have the benefit of improved camera technology; for example, use of the red button, Hawk-Eye, player cams, post/stump cameras.

Spectators are also now much better informed about the activity through the on-screen information that can be supplied; for example, number of shots on target. This makes the sport much more interactive for the spectator.

Positive and negative impacts of technology on sponsors

Technology has assisted sponsors in how they are able to advertise their products. More cameras mean more chance of the sponsor's logo being seen. Logos are often painted onto the pitch to advertise sponsors. In some sports, especially in the USA, camera technology means that logos can be shown on-screen without being present on the pitch.

More advertising usually leads to more sales and more profit, which is usually what the sponsor intended.

However, the negative effects of technology, such as injuries, cheating and losing, can also negatively affect the sales of a sponsor's product because that product is linked to the performer/sport that involves injuries, cheating and losing.

✔ Check your understanding

18 State three benefits of technology to a sport.
19 Suggest why football does not use a TMO.
20 State three benefits of technology to sponsors.

Answers are on page 196.

Summary

- There is a clear relationship – the golden triangle – between sport, sponsorship and the media; each now relies heavily on the other.
- There are both positive and negative impacts of commercialisation on those involved in sport.
- Technology is having an ever-increasing influence, both positive and negative, on those involved in sport.

Chapter objectives

- Understand how the conduct of performers may vary
- Understand the different prohibited substances and the methods that certain types of performers may use
- Understand the positive and the negative effects of spectators at events

Players' conduct

The way people play sports is fixed by the rules, but there are also unwritten rules which people try to abide by, whether they are playing or spectating. These rules are about behaviour and are known as **etiquette**.

▲ **Figure 5c.1** Etiquette.

For example, in football, players usually kick the ball out of play if another player is injured so that they can get treatment. The team that kicked the ball out then get the ball back when the opposition throw it to them when play restarts. In many games, players shake their opponents' hands and those of the officials after the match. In some sports, such as golf, players are expected to officiate themselves and even own up to breaking the rules.

These are examples of **sportsmanship**, sometimes called fair play. Sportsmanship is playing fair, showing respect for the opposition, and gracious behaviour in winning or losing. On the other hand, **gamesmanship** is coming close to breaking the rules, without getting punished. For example, time-wasting when you are winning is not against the rules, but is probably not fair play. In tennis, players sometimes try to break their opponent's concentration by retying their shoelaces when an important serve is about to happen.

Activity 1

Work with a partner. One of you has to argue that sportsmanship is good for a sports performer, while the other has to argue that sportsmanship is not good for a sports performer. Afterwards, discuss the points you made and decide which argument was most convincing.

▲ **Figure 5c.2** Sportsmanship.

Key terms

Etiquette The unwritten rules concerning player behaviour.

Sportsmanship Appropriate, polite and fair behaviour while participating in a sporting event.

Gamesmanship The use of dubious methods, that are not strictly illegal, to gain an advantage.

PRACTICE QUESTIONS

1 Is diving in football gamesmanship or bad sportsmanship? Explain your answer.   (3 marks)
2 How is the ethic of sportsmanship encouraged and maintained at the highest level of sport?   (2 marks)
Answers are on pages 198–9.

▲ **Figure 5c.3** Diving is a common occurrence in football, but is it fair play?

The **contract to compete** is linked to the idea of sportsmanship and is the agreement that in sport players try to win, play within the rules and with etiquette, and allow the opposition a free and fair opportunity to win. The contract to compete is usually in the performer's head rather than written down. It is occasionally seen to be agreed; for example, when players shake hands before a football match. The contract to compete is about trying your hardest and allowing the opposition to play.

▲ **Figure 5c.4** Shaking hands before a match means 'we agree to the contract to compete'.

Check your understanding

1 What is etiquette?
2 Give three examples of sportsmanship from a team game.
3 What is gamesmanship?
4 What is the contract to compete?
Answers are on page 198.

Key terms

Contract to compete Agreeing to play by the rules, trying to win but also allowing your opponent to play.

Ergogenic aid A technique or substance used for the purpose of enhancing performance.

National Governing Body Organisation with responsibility for managing its specific sport.

International Olympic Committee The independent authority of the worldwide modern Olympic movement. It organises the Olympic Games.

Prohibited substances

There are a large number of products which may be taken to help sports performance in some way. These are known as **ergogenic aids** or performance-enhancing drugs (PEDs). PEDs are banned by **National Governing Bodies** of sport and the **International Olympic Committee**.

Activity 2

Use the internet to research the top three sports that are responsible for the most drug-test failures. Why do you think these sports have such high rates of prohibited drug use?

Stimulants

Stimulants are substances that speed up parts of the brain and body. **Adrenaline** is an example of a naturally occurring stimulant in the body. Some athletes may use stimulants in an attempt to increase alertness, reduce reaction time, reduce tiredness and increase their aggressiveness.

Examples of stimulants are amphetamines and caffeine. They are highly addictive and have side effects including high blood pressure, strokes and heart and liver problems. They can also increase the risk of injury because the performer is more tolerant to pain and will continue to train or compete with an injury.

Performers who are injured and want to return to competition or full-time training may be tempted to use stimulants to deaden pain. The most likely users, however, would be those performers who need to be more alert, such as sprinters and speed swimmers, who need a fast reaction time at the start of a race.

Narcotic analgesics

Narcotic analgesics are very strong painkillers which performers could use to mask pain from an injury or overtraining. They are highly addictive and cause withdrawal symptoms when you stop using them.

Examples of narcotic analgesics include heroin and morphine. Constipation and low blood pressure are side effects, as is loss of concentration and possible coma. Performers who need to recover from excessive overtraining or compete with an injury may be tempted to use these.

Anabolic agents

Athletes may use **anabolic agents** to increase the rate and amount of muscle growth. The most common type is the anabolic steroid. These also speed up recovery so performers are able to train harder and more frequently. Common examples include Nandrolone and Danazol.

Performers take anabolic agents to build up body weight and to increase the size of muscles and, therefore, their strength. These drugs may also make the user more aggressive and competitive. Like many other banned substances, they are also addictive.

Heavy, regular use of anabolic agents can shrink the testicles in men, cause high blood pressure and damage the liver, kidneys and heart. Women may develop more body hair, smaller breasts and a deeper voice.

Peptide hormones (EPO)

These are naturally occurring substances that can improve muscle growth and increase production of red blood cells, which increases oxygen delivery to muscles.

One **peptide hormone** is **EPO** (erythropoietin), which will increase the number of red blood cells in the body, and therefore increase the ability of an athlete's blood to transport oxygen to cells that are producing energy during exercise. This additional oxygen reduces the fatigue felt in muscles

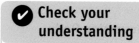

▲ **Figure 5c.5** Drugs can improve performance.

Key terms

Stimulants Make athletes more alert and mask effects of fatigue.

Adrenaline Naturally occurring hormone that prepares the body for 'fight or flight'.

Narcotic analgesics Painkillers that mask pain caused by injury or fatigue, which can make the injury worse.

Anabolic agents Drugs that help athletes to train harder and build muscle.

Peptide hormones (EPO) Naturally occurring chemicals. EPO increases numbers of red blood cells and therefore improves oxygen delivery to muscles.

> **✔ Check your understanding**
>
> 5 Why might a performer use stimulants?
> 6 What type of performer might use anabolic agents?
> 7 What are the side effects of narcotic analgesic use?
>
> Answers are on page 198.

PRACTICE QUESTIONS

3 Taking EPO is a form of blood doping. What are the supposed benefits of this practice and what type of performer might take EPO? (3 marks)

4 Suggest why a performer might take anabolic agents. (2 marks)

Answers are on page 199.

Key terms

Diuretics Drugs that remove fluid from the body.

Dehydration A condition that occurs when the body loses more water than it takes in.

Blood doping Artificially increasing the number of red cells in the blood.

Viscosity How 'thick' a liquid is.

Embolism When a blood clot blocks a blood vessel.

Beta blockers Drugs taken to calm the performer down by reducing the effects of adrenaline.

in long-distance events such as marathon running and cycling. The side effects of EPO are caused by the thickening of the blood, which requires the heart to pump harder and can lead to an increased risk of stroke or heart attack.

Diuretics

Diuretics are drugs such as Frusemide that are taken to remove excess water from the body. They are not used to improve actual performance; they are used for other reasons. First, to lose weight rapidly in sports that require the performer to be within a set weight limit; for example, boxers and jockeys. Second, to dilute the presence of illegal substances and aid their removal from the body in urine.

Diuretics cause severe **dehydration**, low blood pressure and muscle cramp, and may be taken by any performer to hide other PED use.

Blood doping

Blood doping is the use of techniques and/or substances to increase a performer's red blood cell count.

The simplest form of blood doping involves the removal of about two pints of blood from the athlete several weeks before a competition. In the time before the competition, the body will make more blood to replace the amount taken out. The removed blood is frozen until 1–2 days before the competition, when it is thawed and injected back into the athlete. The use of EPO is really a form of blood doping.

Blood doping is most commonly used by endurance athletes, such as marathon runners and cyclists. By increasing the number of red blood cells, the blood can carry more oxygen to the muscles where it can be used for energy.

The following side effects can occur with blood doping:

- increased thickening (**viscosity**) of blood
- potential for heart attacks
- risk of blood-borne diseases such as HIV and hepatitis
- **embolism** (a blockage of a blood vessel).

Beta blockers

Beta blockers reduce the effects of adrenaline on the body. They reduce the heart rate and reduce muscle tension and blood pressure. By doing this, they improve a performer's fine motor control and will increase precision when using motor skills. Beta blockers could be taken by performers who need to reduce the effects of nerves and use fine motor skills, such as players in target sports.

The side effects of beta blockers include nausea, poor circulation leading to heart problems, tiredness and weakness. Sports performers may only take beta blockers if they have been prescribed by a medical professional.

✔ Check your understanding

8 What are the effects of taking EPO?
9 What effects do diuretics have?
10 What type of performer might use blood doping?
11 What are beta blockers?
Answers are on page 198.

Activity 3

Copy and complete Table 5c.1.

▼ **Table 5c.1**

Effects on athlete	Type of PED	Sport that might benefit
Enhance alertness	Stimulant	
Reduce heart rate		Archery
	EPO	Cycling
Mask drug use	Diuretics	
	Anabolic agents	Weight-lifting
Mask pain		Football

Answers are on page 199.

The advantages and disadvantages to the performer of taking PEDs

The reasons athletes use performance-enhancing drugs (PEDs) is that they have a lot of benefits which allow the performer to play better, keep their career going and keep them employed.

Athletes are under pressure to perform, and PEDs can be a way for them to keep up with the competition. Since their income depends on performance, it's not a surprise that some sportspeople may take advantage of the benefits of PEDs.

The potential advantages of PEDs are better performance and, therefore, an increased chance of success. As a professional performer, hand in hand with the success will come the increase in income, and linked to this will be greater recognition or fame for the performer.

One often mentioned reason for the taking of PEDs is the performer's thoughts that everybody else is taking them, so why not join in? In doing so, the performer probably thinks they are simply keeping a level playing field.

Some of these PEDs may come with associated health risks, but they also have several disadvantages that need to be considered.

First, it is cheating. It is immoral and is against the whole idea of what sport is and the concepts of sportsmanship and etiquette. Taking PEDs is against the contract to compete.

Second, as testing procedures become ever more accurate and regular, it becomes more and more likely that the cheats will be caught. Performers who test positive for banned substances usually face a two-year ban from their sport. They will also be fined. Perhaps the biggest disadvantage concerning being caught taking PEDs is the damage to the performer's reputation and the long-term negative publicity they will face.

Rapid recall

An acronym for reasons for drug-taking is **FILS**:
Fame
Income
Level playing field
Success.

Rapid recall

Construct a mnemonic for the disadvantages of taking PEDs; e.g. Clear Bans For Risking Heroin?
Cheating
Bans
Fines
Reputation
Health risks.

Activity 4

Make a list of the advantages and disadvantages to a performer of taking PEDs.
Answers are on page 199.

✔ **Check your understanding**

12 Suggest three possible benefits to the performer of taking PEDs.
13 Identify three disadvantages to the performer of taking PEDs.
14 List two effects on a sport that a positive drugs test might have.

Answers are on page 198.

PRACTICE QUESTIONS

5 Some performers may take PEDs to improve performance. Suggest two potential advantages and two potential disadvantages of a performer taking drugs.

(4 marks)

Answers are on page 199.

Key term

Home-field advantage The psychological advantage that the home team has over the visiting team as a result of playing in familiar facilities and in front of supportive fans.

The disadvantages to the sport of performers taking PEDs

Despite the fines, bans, health risks and damage to their reputation, some performers still take PEDs. Certain sports have lost their reputation because of the number of positive tests that have occurred. Spectators become quite cynical about exceptional performances and are inclined to think 'Was that due to drugs?' rather than 'That was an outstanding performance'. Some sports, such as cycling and athletics, begin to lose their credibility because of regular positive drugs tests.

Sports could lose income through reduced numbers of spectators or through loss of sponsorship. Participation levels could fall.

Spectator behaviour

The whole basis for sports is the idea of playing for fun. But as interest in sport grew, people began paying to watch, and so sports became commercialised as people paid to watch the matches/events. Paying spectators enabled various sports clubs to make a profit and use this money to develop the sport.

Some sports with large spectator bases were able to pay for better performers and so encourage an increase in spectating. These sports became professional in that they paid their players to play.

The increased interest in spectating led to increased media attention. The early media that embraced a massed audience were newspapers and the radio, but TV provided the spur to the dramatic increase in the commercialisation of sport that we now see.

The televising of sport works in two ways. First, it provides a relatively cheap form of production that can be shown live or in a highlights package. Second, it dramatically increases the number of spectators from thousands at the event to millions in their homes.

While spectators do not have any effect on a performer's physical ability, they can make or break some performers' concentration. Spectators don't just watch, they are actively and vocally involved in the experience. Many cheer for the team or individual they are backing and whistle or boo the opposition. This creates an atmosphere at the event.

It is commonly accepted that cheering positively influences a team's performance. When playing a match, the home team receives much more support from the crowd in attendance. This is called **home-field advantage** and explains why most teams have better results at home than when playing away.

If the atmosphere created by the loud support for the home team is an advantage, there are also negative aspects to spectating. The atmosphere itself can be intimidating, especially if a performer is not used to it. The positive effects of home-field advantage must also act as negative effects on the away team, hindering performance. The same thing could happen to the home players, however, with the spectators expecting a positive result and increasing the pressure to perform.

If spectators become over-involved in the expectation of success at a match, this can lead to crowd trouble. This has been a problem for football for the last 50 years. Although acts of **hooliganism** can be serious, they are often sensationalised by the media.

The vast majority of football fans or spectators are not hooligans. This majority expect to attend matches in safety, but this costs money. Crowd trouble at matches needs to be controlled and this causes major concerns for the clubs and footballing authorities.

The potential for crowd trouble has a negative effect for those watching, especially younger spectators. They could easily be dissuaded from participating in a sport where such activity is commonplace.

▲ **Figure 5c.6** Crowd trouble at a football match.

Reasons for hooliganism

Hooliganism can occur in the football grounds, but also in the streets near the ground, in local pubs, on public transport or in city centres. A range of reasons has been suggested for the cause of hooliganism, but none seems to give a full explanation.

One possible cause of hooliganism is rivalry between local teams. Derby matches can inflame the passions of fans, which could spill over into violent behaviour. This is often picked up on by the newspapers and hyped in an attempt to increase sales. However, all sports have derby matches that are played without disturbances between rival fans. In many sports, rival fans often sit together and enjoy the banter.

Crowd trouble has also been linked to alcohol consumption, the argument being that alcohol or drugs lessen inhibitions and make people more open to suggestions. Alcohol is banned at many football stadiums.

Hooliganism is also thought to be a form of behaviour linked to a gang culture. The group thinks they are protecting their local area or 'patch' from the away fans. This can lead to predetermined, organised violence against another group or gang of fans.

Some forms of spontaneous hooliganism have been blamed on frustration. This could be frustration about their own team's performance, refereeing decisions or the particular circumstances at that club.

Key term
Hooliganism Rowdy, violent or destructive behaviour.

Activity 5
Summarise the possible causes of hooliganism as single words. Then rearrange those words into a sports-related phrase that forms an acronym.
Answers are on page 200.

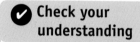 **Check your understanding**
15 What are the main benefits to a sport of more spectators?
16 What is home-field advantage?
17 What is hooliganism?
Answers are on page 198.

Study hint
Make sure you know three or four reasons for hooliganism.

Finally, there is some evidence that hooliganism is a type of ritualised behaviour that provides the opportunity for a display of masculinity, and being part of a group. But hooliganism is more than ritualistic, does not solely concern males and does not always involve group membership.

Realistically, there is no single cause of hooligan behaviour in football. It has multiple causes, with each explanation adding something to our understanding of what may cause such behaviour.

Combating hooliganism

During the 1970s and 1980s, hooliganism became such a problem for the football authorities that the government, the football governing bodies and the police co-operated to put in place a range of strategies that have resulted in a significant reduction in football-related violence. However, these strategies have come at a cost to the authorities.

These strategies are as follows:

▲ **Figure 5c.7** Tackling hooliganism.

- Preventing known hooligans from travelling to matches by requiring them to report to police stations during match times, or by applying banning orders. But this means that the authorities have to create a list of troublemakers and have knowledge of their existing locations and intentions – all of which costs money.

- Alcohol is not served within most football grounds. Sometimes matches are arranged to kick off early so as to prevent excessive alcohol consumption. The police may require local pubs to close early to prevent alcohol consumption, but this means loss of income for those pubs.

- The introduction of all-seater stadiums for teams playing in the higher divisions reduces the ability of people to move within a stand and allows better control over ticket distribution. But again, there is a cost involved in introducing such facilities.

- Segregation of fans travelling to the match and within the grounds. But there is a policing/stewarding cost and possibly a loss of revenue for the home team where spaces are maintained between rival fans and empty seats on the away side cannot be sold.

- Improved levels of policing and stewarding, allied to better training of stewards, improves crowd control and can lower tension. But the cost to a club of policing home matches in the Premiership can be in the region of £1 million per year.

- Introduction of CCTV cameras at grounds and entrances to stadiums has resulted in more information being gathered about individuals engaged in hooligan behaviour. Known hooligans can be identified and, if appropriate, prevented from entering the ground. But again, there is a cost.

- Poor behaviour by the fans or supporters of a club can result in banning or removing them from competitions, fines, or being forced to play matches away or behind closed doors.

- The football authorities have used high-profile role models to appeal for better supporter behaviour, and have also, through campaigns such

Study hint
Make sure you know three or four strategies to combat hooliganism.

as 'Kick It Out', attempted to lessen the influence of racist movements among football supporters.

All of the strategies used have cost the authorities and the clubs money. However, the cost is a small price to pay for spectator safety.

▲ **Figure 5c.8** Opposing football fans have to be kept separated.

PRACTICE QUESTIONS

6 Hooliganism at football matches, both inside and outside stadiums, is a recurring problem.

    a) Describe three steps that have been taken to prevent such acts.   (3 marks)

    b) Identify three reasons that have been suggested as to why football should suffer from hooliganism.   (3 marks)

7 Evaluate the effectiveness of strategies to combat hooliganism at football matches.   (6 marks)

Answers are on page 199.

Activity 6

Read about the Kick It Out campaign at www.kickitout.org. Describe three practical ways that it is fighting racism in football.

✔ Check your understanding

18 Identify three possible negative effects of spectators at matches.
19 Suggest four possible reasons for hooliganism.
20 Give four strategies that have been put in place to reduce hooliganism.

Answers are on page 198.

Summary

- There is a variety of ethical issues within sport.
- Some performers may take prohibited substances, each of which has both positive and negative effects on the performer.
- Blood doping is a prohibited method of improving performance.
- There are various drugs that are banned by the sporting authorities.
- There are advantages and disadvantages to the performer and the sport of taking PEDs.
- Spectators have both positive and negative influences at sporting events.
- There are various reasons suggested as to why hooliganism occurs.
- There are various strategies that have been put in place to prevent and combat hooliganism.

Chapter 6 Health and fitness

Chapter objectives

- Linking participation in physical activity, exercise and sport to fitness, health and wellbeing
- How exercise can suit the varying needs of different people
- The consequences of a sedentary lifestyle
- Obesity and how it may affect performance in physical activity and sport
- The most suitable body type (somatotypes) for particular sports (or positions within a sport)
- How energy is gained from food and used
- Reasons for having a balanced diet
- The role of carbohydrates, fat, protein, vitamins and minerals
- Reasons for maintaining water balance

Physical, emotional and social health, fitness and wellbeing

There are several terms and definitions that you need to know in order to fully understand the link between taking part in an activity and what effect it has on health, wellbeing and fitness.

Although the terms 'health' and 'fitness' are also defined in Chapter 3 on physical training, it is perhaps best to confirm these definitions here:

Health (as per the World Health Organization's definition: 1948) – 'A state of complete physical, mental and social wellbeing and not merely the absence of disease or infirmity.'

Be aware that 'ill health' refers to being in a state of poor physical, mental and/or social wellbeing.

Fitness – The ability to meet/cope with the demands of the environment.

By looking at the terms 'health' and 'fitness', you can see that there is a link between the two. As being 'healthy' includes a 'physical component', you would expect that a healthy person has a well-developed or appropriate level of fitness to allow them to cope with the demands of the environment in which they live and work. This relationship is fully explored in Chapter 3, Physical training.

Health and wellbeing

Health has three distinctive components:

- physical health
- mental health
- social health.

When discussing these three components, it is often useful to group them with the concept of '**wellbeing**'.

Key terms

Health A state of complete physical, mental and social wellbeing and not merely the absence of disease or infirmity.

Fitness The ability to meet/cope with the demands of the environment.

Wellbeing A mix of physical, social and mental factors that gives people a sense of being comfortable, healthy and/or happy.

Thus we often talk about:

- physical health and wellbeing
- mental health and wellbeing
- social health and wellbeing.

Wellbeing

Very simply, 'wellbeing' involves physical, mental and social elements. It is the dynamic mix of the three parts that gives people a sense of being comfortable, healthy and/or happy. Your wellbeing can refer to how content and/or fulfilled you are in your life socially; for example, are you happy with your social life, friends, etc.?

▲ **Figure 6.1** Health and wellbeing have three components: physical, mental/emotional and social.

Physical health and wellbeing

Physical health and wellbeing refers to the idea that all of the body's systems are working well, so you are free from illness and injury. You therefore have an ability to carry out everyday tasks. Being active and taking part in exercise can therefore directly benefit your physical health and wellbeing. In other words, exercise can have a positive impact on the workings within your body.

Taking part in activity/exercise positively affects physical health and wellbeing as it can:

- improve your heart function
- improve the efficiency of the body systems – cardio-vascular system
- reduce the risk of some illness; for example, diabetes
- help to prevent the onset of obesity
- enable you to carry out everyday tasks without getting tired
- provide a feeling that you can comfortably carry out activities and enjoy them.

Study hint

You need to understand the differences between physical, mental and social wellbeing. The three together contribute to a person's health. You do not, however, have to distinguish between health and wellbeing; for example, the effects of exercise on physical health and wellbeing should be learnt together, rather than the health effects and wellbeing effects separately.

✔ **Check your understanding**

1 Define the terms 'health', 'fitness' and 'wellbeing'.

Answers are on page 200.

Key term

Physical health and wellbeing
All body systems working well, free from illness and injury. Ability to carry out everyday tasks.

▲ **Figure 6.2** Participating in aerobics at a leisure centre or playing recreational sport provides similar benefits to your physical health and wellbeing, as stated previously. Your body adjusts to the exercise and adapts, allowing the body's systems to work more efficiently (physical health). The feeling of being able to comfortably complete and enjoy exercise provides physical wellbeing.

Mental (emotional) health and wellbeing

Key term

Mental (emotional) health and wellbeing Defined by the World Health Organization as: 'a state of wellbeing in which every individual realizes his or her own potential, can cope with the normal stresses of life, can work productively and fruitfully, and is able to make a contribution to her or his community'.

Mental health has been defined by the World Health Organization as: 'a state of wellbeing in which every individual realises his or her own potential'. An individual with good **mental health and wellbeing** can cope with the normal stresses of life, can work productively and fruitfully, and is able to make a contribution to her or his community. Taking an active part in exercise can positively affect your mental health and wellbeing. Your general state of mind can improve (mental health) and you may 'feel good' about yourself after taking part in a session of suitable exercise (mental wellbeing).

Taking part in activity/exercise positively affects mental health and wellbeing as it can:

- reduce stress/tension levels
- release feel-good hormones in the body, such as serotonin
- enable a person to control their emotions and work productively.

▲ **Figure 6.3** Many people take part in physical activity to 'remove or release stress from everyday life', thus improving their mental health and wellbeing. For example, this may be done by visiting the gym after work or meeting friends for a recreational game of badminton at the local leisure centre.

Social health and wellbeing

So far we have covered two of the three aspects of health and wellbeing. The third, **social health and wellbeing**, refers to the idea that:

- basic human needs are being met (food, shelter and clothing)
- the individual has friendship and support, some value in society and is socially active
- the individual suffers little stress in social circumstances.

Through participating in sport and exercise, individuals get the chance to mix together and socialise. Becoming familiar with people and enjoying friendship allows an individual to feel at ease when being around people and holding conversations. Similarly, organised sport usually takes place in an environment that facilitates some aspects of social health; for example, clothing in the form of a team strip. Social health and wellbeing is deemed to be a vital component of one's health.

Taking part in physical activity/exercise positively affects social health and wellbeing as it can:

- provide opportunities to socialise/make friends
- encourage co-operation skills
- encourage team-working skills
- ensure that essential human needs are met.

> ✅ **Check your understanding**
>
> 2 Explain how wearing a team strip helps your social health and wellbeing.
> Answers are on page 200.

▲ **Figure 6.4** Socialising through sport and exercise is good for social health and wellbeing.

Key term

Social health and wellbeing
Basic human needs are being met (food, shelter and clothing). The individual has friendship and support, some value in society, is socially active and has little stress in social circumstances.

Fitness

As mentioned at the start of the chapter, fitness is the 'ability to meet or cope with the demands of the environment'. Thus, the fitter you are, the more easily you can cope with the demands of your everyday life. These demands may include being productive at work, walking the dog or even running to catch a bus. As you exercise and take part in activities, your body adapts to the demands of the exercise and improves in fitness. This adaptation also lowers the chance of injury occurring. Therefore, as your fitness improves, you are able to meet the demands of the environment more easily without suffering from fatigue (tiredness).

Improvements in fitness will:

- improve your ability to cope with the demands of your environment
- reduce the chances of you suffering injuries
- make it easier for you to complete physical work; for example, some people work on their feet all day or carry out manual labour
- make you feel more content/happy (increased wellbeing).

▲ **Figure 6.5** A person who has to carry out manual tasks as part of their job needs to be of an appropriate fitness level to cope with the demands of their work.

Study hint
Remember that all three of the above components of health and wellbeing (physical, mental and social) work together.

Activity 1

Individually or in small groups, match the term in the table to its correct definition.

▼ **Table 6.1**

Term	Definition
Health	Basic human needs are being met (food, shelter and clothing). The individual has friendship and support, some value in society, is socially active and has little stress in social circumstances
Fitness	All body systems working well, free from illness and injury. Ability to carry out everyday tasks
Social health and wellbeing	A state of complete, physical, mental and social wellbeing and not merely the absence of disease or infirmity
Mental health and wellbeing	The ability to meet/cope with the demands of the environment
Physical health and wellbeing	A 'feel-good' chemical released during exercise
Wellbeing	A state of wellbeing in which every individual realises his or her own potential, can cope with the normal stresses of life, can work productively and fruitfully, and is able to make a contribution to his or her community
Serotonin	Involves physical, mental and social wellbeing. It is the dynamic process of the three parts that gives people a sense of being comfortable, healthy and/or happy

Answers are on page 203.

Study hint
Make sure you are able to link participation in physical activity, exercise and sport to the different types of health/wellbeing and fitness; for example, how can taking part in activities improve your social health and wellbeing?

PRACTICE QUESTIONS

1 Explain two named components of wellbeing.   (4 marks)
2 Define 'health' and define 'fitness'.   (2 marks)
3 Which *one* of the following is an aspect of physical health and wellbeing?
   A Can cope with the normal stresses of life   ☐
   B Individual has friendship and support   ☐
   C All body systems working well   ☐
   D High level of self-confidence   ☐ (1 mark)

Answers are on page 201.

The consequences of a sedentary lifestyle

'Lifestyle choices' are simply the choices we make about how we live our lives. These could include:

- whether to smoke or not
- whether to drink alcohol or not

- whether to exercise or not
- whether to eat a balanced diet or not
- whether to actively seek an education or not.

Individuals of a suitable level of health are able to actively make choices that directly affect the amount of sport and exercise they take part in. Some people choose to do very little exercise. The lifestyle choice about whether to exercise or not significantly affects the health and fitness of an individual.

Sedentary lifestyle

The term 'sedentary' refers to a person's choice to engage in little, or irregular, physical activity. A 'sedentary adult' tends to make an active choice not to take part in exercise or sport. Such a choice can have far-reaching consequences for a person's health and fitness, as detailed below.

▲ **Figure 6.6** Leading a sedentary lifestyle is usually a choice; i.e. you could choose to be more active.

Here are some potential consequences of choosing a sedentary lifestyle:

- gaining weight/becoming obese (physical health and wellbeing)
- heart disease (physical health and wellbeing)
- hypertension (physical health and wellbeing)
- diabetes (physical health and wellbeing)
- poor sleep/insomnia (physical health and wellbeing)
- poor self-esteem/confidence (mental health and wellbeing)
- feeling tired and lethargic (physical/mental health and wellbeing)
- lack of friends/poor communication skills (social health and wellbeing).

The negative effects of a sedentary lifestyle are numerous, yet society still struggles to deal with those people who do not make positive choices in relation to their health and exercise levels. As you have seen previously, a person who follows a sedentary lifestyle may suffer weight gain and become obese.

Key term

Sedentary lifestyle A person's choice to engage in little, or irregular, physical activity.

▲ **Figure 6.7** A person who chooses to follow a sedentary lifestyle may experience an inability to sleep (insomnia) and/or lack of self-esteem.

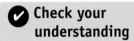

✔ Check your understanding

3 Describe some of the negative effects of choosing to have a sedentary lifestyle.

Answers are on page 200.

PRACTICE QUESTIONS

4 Describe what is meant by the term 'sedentary lifestyle'. (1 mark)

5 Describe three possible negative effects of choosing to have a sedentary lifestyle. (3 marks)

Answers are on page 201.

Key term

Obesity A term used to describe people with a large fat content – caused by an imbalance of calories consumed to energy expenditure. BMI of over 30 or 20 per cent or more above ideal weight for height.

Activity 2

In pairs or small groups, discuss the lifestyle choices you make in relation to the amount of activity you do. Answer the following questions:

- Do you exercise regularly (more than three times a week)?
- What stops or prevents you from making the lifestyle choice to take part in more activity/exercise?
- Do you struggle to sleep or sometimes feel tired for no obvious reason? Could this be because you actually choose not to exercise and therefore often suffer the negative consequences?

Obesity and how it may affect performance in physical activity and sport

'**Obesity**' is a term used to describe people with a high body fat content – usually over 40 per cent body fat. It is caused by an imbalance of calories consumed compared to energy expenditure. Obesity is used to classify people with a body mass index (BMI) of over 30, or 20 per cent or more above ideal weight for height. In simple terms, BMI compares your weight to your height.

Although body mass index is not something you specifically need to know, it is a good measure of whether someone is obese or not. A body mass index chart can show you if you are the correct weight for your height, as shown on the next page.

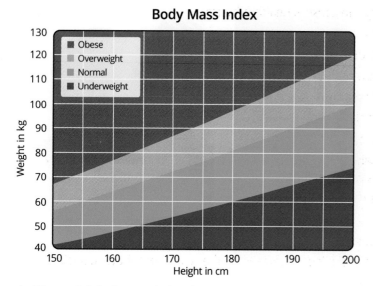

▲ **Figure 6.8** Body mass index chart.

The general classifications for an individual's BMI are:

- a score of less than 20 = underweight
- a score of 20–25 = correct weight
- a score of 25–30 = overweight
- a score of 30+ = obese.

Being significantly overweight can affect sporting performance, but it can also affect all three aspects of health and wellbeing (physical, mental and social).

Obesity and its effects on fitness

It may seem obvious, but carrying a large fat content can affect performance. Although performance in some activities can actually improve due to a large fat content (for example, sumo wrestling), the effect of being obese is generally negative as it can limit different components of a person's fitness.

Obesity can affect fitness by:

- limiting stamina/cardio-vascular endurance – thus making it difficult to perform any activities of a long duration
- limiting flexibility – making it difficult for performers to use a full range of movement at joints when attempting to perform skills
- limiting agility – making it difficult to change direction quickly
- limiting speed/power – making it hard to react quickly enough or to produce force.

Obesity and its effects on health and wellbeing

Just as obesity can negatively affect fitness, it also has far-reaching negative effects on a person's health and wellbeing. Being obese will affect all three components of health and wellbeing (physical, mental and social).

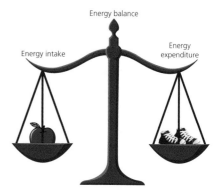

▲ **Figure 6.9** In simple terms, you will increase in body weight if your energy intake is greater than your energy expenditure.

How obesity can cause ill health (physical):

- It contributes to the development of cancer.
- It contributes to heart disease/heart attacks.
- It contributes to an increase in blood pressure.
- It contributes to the development of diabetes.
- It causes cholesterol levels to rise.
- It can lead to injury.
- It can make the individual feel that they cannot comfortably enjoy activities (wellbeing).

How obesity can cause ill health (mental/emotional):

- It can lead to depression.
- It can cause a loss of confidence.
- It can make the individual feel like they can't contribute to society (wellbeing).

How obesity can cause ill health (social):

- It can lead to an inability to socialise.
- It may make the individual feel unable to leave home.
- It may make the individual conscious of how they look and, therefore, uncomfortable in social situations (wellbeing).

Rapid recall

As you can see, the physical effects of obesity are numerous. However, you can remember that the physical effects of obesity are **BAD**:

Blood pressure increases
Attacks of the heart can occur
Diabetes may develop

✔ Check your understanding

4 In pairs, try to remember one negative effect that obesity may have on each of the three aspects of health and wellbeing (physical/mental/social). Then aim to make a list of negative effects.

PRACTICE QUESTIONS

6 Define 'obesity' and explain one negative effect that it could have on mental health and wellbeing. (2 marks)

7 Explain one negative consequence that obesity can have on a person's fitness. (1 mark)

8 Evaluate the effects of a sedentary lifestyle for someone who decides to start taking part in a team game activity. (6 marks)

Answers are on pages 201–2.

Key term

Somatotype A classification of body type – ectomorph, endomorph or mesomorph.

Somatotypes

Using **somatotypes** is a method of classifying body types. Three distinctive somatotypes (body shapes) were proposed by William Herbert Sheldon in the 1940s. The particular types of human body shape/physique were classed into the following somatotypes:

- ectomorph
- endomorph
- mesomorph.

These three somatotypes are extremes; that is, most people do not necessarily display extreme levels of one body type. Many people have characteristics of two or possibly a mixture of all three of these shapes.

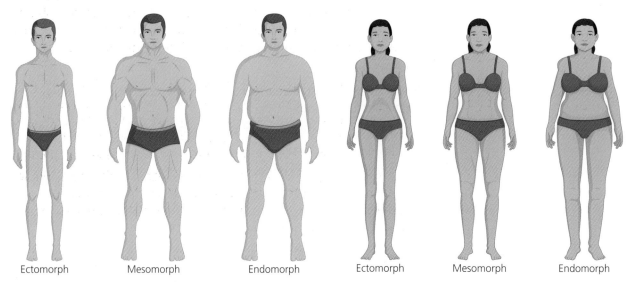

Ectomorph   Mesomorph   Endomorph   Ectomorph   Mesomorph   Endomorph

▲ **Figure 6.10** Somatotypes in men and women.

Somatotypes for sport

In trying to understand what specific body type is best for an activity, you need to appreciate the characteristics of each somatotype classification and the demands of any given activity. It can be argued that modern-day sport often necessitates a particularly well-developed level of specific fitness with a greater need for strength. Therefore, the link of extreme body shapes to particular sports can be tenuous, as most athletes will display a mixture of characteristics. However, the demands of an activity often lead it to suiting a particular body type.

Ectomorph

An ectomorphic body shape is usually characterised by:

- very thin and lean (usually tall)
- narrow shoulders, hips and chest
- not much fat/muscle
- long arms and legs
- thin face and high forehead.

The thin, lean and tall body shape of an ectomorph is often beneficial for activities where the characteristics of being tall and lean are advantageous. Activities which tend to suit an ectomorphic body shape include:

- high jump
- long jump
- tennis
- endurance activities; for example, marathon.

Study hint
You should be able to identify the most suitable body type for particular sports (or positions within a sport) and provide reasons for your choice. Remember that body types can be mixed, e.g. swimmers are often ecto/mesomorphic (tall and muscular).

Key terms
Ectomorph A somatotype characterised by being tall and thin with narrow shoulders and hips.

A marathon runner may well benefit from having ectomorphic characteristics as they do not carry much weight (fat and/or muscle). However, for an activity like long jump, which requires power and speed, athletes may well have worked on developing some muscular bulk and therefore display an element of being slightly mesomorphic as well. Equally, an endomorph body type may suit the demands of events like shot put or discus, whereby the bulk of the body can be used to create force behind the object being thrown.

Modern sprinters, tennis players and some team-sports performers often display the characteristics of an ecto/mesomorph. Ex-Olympian Usain Bolt is 195 cm (6 ft 5 inches) tall and his long frame characterises elements of an ectomorph. He did, however, work on building up some muscular bulk to provide him with the mesomorphic characteristics he needed for sprinting.

Modern-day tennis players are taller and leaner than ever. The characteristics of an ectomorph are beneficial in that serving has become an ever-increasingly important part of the game and serving from height can provide distinct advantages.

▲ **Figure 6.11** Ectomorph characteristics are frequently found in professional tennis players, such as (clockwise) Andy Murray, Ashleigh Barty, Rafael Nadal and Simona Halep.

Endomorph

An endomorphic body shape is usually characterised by:

- pear-shaped body
- higher content of fat
- fat round middle, thighs and upper arms.

The pear-shaped appearance of an endomorph can be beneficial for some activities that simply require bulk. Front row forwards in rugby are often an endomorphic shape, which benefits them when pushing the opposition in the scrum. Similarly, shot putters often display the characteristics of an endomorph, whereby sheer bulk is used in a powerful release of the shot. This is also the case for an activity like sumo wrestling.

▲ **Figure 6.12** Retired rugby prop Adam Jones used his endomorph characteristics on the field of play.

Mesomorph

A mesomorphic body shape is usually characterised by:

- a wedge or rectangular shape in men; an hourglass shape in women
- higher muscle content
- broad shoulders and thin waist.

The muscular nature of a mesomorph is excellent for producing power and strength. They are not necessarily overburdened with muscle (that is, can hardly move due to having so much muscle) but tend to have distinctive muscle definition in the chest and shoulders, creating a wedge-like body shape. Such a shape is beneficial in sprinting, whereby the force generated at the shoulders can allow the arms to 'pump' (allowing the legs to move faster). Equally, a weight-lifter will have high upper-body muscle bulk to provide the force to lift and hold a very heavy weight. Many rugby players (league and union) display mesomorphic characteristics, allowing them to generate force when making contact with their opponents.

Key terms

Endomorph A somatotype characterised by a pear-shaped body with high fat content, wide hips and narrow shoulders.

Mesomorph A somatotype characterised by muscular appearance with wide shoulders and narrow hips.

Activity 3

In small groups, learn to appreciate the importance of the muscular upper body of a sprinter (mesomorph). Jog slowly on the spot. Start to pump your arms with power whilst trying to keep your legs jogging slowly. You should realise that the faster and more powerfully the arms work, the faster and more powerfully the legs work.

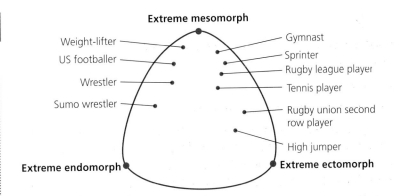

Extreme mesomorph

Weight-lifter
US footballer
Wrestler
Sumo wrestler

Gymnast
Sprinter
Rugby league player
Tennis player
Rugby union second row player
High jumper

Extreme endomorph   Extreme ectomorph

▲ **Figure 6.13** A representation of which somatotype tends to suit certain sports.

Rapid recall

A simple way to remember the body types is by using the following:
- **M**esomorphic body shapes have a high **m**uscle **m**ass.
- Endomorph (end-**o**-morph) – you can accentuate the 'o' to suggest the body shape is like an 'O', or you can remember Homer Simpson, who regularly says 'Doh' and has an endomorphic body shape.
- Ectomorph (Ec-to) – referring to your neck to toe being a long distance; that is, it's a long (thin) distance from your 'Ec' (neck) to your 'to' (toe).

✔ Check your understanding

5 Describe the three somatotypes.
Answers are on page 200.

PRACTICE QUESTIONS

9 Explain, with reference to a sporting activity of your choice, why an ectomorph body type may be beneficial.   (3 marks)

10 Sprinters often have wide muscular shoulders and a low fat content. What body type is this?
   A Mesomorph ☐
   B Ectomorph ☐
   C Endomorph ☐
     (1 mark)

11 Justify why an ectomorph body type may be suited to long-distance running.
     (2 marks)
Answers are on page 202.

Study hint
Make sure you know how many calories the average adult male and female need per day.

Activity 4

1 What body type would you say you were? Therefore, what sporting activities does your body shape stereotypically suit? Do you actually play/perform in these activities? Compare with classmates.

2 For the following sporting activities, suggest the stereotypical body shape that would suit that activity.

▼ **Table 6.2**

Activity	Body type required
Hammer throw	
Pole vault	
400 m sprint	
Marathon	

Answers to question 2 are on page 203.

Energy use, diet, nutrition and hydration

Kilocalories or calories (energy from food) are important for providing energy to carry out everyday activities and allow the body to function normally. Our bodies require energy for everything we do – for growth, repair, development and movement, especially when performing activities like running, swimming and walking.

Energy is measured in calories or kilocalories (kcal). These calories are obtained from the food and drink we consume. Therefore, the more calories we consume through our food, the more energy we have to use. If we do not use the calories, they get stored in the body, causing weight gain.

Average calorie requirements

The average adult male requires 2500 kcal/day and the average adult female requires 2000 kcal/day. However, these figures are dependent upon several factors:

- age of the individual (after age 25, the calorie needs of individuals start to fall)
- gender (as you can see, men usually need more calories)
- height of the individual (taller people tend to require more calories)
- energy expenditure (in other words, how much exercise the individual does – the more exercise, the more calories are required)
- basal metabolic rate (BMR). This is basically how fast energy is being used. It can vary from individual to individual.

It may seem obvious, but the calorie intake required to provide energy for a day will vary depending on what you are doing that day. Some top-class athletes need to eat much more than the average suggested intake in order to cope with the demands of their training schedule.

> ✔ **Check your understanding**
>
> 6 What is the suggested calorie intake per day for an average adult male and adult female?
>
> Answers are on page 200.

It is interesting to note that an individual uses approximately 1 calorie per minute when sleeping, 3–4 when walking and 8–10 when jogging fast.

Nutrition – reasons for having a balanced diet

The food and drink you consume contain calories but are also made up of varying constituents. A **balanced diet** is eating the right amount of calories to deal with the energy that will be needed (suitable intake to match energy expenditure/exercise). However, it is also eating different food types to provide suitable nutrients, **vitamins** and **minerals**. Minerals are inorganic substances which assist the body with many of its functions; for example, calcium for bone formation. Vitamins are organic substances that are required for many essential processes in the body; for example, Vitamin A for structure and function of the skin.

▲ **Figure 6.14** Olympic swimming legend Michael Phelps was rumoured to consume as many as 12 000 calories a day during his gruelling training schedule in preparation for the Olympics.

Key terms

Balanced diet Eating the right amount (for energy expended)/ the right amount of calories/ eating according to how much you exercise/eating different food types to provide suitable nutrients, vitamins and minerals.

Vitamins Organic substances that are required for many essential processes in the body.

Minerals Inorganic substances that assist the body with many of its functions.

▲ **Figure 6.15** An English breakfast, Cornish pasty for lunch and fish and chips for an evening meal. These are popular British meals but would they constitute a 'balanced diet', providing the body with the nutrients, vitamins and minerals it needs?

Aiming for a balanced diet

Unfortunately, there is no one food that contains all the nutrients the body needs. Some foods have particular properties which benefit the body:

- High-fibre cereals and whole grains provide fibre, which prevents constipation and can help reduce blood cholesterol (fatty deposits).
- Milk, cheese and other dairy products provide calcium (a mineral), which is good for nerve and muscle function as well as teeth and bone growth and repair.
- Foodstuffs rich in iron (a mineral) like liver help the immune system and assist in the production of red blood cells, which carry oxygen.
- Vitamin A (for skin function and growth) is found in dairy products like cheese.
- Oily fish, eggs and butter provide vitamin D to help strengthen bones.
- Vitamin C is found in citrus fruit, broccoli and liver and aids the immune system, skin elasticity and blood vessel function.
- Various types of vitamin B are found in whole grains, nuts, eggs and fish and assist with the functions of the body.

A truly 'balanced' diet contains lots of different types of food and would normally involve an individual consuming a mixture of carbohydrate, protein and fat from a variety of sources. The ideal mix of different foods should also include green vegetables and fruit to provide the suitable nutrients, vitamins and minerals required. As a rough guide, you should aim for five portions of fruit and vegetables per day. When measuring vegetables, a 'fist-sized' portion is often regarded as one portion. The ideal mix of foods is sometimes referred to as the 'seven classes of food': carbohydrate, fat, protein, fibre, vitamins, minerals and water.

Activity 5

Discuss last night's evening meal with a partner. Did either of you consume all seven of the classes of food? Did you manage to consume five portions of fruit and vegetables yesterday? In France, the government recommends ten portions of fruit and vegetables a day!

▲ **Figure 6.16** A mix of fruit and vegetables provides the body with vitamins and minerals.

So why should you strive to have a balanced diet?

- Unused energy is stored as fat, which could cause obesity (particularly saturated fat found in deep-fried food).
- Suitable amounts of energy should be consumed to be made available for the exercise and activity carried out.
- The human body needs nutrients for energy, growth and hydration (see 'Water' on page 152).

PRACTICE QUESTIONS

12 An adult man averages a daily intake of 3500 kcal per day. Is this too much or too little based on recommended guidelines? Justify your answer. (2 marks)

13 If an adult female is in training for an event, why might she eat and drink more calories than the recommended daily intake? (2 marks)

Answers are on page 202.

Answers are on page 200.

> **✔ Check your understanding**
>
> 7 What are the seven classes of food? What is a truly 'balanced' diet?
>
> Answers are on page 200.

▲ **Figure 6.17** Pasta is a food source rich in complex carbohydrate – providing energy.

Carbohydrates, fat, protein, vitamins and minerals

As you have discovered already, a balanced diet contains seven elements: carbohydrate, fat, protein, fibre, vitamins, minerals and water. With specific reference to carbohydrates, fat and protein, the recommended percentages that your diet should contain are:

- 55–60 per cent carbohydrate
- 25–30 per cent fat, and
- 15–20 per cent protein.

Carbohydrates

Carbohydrates are the main and preferred energy source for all types of exercise, of all intensities. The body requires a supply of glucose as an energy fuel and carbohydrate acts as the main source of glucose. Thus, for an athlete requiring energy, carbohydrate is a very important part of their diet. There are many types of carbohydrate (simple and complex) that can be consumed. Bread, pasta and potatoes provide valuable sources of starch, which is a complex carbohydrate.

Fat

Fat is also an energy source and helps to carry vitamins in the body; for example, vitamin A. It provides more energy than carbohydrates – in fact, more than double the amount that carbohydrate provides. The key, however, is that fat can only be used as an energy source at low intensity; for example, walking, light jogging and so on. Although fat is a concentrated energy source, it does come in two forms – saturated fat (usually animal fat) and unsaturated fat (usually vegetable fat/oils).

> **Study hint**
> Make sure you know the percentage recommendations for carbohydrate, fat and protein.

> **Key terms**
> **Carbohydrate** Food source that acts as the body's preferred energy source.
>
> **Fat** Food source that provides energy at low intensities.

Study hint

Don't forget that fat can provide more energy than carbohydrate BUT only when you are working at a low intensity.

Although many people perceive fat as a bad or unhealthy part of a diet, you do in fact need to consume 25–30 per cent fat within your normal diet. However, a high fat intake (particularly saturated fat) is strongly linked to many health risks. These include:

- high cholesterol
- heart disease
- narrowing of arteries due to fat deposits.

▲ **Figure 6.18** Saturated fat tends to be derived from animal sources and can cause health risks.

Protein

Protein is used predominantly for growth and repair of body tissues. It also has a small part to play in providing energy. The main sources of protein within the diet are meat, eggs, fish, dairy products, nuts and cereals. For some athletes, particularly those who lift weights and do strength/power activities, a diet rich in protein is beneficial to help them with the development and repair of muscle tissue.

▲ **Figure 6.19** Eggs and dairy products are rich in protein.

Key term

Protein Food source which is predominantly for growth and repair of body tissues.

> **Activity 6**
>
> Take note of your daily intake of food. Using the wrappers and packaging, try to keep track of the amount of carbohydrate, fat and protein you consume. Does your intake conform to the recommended levels? You could also try to design a suitable daily intake containing the recommended percentages of carbohydrate, fat and protein.

Vitamins and minerals

Vitamin and mineral intake comes from foodstuffs such as fruit and vegetables. Vitamins and minerals are needed for maintaining the efficient working of body systems and general health.

Vitamins are organic substances that are required for many essential processes in the body; for example, vitamin A for structure and function of the skin. Minerals are inorganic substances which assist the body with many of its functions; for example, calcium for bone formation.

Water

Water consumption is often neglected by many people, but it is a vital component of a healthy diet. As water makes up more than half of the human body, it is necessary to maintain **hydration** levels (water balance) as it assists in how the body functions generally. It helps with reactions and lubrication and also plays a big part in maintaining correct body temperature. It is also important to note that the amount of water you should drink a day depends on several factors:

- the environment you are in – for example, you would need more water in a desert
- the temperature – the hotter it is, the more you sweat and therefore you need more water
- the amount of exercise/activity you are doing – exercising means that you need to replace water (**rehydration**).

It is vital that water consumption prevents **dehydration**. This is when there is an excessive loss of body water, interrupting the functioning of the body.

It is important to remain hydrated as it prevents the effects of dehydration. Dehydration in the body has many harmful effects:

- The blood thickens (increased viscosity), which slows blood flow.
- The heart rate increases, which means that the heart has to work harder. This can cause an irregular heart rate (rhythm).
- The body temperature is likely to increase, meaning that the body may overheat.
- Reaction time increases. In other words, it gets slower and general reactions are poorer. This, of course, means that decisions made may be negatively affected.
- An individual may suffer muscle fatigue and/or muscle cramps.

Study hint
Make sure you are aware of why hydration is necessary.

Study hint
Although this section provides examples of vitamins and minerals, you are not required to know about the role of specific vitamins and minerals.

Key terms

Hydration Having enough water (water balance) to enable normal functioning of the body.

Rehydration Consuming water to restore hydration.

Dehydration Excessive loss of body water, interrupting the functioning of the body.

▲ **Figure 6.20** The recommended daily intake of water is approximately eight large glasses a day to maintain hydration levels.

Rapid recall

Remember the dangers of dehydration as **THRST** (no 'I'):
TH – **TH**ickens (blood)
RS – **R**eactions **S**low
T – **T**emperature increases

PRACTICE QUESTIONS

14 Fat makes up 40 per cent of an adult's diet in a day. Suggest whether this conforms to the recommended daily intake. Justify your answer.
(2 marks)

15 Explain three different negative consequences of becoming dehydrated.
(3 marks)

16 Explain the main roles of carbohydrate, fat and protein.
(3 marks)

17 Evaluate the importance of eating carbohydrates, fats and protein to a team sports performer.
(6 marks)

18 Evaluate the importance of hydration to a discus thrower and a long-distance road cyclist.
(9 marks)

Answers are on pages 202–3.

Activity 7

1 In the table below, match the correct term with the correct definition.

▼ **Table 6.3**

Term	Definition
Dehydration	Consuming water to restore hydration.
Hydration	Excessive loss of body water, interrupting the function of the body.
Rehydration	Having enough water (water balance) to enable normal functioning of the body.

2 Take note of the amount of water you consume in a 24-hour period. Does it conform to the recommended daily intake of eight large glasses? Compare your results with classmates.

Answers to question 1 are on page 203.

✔ Check your understanding

8 What are the recommended percentages for carbohydrate, fat and protein within your daily diet?
9 What is the role of vitamins and minerals within the diet?
10 What do the terms 'hydration', 'dehydration' and 'rehydration' mean?
Answers are on page 200.

Summary

- Exercise can be used to suit the varying needs of different people.
- Exercise can affect physical, mental and social health and wellbeing.
- A sedentary lifestyle is a choice and has many negative effects.
- Obesity is a consequence of a sedentary lifestyle and can affect all aspects of health and performance.
- There are stereotypical and suitable body types (somatotypes) for particular sports (or positions within a sport).
- Energy is gained from food. If more energy is taken in than used, there will be weight gain (and vice versa).
- A balanced diet contains the seven classes of food: carbohydrate, fat, protein, fibre, vitamins, minerals and water.
- The following have specific roles: carbohydrates (energy), fat (energy), protein (growth and repair), vitamins and minerals (efficient functions).
- Water balance prevents dehydration and the resultant consequences; for example, thicker blood.

Chapter 7 Use of data

As part of your GCSE in Physical Education, you will be required in both of your examinations to show knowledge and understanding of data analysis. In simple terms, the skills you will need to show can be summarised as:

- Show an understanding of the types of data.
- Show an understanding of how data is collected.
- Demonstrate an ability to present data in various formats.
- Demonstrate an understanding of how to analyse data; for example, break it down into smaller parts.
- Demonstrate an understanding of how to evaluate data; for example, does the data show anything, any trends, any interesting points?

It is important to note that there is no one topic area that will definitely be examined using data. All topic areas within the specification could be referred to with data-based questions. This chapter provides you with some further information to help to prepare you for your examinations.

Show an understanding of the types of data

Your ability to show an understanding of the types of data is with particular reference to the terms:

- quantitative data
- qualitative data.

Quantitative data deals with numbers. You can remember the meaning of this by using the expression 'Quantitative data deals with quantities'.

By definition, quantitative data is a measurement that can be quantified as a number; for example, time in seconds, or goals scored. There is no opinion expressed (qualitative); it is a fact/objective.

Most topic areas within the specification could potentially be examined through questions which refer to numbers/quantities/amounts.
For example:

- Fitness tests produce numerical scores.
- Heart rate is measured in beats per minute and can therefore be plotted on a graph.
- Engagement patterns of different social groups could actually be shown as numerical amounts or percentages.

Qualitative data on the other hand deals with opinions. It is subjective as it allows for different people to express different viewpoints.

By definition, qualitative data is more of a subjective than an objective appraisal. It involves opinions relating to the quality of a performance rather than the quantity. Whereas a fitness test could produce a numerical score (quantitative), the person carrying it out may well suggest that they 'did poorly'. This expression of opinion is qualitative.

Key terms

Quantitative data Data that can be quantified as a number, e.g. time in seconds, or goals scored. There is no opinion expressed (qualitative); it is a fact.

Qualitative data Data which is subjective, involving opinions relating to the quality of a performance rather than the quantity.

Most topics within the specification could include qualitative data within the examinations. For example:

- the opinions expressed about the positive or negative impact of commercialisation on a spectator
- the opinions expressed about the merits of extrinsic motivation
- the opinions expressed by different people about what a diet should contain.

Show an understanding of how data is collected

It is also important that as a student of GCSE Physical Education you can identify how quantitative and qualitative data are collected.

Quantitative data involving quantities and amounts tends to be gathered using the following methods:

- questionnaires – a series of questions, whereby the number of people who give a certain answer can be expressed as a quantity
- surveys – for example, in the television programme *Family Fortunes*, the host uses the number of people who expressed a particular answer.

However, with specific reference to physical education, it is also likely that other data collection could be used. For example:

- heart-rate monitors to measure heart rate
- stop-watches to gain a time; for example, in the Illinois agility test
- metre ruler to gain a score; for example, in the reaction time test.

Qualitative data involving opinions is generally gathered through the following methods:

- interviews
- observations.

With specific reference to physical education, you may well see from an observation that a performer appears to be over aroused, or you may interview a participant who expresses their delight at their score after a fitness test.

Demonstrate an ability to present data in various formats

As previously mentioned, you may be required to present data as part of your examinations. In simple terms, this could involve looking at information provided to you and turning it into a different format. The specification states that those formats could include:

- plotting a basic line chart
- plotting a basic bar chart
- labelling the *x*- and *y*-axis correctly on a chart.

At this point, it is perhaps best to provide some detail about line charts, bar charts and labelling axes.

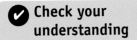

Check your understanding

1 Explain what qualitative and quantitative data are and identify some methods to collect the data.

Answers are on page 204.

Activity 1

In pairs, discuss the last time you carried out fitness tests. What did you score in the test (quantitative) and how was the data collected? How did you feel you did in those tests (qualitative)? Interview each other to collect the qualitative data.

PRACTICE QUESTIONS

1 Define the terms 'qualitative data' and 'quantitative data'.
(2 marks)

Answers are on page 204.

A **line chart** involves plotting points (markers) onto graph paper so that the points (markers) can be joined together. An example is shown below; it shows the results when a performer's heart rate was measured at different times before, during and after exercise.

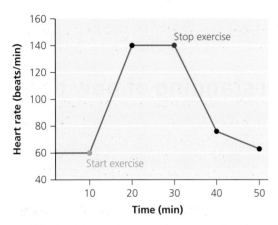

Key terms

Line chart The use of plotted points (markers) to show data, which are joined together by a line.

Bar chart The use of rectangular bars which show the data quantities.

▲ **Figure 7.1** A line chart showing changes in heart rate before, during and after exercise.

A **bar chart** is similar to a line chart; however, the amount up to the plotted point is shaded in to show a 'bar area'. The rectangular shaded areas show the amount. An example is shown below, which shows participation rates in the UK for different sports.

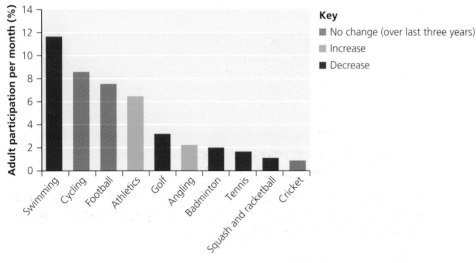

Key
- No change (over last three years)
- Increase
- Decrease

▲ **Figure 7.2** A bar chart showing the participation rates of different sports in the UK.

Source: Sport England

In terms of labelling axes, it is important to remember a couple of terms:
- The **x-axis** goes across – so remember X (a cross).
- The **y-axis** goes up the side – the letter Y points up.
- If you need to decide which set of values goes on the x-axis and which goes on the y-axis, then you need to understand the difference between independent and dependent variables. The **independent variable** goes on the x-axis (the bottom, horizontal

Key terms

x-axis Shows the independent variable.

y-axis Shows the dependent variable (the thing you are measuring, e.g. heart rate).

Independent variable In a graph or chart, the factor (variable) that you purposely change or control in order to see what effect it has.

Key terms

Dependent variable In a graph or chart, the factor that changes in response to the independent variable.

Pie chart Displays the proportions of data as sections of a circle.

one) and the **dependent variable** goes on the *y*-axis (the left side, vertical one). In the line chart above, time is the independent variable because the experimenter decides what time to measure heart rate. Heart rate is the thing you really want to know, so it is the dependent variable.

- In the bar chart above, the independent variable (*x*-axis) is the type of sport. The dependent variable (*y*-axis) is the percentage of people who play that sport.

Whether you should use a line chart or bar chart depends on whether the dependent variables are related. Use a line chart if the values are linked and form an orderly sequence. In the line chart above, the periods of time follow on from each other; therefore, we use a line chart. In the bar chart above, there is no relationship between the dependent variables. Participation in football does not depend on participation rates in cycling.

A pie chart is another way of displaying data. Pie charts use different-sized sectors of a circle to represent data. The angle of each sector represents the data value.

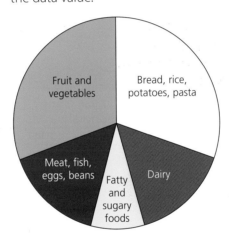

▲ **Figure 7.3** Pie chart showing the Eatwell Plate, the UK government's recommended dietary proportions.

Within this chapter we are going to use an example from the topic area of motivation. Given the information below, it is suggested that you practise carrying out the tasks on graph paper.

> ### ✔ Check your understanding
>
> 2   In an experiment, a performer's heart rate is measured as an indicator of their levels of arousal. The performer is then faced with different types of audiences.
>   The results of the experiment give values for the performer's heart rate in front of different types of audiences.
>   a)   Which of the two sets of values are the dependent variables?
>   b)   Which set of values should be on the *x*-axis?
>   c)   Should the results be presented as a bar chart or a line chart? Explain your answer.
>
> Answers are on page 204.

PRACTICE QUESTIONS

2 A class of PE students were given a question to answer:
During today's training, what do you think is motivating you more to train harder – intrinsic reward (for example, personal pride) or extrinsic reward (for example, winning a medal)?
The following quantitative responses were gained as scores out of 10.

N.B. As the level of motivation is the thing being studied, this is the dependent variable – y-axis.

▼ **Table 7.1**

Week	Answers given
1	Intrinsic 3 Extrinsic 7
2	Intrinsic 4 Extrinsic 6
3	Intrinsic 5 Extrinsic 5
4	Intrinsic 5 Extrinsic 5
5	Intrinsic 8 Extrinsic 2

a) Plot the data onto the graph paper below, showing athlete responses over the five-week period. You should use a line graph method and should label the axes appropriately.

(2 marks)

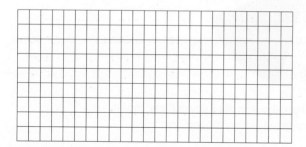

b) Plot the same data onto the graph paper below, showing athlete responses over the five-week period. You should use a bar chart method and should label the axes appropriately.

(2 marks)

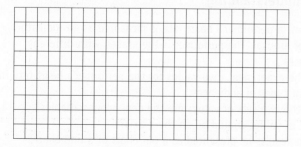

Answers are on page 204. Compare your responses to those on page 204 and try again if necessary. Have plenty of goes using different data sources.

Demonstrate an understanding of how to analyse and evaluate data

Key terms

Analyse Break things down into smaller parts or identify the relevant parts.

Evaluate Use the information provided to decide upon the worth of or reasons for something.

In your exam, you may be asked to **analyse** and/or **evaluate** data. Analyse means to break things down into smaller parts or identify the relevant parts. Evaluate means deciding upon the worth of or reasons for something.

To make this simpler, look at the following example:

An athlete's heart rate was recorded before and during exercise at one-minute intervals.

▼ **Table 7.2**

TIME	HEART RATE IN BEATS PER MINUTE (BPM)
2 minutes before	68 bpm
1 minute before	74 bpm
At the start	78 bpm
1 minute into exercise	84 bpm
2 minutes into exercise	88 bpm
3 minutes into exercise	105 bpm
4 minutes into exercise	106 bpm
5 minutes into exercise	106 bpm
6 minutes into exercise	107 bpm

Analyse the data shown to plot a line chart – because the independent variable values (different times) are related – showing the heart rates 1 minute before exercise, at the start of exercise, and 1, 2, 3, 4, 5 and 6 minutes into exercise.

In this specific example, your graph would look like the following:

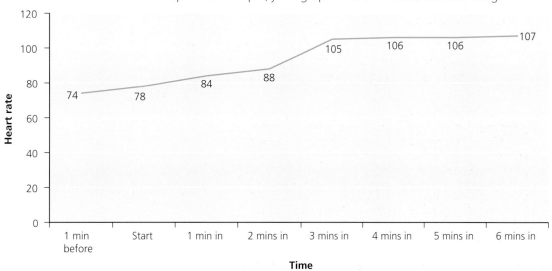

▲ **Figure 7.4** Line chart showing heart rate against time.

An evaluation of this chart could well ask you to evaluate what the data shows. For example, 'Looking at the heart rate during exercise, describe what intensity the athlete has been working at.'

In this case, the data demonstrates a slight rise in intensity at the start of exercise, which appears to be levelling off at 3 minutes.

The following chart shows the percentage of females/males (of differing ages) that participate regularly in sporting activity.

Study hint
Remember that analysis involves breaking data down into smaller parts or picking out the relevant data. Evaluation involves looking at something's worth or what it actually shows.

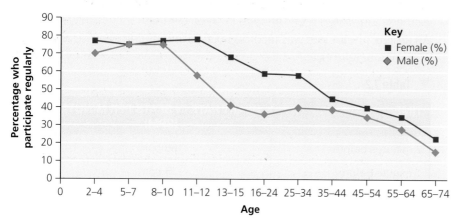

▲ **Figure 7.5** Line chart showing participation rates against age.

With this kind of chart, you could be asked a range of questions. For example, you may encounter ones which involve evaluation:

1 At what age do participation rates of females match those of males?

2 At what age are participation rates for males the highest?

3 At what age are participation rates for females the lowest?

Answers:

1 5–7 years

2 11–12 years

3 65–74 years

Chapter 8 Non-examined assessment

As part of your GCSE in Physical Education, you are required to complete a non-examined assessment (or NEA for short). You may well refer to this as your 'practical'.

Your NEA contributes 40 per cent of your overall mark, with your examinations making up the remaining 60 per cent. You will have to choose to be assessed in three different activities from the official activity list below and complete an analysis and improvement task (about yourself or another person) on one of the activities from the list.

In choosing from the list below, be aware that you must choose:

- an individual activity
- a team activity, and
- another activity of your choice; for example, badminton (individual), football (team), tennis (other).

Team activities

- Acrobatic gymnastics (cannot be assessed with gymnastics)
- Association football (cannot be five-a-side; cannot be assessed with futsal)
- Badminton doubles (cannot be assessed with singles badminton)
- Basketball
- Camogie (cannot be assessed with hurling)
- Cricket
- Dance (can only be used for one activity; cannot be assessed with figure skating)
- Figure skating (can only be used as one activity – that is, not as team and individual figure skating; cannot be assessed with dance)
- Futsal (cannot be assessed with association football)
- Gaelic football
- Handball
- Hockey (must be field hockey; cannot be assessed as ice hockey or inline roller hockey)
- Hurling (cannot be assessed with camogie)
- Ice hockey (cannot be assessed with inline roller hockey)
- Inline roller hockey (cannot be assessed with ice hockey)
- Lacrosse
- Netball
- Rowing (cannot be assessed with sculling, canoeing or kayaking; can only be used for one activity)
- Rugby league (cannot be assessed with rugby union or rugby sevens; cannot be tag rugby)
- Rugby union (can be assessed as sevens or fifteen-a-side; cannot be assessed with rugby league and cannot be tag rugby)

- Sailing (can only be used as one activity; RYA-recognised sailing boats only; role of helm only)
- Sculling (cannot be assessed with rowing, kayaking, canoeing or individual sculling)
- Squash doubles (cannot be assessed with singles squash)
- Table-tennis doubles (cannot be assessed with singles table tennis)
- Tennis doubles (cannot be assessed with singles tennis)
- Volleyball
- Water polo

Individual activities

- Amateur boxing
- Athletics (two different events/groups; for example, sprint and jump)
- Badminton singles (cannot be assessed with doubles badminton)
- Canoeing/kayaking (slalom; cannot be assessed in both canoeing and kayaking; cannot be assessed with canoeing/kayaking sprint, rowing or sculling)
- Canoeing/kayaking (sprint; cannot be assessed in both canoeing and kayaking; cannot be assessed with canoeing/kayaking slalom, rowing or sculling)
- Cycling track, road cycling or BMX racing only (cannot be assessed in two types of cycling)
- Dance solo (can only be used for one activity; cannot also be assessed in figure skating)
- Diving (platform diving only)
- Figure skating (can only be used as one activity – that is, not as team figure skating as well as individual; cannot also be assessed in dance)
- Golf
- Gymnastics (artistic; floor routines and apparatus only; cannot be rhythmic gymnastics specialism and dance in combination)
- Equestrian
- Rock climbing (can be indoor or outdoor climbing)
- Sailing (can only be used as one activity; RYA-recognised sailing boats only; role of helm only)
- Sculling (cannot be assessed with rowing, kayaking, canoeing or team sculling)
- Skiing (outdoor/indoor on snow; cannot be assessed with snowboarding; must not be on dry slopes)
- Snowboarding (outdoor/indoor on snow; cannot be assessed with skiing; must not be on dry slopes)
- Squash (cannot be assessed with doubles squash)
- Swimming (cannot be synchronised swimming; cannot be personal survival; cannot be lifesaving)
- Table tennis (singles; cannot be assessed with doubles table tennis)
- Tennis (singles; cannot be assessed with doubles tennis)

- Trampolining
- Windsurfing

Disability/specialist activities

N.B. Students without a disability cannot be assessed in these activities.

- Blind cricket
- Goalball
- Powerchair football (cannot be assessed with wheelchair football)
- Table cricket
- Wheelchair basketball
- Wheelchair football (cannot be assessed with powerchair football)
- Wheelchair rugby

Specialist individual activities

- Boccia
- Polybat

Choosing your activities

In choosing your three activities, remember that you can only perform (play) in these activities. You are not able to coach or officiate. Therefore, you must choose wisely, with the intention to maximise the marks that you will eventually be given. Please also note that there are a few activity combinations that are not possible. These are included in the list above – for example, you cannot do rugby union and rugby league or singles and doubles badminton.

All activities are scored out of 25, with:

- 10 marks being awarded for Part 1: your performance in progressive drills/practices
- 15 marks being awarded for Part 2: your ability to perform in a fully competitive context.

Please see AQA's specification for full details of how marks are awarded.

▲ **Figure 8.1** Choose from an individual activity.

▲ **Figure 8.2** Choose from a team activity.

▲ **Figure 8.3** Choose another activity of your choice.

There are a few key points to consider:

- The skills being performed in **Part 1** should allow you to show yourself in the best possible light; for example, a simple passing drill in football will not score very high marks. You may start with a simple drill but it must progress to challenge you and show your ability to, for example, receive the ball on the move and pass accurately to other players on the move over varying distances.

- When performing **Part 2**, the level of the competition will be taken into account when assessing you. Therefore, if you are playing against very easy opposition, it may not help you to score a high mark. It is beneficial to show yourself playing at the highest standard possible for Part 2. This may require you to collect unedited video evidence.

Assessment

Assessment of your three chosen activities will be carried out by your teachers but will also be moderated by external AQA staff.

If selected for moderation, you will need to show Part 1 (skills) and Part 2 (full context) in the activity selected by the moderator. You will also need to hand in your analysis and evaluation coursework. Although evidence for moderation is often shown live, some evidence is shown via digital footage.

It can be difficult capturing footage of yourself performing at your best. If you are asked by your teacher to do so, please remember a few simple rules:

- You should be seen performing at the highest level possible – ask your coach to make the practices harder and harder to show you being tested in Part 1.

- Don't forget, it must be the full recognised version of the activity for Part 2 – for example, five-a-side football will not do!

- It must be clear and the person watching it must be able to actually see you.

- You may need to gain several examples from several different drills in training and several different competitive contexts. If it is a team sport, it can be several different halves or quarters.

- Team sports require a 'player cam' approach for Part 2 – that is, the camera should follow you but also be on a wide enough setting to see what is going on in the game. If you go out of shot for a moment, do not worry as this will not be held against you.

- The mark awarded will not be based purely on the level you are performing at – for example, even if you are an international performer, there must be an appropriate amount of evidence of you actually performing.

- It is sometimes advisable to include 'voice-over' on top of the footage. For example, in a game of rugby there may be 30 bodies covered in mud! In this case, it will help if you commentate as to where you are and what you are doing. The alternative, and perhaps an easier approach, is to provide a written commentary of when you are involved in the footage and what you are doing.

Part 1

The main factors that you will be assessed on in Part 1 are:

- the quality of technique shown and whether it is maintained for all skills and throughout all practices
- your ability to make decisions in both predetermined (expected) and spontaneous (unexpected) situations
- the number of errors in your skill production
- how adaptive you are (in other words, how you change what you are doing) when faced with progressively challenging situations; for example, as the practice progresses
- your fitness level (in sports like cycling and rowing)
- how well you cope and maintain consistency when faced with increasingly demanding and competitive scenarios.

▲ **Figure 8.4** Skill drills being performed for Part 1.

When performing the Part 1 skill drills, it is vital that there is more than one drill per skill. Each drill for each skill must progress, to further challenge you. The key is that the evidence for each skill should include:

- progression
- challenge
- an element of competition.

This can be easy for some skills, such as passing and receiving in hockey, whereby a fairly static passing drill quickly progresses to become a more dynamic drill, before incorporating competitive pressure from opponents. For other skills, this can prove quite challenging so here are some examples that are not prescriptive but allow for progression, challenge and competition.

Example: Seat drop in trampolining

Drill one: simple seat drop with controlled bounce.

Drill two: simple seat drop with more height on the bounce to challenge the skill.

Drill three: incorporate a move that transitions into the seat drop and a move that transitions out of the seat drop.

Drill four: choose higher tariff moves before and after the seat drop to challenge the seat drop itself and to replicate a small part of a competitive routine.

Example: 800 m start

Drill one: show a simple 800 m start and run 20 m.

Drill two: show a simple 800 m start but demonstrate the stride pattern that would be used for the first 50 m of a race.

Drill three: show a start at race pace past the 'first turn stagger' to then take lane 1.

Drill four: against a similar-standard competitor, show a start at race pace past the 'first turn stagger' to then take lane 1.

Part 2

The main areas that you will be assessed on in Part 2 are:

- your ability to make successful and effective tactical and strategic decisions, suitable for the standard of the full context. Remember, the higher the standard the better!
- your level of contribution – is it sustained for the whole activity?
- your level of technical consistency in the performance of all skills
- selecting the appropriate skills to use at the right time
- your ability to play a position (in team sports)
- your ability to outwit opponents (where appropriate)
- your choreography skills (in dance).

▲ **Figure 8.5** Full competitive context for Part 2.

Analysis and evaluation task

The analysis and evaluation task is completed as a piece of coursework that you can work on at school/college and/or at home. It can be completed at any point during the two years of your studies at GCSE. It is submitted towards the end of the second year (usually Year 11).

The analysis and evaluation task that you have to complete is marked out of 25. This is split into two separate sections:

- analysis (15 marks)
- evaluation (10 marks).

For this element of coursework, you are required to analyse and evaluate a performance in one activity from the specification. This can be an analysis/evaluation of one of your own performances or it could be on the performance of another person. It must, however, be in relation to an activity that is from the specification.

N.B. You can choose to present your work in a written format or a verbal format. If you use a verbal format, your teacher will take video evidence of you carrying out the verbal task. You will be allowed to take notes into this assessment but cannot simply read a script.

▲ **Figure 8.6** Students undertaking written assessment.

▲ **Figure 8.7** A student carrying out a verbal interview.

Analysis – 15 marks

Whether you analyse your own or another person's performance, you are required to analyse the performance to suggest two strengths and two weaknesses, referring to recent competitive performance(s) in the chosen activity.

The key to your analysis is to justify why you have chosen the strengths and weaknesses. The justifications should be *personal* to you as a performer and be backed up with examples from *recent performances*.

- **Strength 1** should be a fitness component (for example, speed, or something relevant to the chosen activity). You will need to justify how it has helped in two different performances, thus justifying why you have chosen it as a strength. The fitness components you can choose to highlight as your strength are listed in the specification as follows:
  - agility
  - balance
  - cardio-vascular endurance (aerobic power)
  - co-ordination
  - flexibility
  - muscular endurance
  - power/explosive strength (anaerobic power)
  - reaction time
  - strength (maximal, static, dynamic and explosive)
  - speed.
- **Strength 2** should be a specific skill/technique (from those listed in the activity criteria) or tactic/strategy/aspect of choreography (as appropriate). If you choose a skill (for example, shooting in football), you should refer to the technique used and how that technique benefited performance (for example, kept head over the ball to keep the shot low). If you choose to use a tactic/strategy, you must explain how it benefited performances. If an aspect of choreography is chosen, reference can be made to how the choreographed movement benefited performance of the dances.

- In choosing these strengths, it is very important that you fully justify your two choices; for example, what impact did they have on performance? Where possible, try to use activity-specific terminology/terms within your answer. Remember that Strength 1 should be justified with reference to *two* recent performances and so should Strength 2. The performances referred to can be different performances.
- **Weakness 1** should be a fitness component (for example, power, or something relevant to the chosen activity – from the list above). You will need to justify how it has negatively affected two performances.
- **Weakness 2** should be a specific skill/technique (from those listed in the activity criteria) or tactic/strategy/aspect of choreography (as appropriate). Again, the justification for this weakness should be personalised and related to two recent performances.

Key tips for your analysis

- Avoid any unnecessary and irrelevant text. For example, an overview of the history of the activity is irrelevant. Get straight into justifying your strengths and weaknesses.
- Ensure that all your strengths and weaknesses are clear and given in equal detail.
- Show that you know and understand the activity you are discussing by using key terms and activity-specific terminology in your justifications.
- Justification is key! You get very little credit for actually choosing the strengths and weaknesses. It is best to provide detailed justifications of the choices. Each strength and weakness should ideally relate to two recent performances.

Evaluation – 10 marks

Your evaluation section will focus solely on the weaknesses you have identified in your analysis section. You are now required to devise an action plan that evaluates how the weaknesses can be improved. All of the evaluation will make use of theoretical topics from the specification. **Remember that improvement does not actually have to happen. You are suggesting what would happen if you were to do these things!**

The process of the evaluation

- Initially, you have to choose a suitable training type to use to improve your stated fitness weakness. You must ensure that the training type chosen is appropriate and could be used to improve upon the weakness. The marks will be awarded for the justification of your training type. Think about: Why would this training type be suitable for you? How will it enable your improvement to take place?

- You then need to design one session of training of the training type chosen. This should be a detailed account but remember it does not actually have to be physically carried out. The session should be personalised and not simply copied. Think about how you design your session to be suitable to your needs. The session should include a warm-up, a cool-down and a calculated intensity. This calculated intensity should be justified to show why this is appropriate for you.

- The final part of the evaluation section involves you choosing one theoretical area of the course. With reference to your identified skill weakness, you should justify how application of the theoretical area could be used to improve the skill weakness. The theoretical area can be any part of the specification except training types. In summary, if you applied the theory you have learned, how could this be used to improve your skill weakness?

▲ **Figure 8.8** Could weight training or continuous training be appropriate training types to improve upon the identified weaknesses?

Key tips for your evaluation

- Your evaluation must be personalised. The training type, training session and application of the theoretical area must be related to you and to why they are suitable for you.

- Think about your personal needs in your training session. Do you have any old or persistent injuries? How can you justify that the chosen intensity is suitable for you? Do you need to consider the facilities you would have available to you?

- When applying the theoretical area, remember it is considering how you would apply it, how it would work for you and what changes you think it would make to you.

Answers

Chapter 1a Applied anatomy and physiology

Check your understanding

Page 3

1 We need support to give our body shape, to keep us upright and to keep the muscles and organs in place.

2 The skeleton produces red blood cells that transport carbon dioxide and oxygen to and from the lungs. White blood cells are produced and help fight off infections.

3 Muscles attach to the bones of the skeleton and pull the bones, which causes movement.

Page 3

4 Joint capsule provides stability; ligaments join bone to bone.

5 Synovial fluid is produced from the synovial membrane and works as a lubricant; bursae are bags of fluid that help reduce friction.

6 Tendons attach muscles to bone.

Page 8

7 Humerus, radius and ulna.

8 Ball and socket joint; for example, hip or shoulder.

9 Dorsiflexion and plantar flexion.

Page 9

10 Tibia and femur.

11 Knee, elbow and ankle.

12 Flexion, extension, adduction, abduction, rotation.

Practice questions

Page 2

1 Flat bones protect (AO1); for example, the cranium protects the brain/ the sternum and ribs protect the heart and lungs/the vertebrae protect the spinal cord (AO2).

Page 3

2 Join bone to bone.

3 Covers ends of bone to protect.

4 Release/produce synovial fluid – lubricates the joint.

Page 9

5 Plantar flexion – toes pointed/move down; dorsiflexion – toes pulled up.

6 Extension.

7 Abduction – arm/limb away from mid-line; adduction – arm/limb towards mid-line.

8 Answer should demonstrate knowledge of structure of hip and shoulder joints (AO1), examples of uses of shoulder and hip joints in netball (AO2) and a comparison of range of movement and stability of hip and shoulder joints (AO3).

Activities

Activity 1, page 4

- Cartilage – on ends of bones – protective covering.
- Capsule – tough fibrous tissue – supports/strengthens joint.
- Synovial membrane – releases synovial fluid – lubricates joint.
- Synovial fluid – lubricant – reduces friction.
- Bursae – fluid-filled bags – reduce friction.
- Ligaments – dense fibrous tissue – join bone to bone.

Activity 2, page 7

- Flexion – move forwards.
- Extension – move backwards.
- Abduction – move away from the body.
- Adduction – move back towards the body.
- Rotation – turn hand/arm in and/or out.
- Circumduction – whole arm moves in a cone shape.

Activity 3, page 9

- Shoulder – flexion – arm forwards, extension, arm back, abduction – arm out to side, adduction – arm back to body from side, rotation – hand/arm turn in/out, circumduction – arm moves in a cone shape.
- Elbow – flexion – arm bends at elbow, extension – arm straightens at elbow.
- Hip – flexion – whole leg moves forward when in standing position, extension – whole leg returns from flexed to standing position, circumduction – leg circles.
- Knee – flexion – leg bends at knee, extension – leg straightens at knee.
- Ankle – plantar flexion – toes pointed away from leg, dorsiflexion – toes pointing up towards leg.

Chapter 1b The structure and function of the cardio-respiratory system

Check your understanding

Page 11

1 Trap dirt and dust.
2 Bronchi conduct air from trachea to lungs; bronchioles conduct air from bronchi to alveoli.
3 Keep trachea open.
4 Provide surface for diffusion of gases/gas exchange.

Page 12

5 Because concentration of oxygen is higher in alveoli than in blood capillaries.

6 Thin cells walls/membranes; short distance between membranes; large surface area; layer of moisture; rich blood supply/lots of capillaries.

7 Transports oxygen (as oxyhaemoglobin; also transports carbon dioxide).

Page 13

8 Diaphragm and intercostal muscles.

9 Pectorals and sternocleidomastoid muscles.

10 The diaphragm and intercostals relax and the chest cavity returns to its normal/resting size.

11 Abdominals.

Page 14

12 Volume of air breathed in or out at rest.

13 Inspiratory reserve volume.

14 Residual volume.

Page 15

15 Recoil/return to shape.

16 Veins.

17 Increasing diameter of artery.

18 Allow diffusion.

Page 17

19 Systole – contraction; diastole – relaxation.

20 Prevent backflow of blood.

21 From right atrium; through atrioventricular valve; to right ventricle; systole; through pulmonary artery to lungs.

22 From lungs through pulmonary veins; into left atrium; through atrioventricular valves; to left ventricle.

Page 17

23 Volume of blood leaving the heart in one minute.

24 Cardiac output = stroke volume × heart rate.

25 Volume of blood leaving the heart per beat.

26 4900 mls/min or 4.9 L/min.

Practice questions

Page 11

1 Trachea; bronchi; bronchioles.

Page 12

2 Gases move from area of high concentration to lower concentration; oxygen out of alveoli; carbon dioxide into alveoli.

Page 13

3 Diaphragm and intercostal muscles contract; chest volume increases; pressure in chest reduces; air moves from higher pressure into the lungs.

4 Inspiration assisted by pectorals and sternocleidomastoid; expiration assisted by abdominals.

Page 14

5 Answer should include a description of mechanics of inspiration (AO1), a description of the effects of exercise/HIIT on the mechanics of inspiration (AO2) and a conclusion linking HIIT effects on inspiration and consequently expiration (AO3).

6 TV increases; IRV decreases; ERV decreases.

Page 17

7 Deoxygenated blood; from RV into pulmonary artery; to lungs; gas exchange/becomes oxygenated; pulmonary veins; left atria.

8 Answer should include a description of systole and diastole (AO1), a description of how running affects heart rate and the duration of systole and diastole (AO2), and the consequences of increase in heart rate on cardiac output (AO3).

Page 18

9 Cardiac output – volume of blood leaving the heart per minute.

Stroke volume – volume of blood leaving the heart per beat.

Cardiac output = stroke volume × heart rate.

Activities

Activity 1, page 11

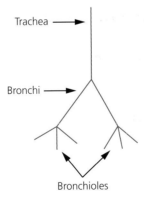

Trachea

Bronchi

Bronchioles

Activity 2, page 11

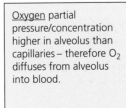

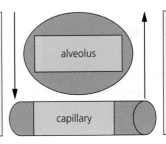

Oxygen partial pressure/concentration higher in alveolus than capillaries – therefore O_2 diffuses from alveolus into blood.

alveolus

capillary

Carbon dioxide partial pressure/concentration higher in capillaries than alveolus – therefore CO_2 diffuses from blood into alveolus.

Activity 3, page 12

Any four from:

- Large surface area – large.
- Thin membranes – thin.
- Short diffusion pathway – short.
- Layer of moisture – moist.
- Rich blood supply – blood.

Activity 4, page 14

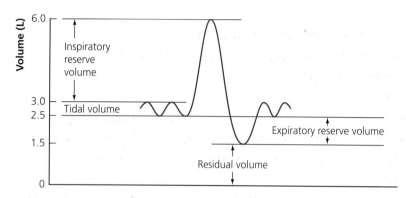

Activity 5, page 16

Right atrium	Left atrium
Right ventricle	Left ventricle

Activity 6, page 16

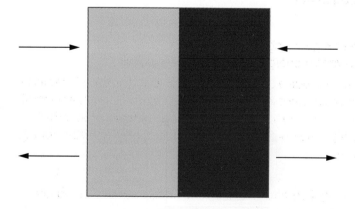

Chapter 1c Anaerobic and aerobic exercise

Check your understanding

Page 20

1 Aerobic – with oxygen; anaerobic – without oxygen.

2 Glucose + oxygen → energy + carbon dioxide + water.

3 Waste product of anaerobic exercise/causes fatigue.

4 Glucose → energy + lactic acid.

Page 21

5 Excess post-exercise oxygen consumption.

6 Use of anaerobic exercise; need to repay oxygen not used.

7 Removes lactic acid.

Page 22

8 Increased heart rate; increased breathing rate; increased temperature.

9 Tiredness/fatigue; nausea/light-headedness; aching/DOMS/cramp.

10 Delayed onset muscle soreness; aching muscles day after strenuous exercise.

11 Strenuous/different exercise/eccentric contractions; tiny muscle tears releasing fluids.

Page 24

12 Water/minerals/carbohydrates.

13 Flush out waste/lactic acid; reduce swelling.

14 Slowly reduces heart rate and breathing rate; relaxes muscles; removes lactic acid.

Page 25

15 Loss of weight; increased muscle/hypertrophy.

16 Hypertrophy; stronger contractions – increased stroke volume; reduced resting heart rate/bradycardia.

17 Increased stamina; strength; speed; suppleness; muscular endurance.

Practice questions

Page 20

1 Aerobic; uses oxygen; long distance/duration; low intensity; Glucose + oxygen = energy + water + carbon dioxide.

2 Answer should include a description of aerobic and anaerobic exercise (AO1), examples of aerobic and anaerobic exercises from either netball or basketball (AO2), and a decision on whether netball or basketball consists mainly of aerobic or anaerobic exercises, giving reasons for this opinion (AO3).

Page 21

3 Extra oxygen required; after exercise; to maintain high breathing rate and temperature/remove CO_2.

4 Your heart beats stronger and faster/stroke volume increases.
Your breathing quickens and deepens/tidal volume increases.
Your body temperature increases.
You start to sweat/go red.

5 Answer should include a description of oxygen use for aerobic exercise and EPOC (AO1), give examples from badminton of aerobic exercises and the need for EPOC because of anaerobic exercise (AO2), and a decision on whether badminton, in your opinion, consists mainly of aerobic or anaerobic exercises; give reasons for your opinion (AO3).

Page 22

6 a) Build-up of lactic acid; excess fluids.

   b) Tiny tears in muscles; excess fluids.

Page 24

7 Jogging/walking/easy movements; (static) stretching.

8 The game lasts four quarters, so enduring aspects are required to last the full game (aerobic).
Short, intense sprints are required to get free using anaerobic energy.

Page 25

9 a) Stamina, muscular endurance; speed; strength; suppleness/flexibility.

   b) Change in body shape; increased stroke volume/hypertrophy; reduced resting heart rate/bradycardia.

Activities

Activity 1, page 20

- Aerobic – marathon, triathlon (possibly cricket).
- Anaerobic – pole vault, trampolining.
- Mixed – netball, cricket (possibly pole vault).

Activity 2, page 20

For example, football.

- Aerobic – standing during break in play, walking to retrieve ball, jogging when not in possession.
- Anaerobic – sprinting into space, jumping up to head ball, shooting at goal.

Activity 3, page 21

- Tired due to production of lactic acid from anaerobic exercise.
- During recovery EPOC occurs and oxygen is used to remove the lactic acid.

Activity 4, page 21

- Heart beats faster.
- Breathing rate increases.
- Body temperature increases, making us hot and sweaty, and we may go red.

Activity 5, page 22

- Fatigue.
- Dizzy/light-headed.
- Nausea/feeling sick.

- Delayed onset muscle soreness (DOMS).
- Cramp.

Activity 6, page 24

- Cool-down.
- Ice baths.
- Massage.

Activity 7, page 25

- HR = 4
- HR = 3

Chapter 2 Movement analysis

Check your understanding

Page 29

1 Third class lever.

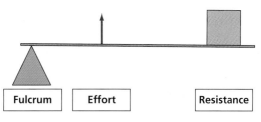

2 First class lever.

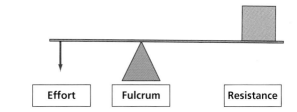

3 Second class lever.

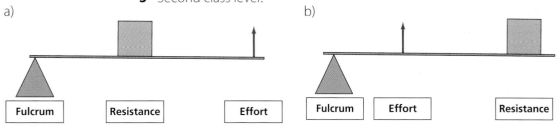

4 Moves heavy weight; permits large force to be applied.

Page 30

5 Isotonic – movement occurs; isometric – static/no movement.

6 Concentric – muscle shortens; eccentric – muscle lengthens.

7 Gymnast balancing; athlete/swimmer on starting blocks; weight-lifter holding finishing position; wicketkeeper waiting for delivery.

Page 33

8 Sagittal plane and transverse axis.

9 Transverse plane and longitudinal axis.

10 Frontal plane and sagittal axis.

Page 33

11 Latissimus dorsi.

12 Extension.

13 Eccentric; triceps.

Page 35

14 Plantar flexion – toes pointed by action of gastrocnemius; dorsiflexion – toes pulled up by action of tibialis anterior.

15 Joint action – extension; agonist – quadriceps.

16 Muscle contraction – eccentric; agonist – quadriceps.

Page 37

17 Flexion and abduction.

18 Frontal plane and sagittal axis.

19 Rotation.

Page 38

20

	TYPE OF CONTRACTION	MAIN AGONIST	JOINT ACTION	PLANE AND AXIS
Upward phase	Concentric	Triceps	Extension	Sagittal and transverse
Downward phase	Eccentric	Triceps	Flexion	Sagittal and transverse

Page 39

21

	TYPE OF CONTRACTION	MAIN AGONIST	JOINT ACTION	PLANE AND AXIS
Hip	Concentric	Hip flexor	Flexion	Sagittal and transverse
Knee	Concentric	Quadriceps	Extension	Sagittal and transverse
Ankle	Concentric	Gastrocnemius	Plantar flexion	Sagittal and transverse

22 Joint action – plantar flexion; type of contraction – isometric.

23 Knee – flexion; ankle – dorsiflexion.

Page 40

24 Transverse plane; longitudinal axis.

25

	TYPE OF CONTRACTION	MAIN AGONIST	JOINT ACTION
Upward phase	Concentric	Quadriceps	Extension
Downward phase	Eccentric	Quadriceps	Flexion

26		TYPE OF CONTRACTION	MAIN AGONIST	JOINT ACTION
	Upward phase	Concentric	Gastrocnemius	Plantar flexion
	Downward phase	Eccentric	Gastrocnemius	Dorsiflexion

Practice questions

Page 29

1 Answer should include a description of the structure of three classes of levers (AO1), the anatomical structure of levers at the ankle for plantar flexion and elbow for flexion (AO2), and a comparison of different mechanical advantages of the two lever systems (AO3).

Page 32

2 Answer should include a description of the three planes and axes (AO1), examples of movements taking place in each plane and axis in a game of football (AO2) and, in your opinion, which plane and axis are most widely used in a game of football (AO3). Give reasons for your answer, as it could depend on what position you play.

Pages 41–2

3 **A** – isometric; **B–C** – isotonic.

4 **a)** Agonist – triceps; antagonist – biceps.
b) Position **A** – isometric; **A** to **B** – eccentric.
c) Sagittal plane and transverse axis.

5 **a)** **(i)** Flexion.
(ii) Flexion.
b) Agonist – biceps; type of contraction – concentric/isotonic.
c) Sagittal plane and transverse axis.

Activities

Activity 1, page 29

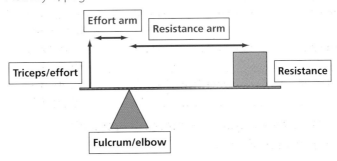

Activity 2, page 29

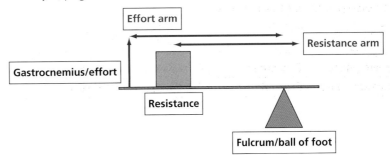

Chapter 3 Physical training

Check your understanding

Page 44

1 Health is a state of complete physical, mental and social wellbeing and not merely the absence of disease or infirmity.
- Fitness is the ability to meet/cope with the demands of the environment.
- Ill health can negatively affect fitness as the individual may be too unwell to train – thus lowering their fitness.
- Ill health may not affect fitness if the person is still well enough to train.
- Increased fitness can positively affect health and wellbeing; for example, you may be less likely to contract certain illnesses and diseases, you may feel more content and happy within yourself and you may have enhanced your social wellbeing through taking part in activities.
- However, increased fitness cannot prevent you from contracting some illnesses and diseases and subsequently your physical health may suffer.
- Increased fitness cannot prevent you from suffering mental health problems or social health problems.

Page 45

2 Answers should provide a reasoned conclusion which links the ability to change direction at speed to the demands of the sports chosen; for example, in football where players need to find space away from opponents to take a shot, or in tennis, where players may need agility to react to their opponent's shot so they can return the ball.

Page 46

3 Balance is maintaining the centre of mass over the base of support.

The two types of balance are: static and dynamic.

Page 47

4 Cardio-vascular endurance is the ability of the heart and lungs to supply oxygen to the working muscles. Cardio-vascular endurance is needed by marathon runners to ensure they have enough oxygen to last for a whole race without suffering fatigue.

5 Co-ordination is the ability to use two or more body parts together smoothly and efficiently. Co-ordination is needed in inline roller hockey to co-ordinate the eyes and hands to move the stick to hit the ball.

6 Flexibility is the range of movement possible at a joint. Flexibility is needed by a trampoline performer to make the shapes required to score a high mark for their routine.

Page 48

7 Muscular endurance is the ability of a muscle or group of muscles to undergo repeated contractions while avoiding fatigue. Muscular endurance is needed by a rower to repeatedly contract the muscles to perform a consistent stroke that maintains the race pace required to win.

8 Power is strength × speed. Power is needed by a long jumper to gain height in the jump to have more chance of recording a longer distance.

Page 49

9 Speed is the maximum rate at which an individual is able to perform a movement or cover a distance. Speed is needed by a sprinter to cover the distance as quickly as possible, therefore having more chance of winning.

Page 50

10 Strength is the ability to overcome a resistance. Strength is needed by a rugby player when faced by a tackler so they can attempt to break free and keep moving forward.

Page 59

11 Refer to the test protocols on pages 52–60.

Page 63

13 The principles of training: specificity, progressive overload, reversibility, tedium.

The principles of overload: frequency, intensity, time, type.

Page 69

14 HIIT training is periods of extreme intensity with periods of rest.

Page 71

15 Static stretching is when a stretch is held (isometrically) for 30 seconds.

Advantages include: increase in range of movement at a joint, easily completed, relatively safe.

Disadvantages include: time-consuming, some muscles easier to stretch than others, can lead to injury (overstretching).

Page 72

16 Strength is high weight/low reps, muscular endurance is low weight/high reps.

17 Positives include increased red blood cell count, increased ability to carry oxygen and improved endurance performance when returning to sea level. Negatives include difficulty in completing training, altitude sickness, potential for detraining to occur and the effects do not last for very long.

Page 77

18 Warming up has three parts: pulse raiser, stretching and skill familiarisation. Cooling down involves gradual reduction in pulse with some stretches.

Practice questions

Page 44

1 **B** Be less likely to catch some illnesses or disease.

Page 47

2 10 000 m would require cardio-vascular endurance as it:
- is of long duration so the anaerobic system will not be able to meet the demands
- requires oxygen/use of the aerobic energy system to keep working at relatively constant intensity for 25 laps.

Page 50

3 It is needed for netball so that the player can dodge or move into space to receive a pass. It is also needed in netball to stay with and mark your player so they do not get the space to receive the ball and continue an attack.

4 Any sporting example that requires reaction to a stimulus; for example, reacting to the gun in sprinting. Answer must contain two elements:
  - the stimulus
  - the time taken to start to initiate the movement.

5 Muscular endurance.

6 Balance can be static (still) or dynamic (whilst moving).
  - It is the ability to maintain the centre of mass over the base of support.
  - It is needed in team games – static; for example, to hold a position ready to take a set shot in basketball (or any other suitably static example), so that the shot is performed with the correct technique and has more chance of going in.
  - It is needed in team games – dynamic; for example, when dribbling a football, so that technique is maintained whilst moving quickly.

7 The maximum rate at which an individual is able to perform a movement or cover a distance in a period of time. Distance divided by time. Needed to find space, sprint for a lost ball, track an opponent, etc.

8 To overcome the resistance from another player to hold someone off to keep the ball/to apply force into a tackle to win the tackle and regain possession, etc.

9 Reference to any non-enduring activity with reasoned justification why cardio-vascular endurance is not needed.

Page 61

10 Cones, 20 m tape measure, recording of the test, record sheet.

11 Any two from:
  - To identify strengths and/or weaknesses in a performance. Are there reasons for performing well or not so well? For example, perhaps your dribbling in a hockey match was poor because of a lack of speed?
  - To inform your training requirements – as a result of initial tests, what components did you score poorly in and therefore may need to improve?
  - To show a starting level of fitness. By testing at the start of a training programme, you can work out what level you are starting at.
  - To monitor improvement. Have the components of fitness you needed to improve actually improved over a period of time?
  - To gauge the success of a training programme. If you have been training specific components of fitness you may well test how well it has gone by undertaking fitness tests.
  - To compare against norms of the group/national averages. You can compare results with your peers or for an informed appraisal. Some tests have national averages that you can compare your scores to.
  - To motivate/set goals. Having knowledge that you will be doing fitness tests may well motivate an individual to try harder or to train in advance of the test so as to score well. It could also be that an

individual is set a specific goal to achieve in the tests, thus providing them with motivation (drive).

- To provide variety to a training programme. Training programmes can be boring and lack variety. Carrying out tests either randomly or on a planned basis may well provide the variety required to keep individuals enthused and motivated.

12 Any two from:
- Tests are often not sport-specific and can be too general. For example, the ruler drop test is not something that is carried out in any sport.
- They do not replicate movements of activities – very few sports involve direct running of 20 m up and down in a straight line like the multistage fitness test.
- They do not replicate competitive conditions required in sports – major sporting events are performed under extreme pressure. Many of the tests can be repeated/retried.
- Many of the tests have questionable reliability. As most tests are maximal, the individual must try their hardest in the test to gain an accurate score, thus motivation levels must be high. Also, as a partner sometimes measures your score, for example, vertical jump test, it is possible that they will get the scoring wrong.
- The tests must be carried out with the correct procedures and protocols, otherwise scores will not be accurate or valid.

13 Yes, because netball needs opponents to change direction at speed, in order to dodge, lose or mark opponents, etc. It is a vital component of fitness for a netball player, so it is worth gaining a test score to improve upon.

14
- Equipment: appropriate weights/resistance machine – usually a bar-bell or bench press machine.
- Lift a weight once, using the correct technique.
- If completed attempt a heavier weight until the heaviest weight the individual can possibly lift once is discovered (one correctly completed repetition).
- If a weight cannot be lifted, a lighter weight should be used to calculate the maximum weight that can be lifted.

15 A measurement which has been quantified as a number; for example, time in seconds, or goals scored. There is no opinion expressed (qualitative). It is a fact. It is often the case that quantitative scores in fitness tests can be compared to national averages.

Page 63

16 Frequency means how often you train.

17 Progressive overload:
- working harder than normal
- whilst gradually and sensibly increasing the intensity of training.

18 Make the training:
- specific to the activity
- specific to the movements used
- specific to the muscles used
- specific to the energy systems used.

Page 64

19 Consider fitness aim, fitness level, number of stations, work : rest ratio, equipment available, space available, etc. so they can develop a better aerobic power.

20 The amount of work done at a station compared to the rest in between stations.

Page 68

21 It would benefit any performer whose sport is enduring/long in duration; for example, marathon runner, long-distance runner, cyclist, games player.

22 60–80 per cent of 220 – age. So, 220 – 17 = 203
60–80 per cent = 122–162 bpm

23 It is not appropriate:
- can build up aerobic base before specific training starts
- 100 m is predominantly anaerobic in nature
- anaerobic sprints may be better suited to interval training.

24 Speed play. Altering the intensity/speed/terrain to improve cardio-vascular endurance. Can improve aerobic and anaerobic systems.

Page 70

25 Power.

26 Advantages (any two from):
- Burns body fat and calories quickly.
- Can be altered easily to suit the individual.
- Can be completed relatively quickly.
- Can improve the anaerobic and aerobic energy systems.

Page 71

27 Any two from:
- Stretching to the limit.
- Holding the stretch (isometrically) for approximately 30 seconds.
- Avoiding overstretching as injury can occur.
- Using the correct technique; for example, avoid dangerous stretches such as straight legged toe touches.
- By making the stretches appropriate to the sport.
- By making sure the muscles stretched are used in the sport.

28 Stretches should make use of muscles/muscle groups used within the sport.

Page 73

29 Muscular endurance – less than 70 per cent of one rep max. Three sets of 12–15 reps.

30 Any sport that is explosive/powerful; for example, shot, discus, javelin, etc. Weights can increase the strength in targeted muscles used during performance.

31 Answer should demonstrate knowledge of the principles of training and what weight training is (AO1). It should apply the principles of training to a weight-lifter; for example, specificity – it will train the muscles used when weight-lifting; tedium – may use weights, machines and kettle bells to vary the training, etc. (AO2). The answer should end with a discussion of why training the appropriate muscles would allow the weight-lifter to improve their performance; for example, as the appropriate muscles increase in strength, so the weight-lifter will be able to lift more weight and will have more chance of winning the event (AO3).

Page 75

32 No. Sprinting is an anaerobic sport. Altitude training is for endurance athletes who use oxygen and who work aerobically. Sprinters work anaerobically.

33 Any three from:
- It can be very difficult to complete training. Some people find it too hard and actually train less than if they were at sea-level.
- This means that fitness can actually be lost.
- Some athletes can experience altitude sickness – a feeling of nausea.
- The benefits are lost quite quickly – that is, when returning to sea-level, red blood cell count starts to decrease again.

34 Answer should demonstrate knowledge of altitude training; for example, that it is above 2000 m, is generally cardio-vascular training, etc. (AO1). It should then explain how altitude in training could be used by an athlete to improve their performance; for example, red blood cell count, adaptation, etc. (AO2). The evaluation should include points relevant to the types of performer; for example, it is more beneficial for a marathon runner as the benefits are to endurance performance. The sprinter will gain no benefits as their event is anaerobic. It may be unsuitable for either if altitude sickness prevents them from training, as there will be no benefit, etc.

Page 76

35 To rest/recover/do light aerobic work to prevent loss of fitness.

Page 78

36 Warm-up should include:
- gradual pulse-raising activity; for example, fast walk/jog/light swim
- stretching – of all relevant muscles
- skill-based practices/familiarisation activities; for example, ball work in football
- mental preparation – starting to get focused, using techniques to control arousal; for example, deep breathing.

37 Benefits of cooling down:
- It allows the body to start to recover after exercising.
- It helps with the removal of lactic acid, carbon dioxide and waste products.
- It can help to prevent the delayed onset of muscle soreness, sometimes referred to as DOMS.

Activities

Activity 2, page 45

EXAMPLE SPORTING SCENARIO	JUSTIFICATION
Rugby player	Needs to change direction to avoid a tackler or to perform a side-step or to perform a side-step so they can be free to run to the try line and score a try
Hockey player	To avoid opponents perhaps using an Indian dribble manoeuvre into shooting or passing position so they can gain the space to shoot at goal
Badminton player	If the shuttle unexpectedly clips the net or if the player is moving one way and the shuttle is hit back the other way so they can remain in the rally
Water polo player	To move in the pool to gain the space to shoot or a position to receive a pass

Activity 3, page 46

GYMNASTIC EXAMPLE	TYPE OF BALANCE	JUSTIFICATION
Handstand	Static	Position of handstand has to be held whilst maintaining control, e.g. no wobbles, which could reduce the score
Headstand	Static	Position of headstand has to be held for several seconds whilst maintaining control, e.g. no wobbles, which could reduce the score
Cartwheel along a beam	Dynamic	Moving along the beam without falling off, as that would make the score significantly lower. Maintain control during the jump/rotation/movement to allow a high tariff to be achieved
Tumble	Dynamic	Carrying out the tumble/somersaults without losing control. Movement must flow, e.g. look controlled and joined together to achieve the highest score

Activity 4, page 46

Basketball is a game with 4 quarters, which each last for 12 minutes (a total of 48 minutes), thus cardio-vascular endurance is needed. Most of the game requires the use of oxygen – the aerobic energy system.

Activity 5, page 49

10 metres per second.

Activity 6, page 50

- Muscular strength – anaerobic, moving heavy objects/weights.
- Muscular endurance – anaerobic repeated exercises.
- Suppleness/flexibility – repeated movements.
- Speed – rapid anaerobic exercises.
- Stamina – rhythmical aerobic exercises.

Activity 13, page 72

Use less than 70 per cent of 50 kg and lift 3 sets of approximately 15 reps.

Chapter 4 Sports psychology

Check your understanding

Page 79

1 Skills are learned whereas abilities are inherited and stable.

Page 80

2 Basic skills can be done by beginners. They can be taught quickly and involve little thinking/decision-making. Complex skills involve much decision-making and can usually only be done by experts.

Page 81

3 Open skills are affected by the environment and can change as a result of, for example, opposition players. Closed skills are unaffected by the environment and are repeatable each time.

Page 82

4 Self-paced skills are controlled by you. You control how quickly you react to a stimulus and how fast you move once you have reacted. Externally paced skills are as a result of external factors; for example, having to run to keep up with an opponent you are marking.

Page 83

5 Gross skills involve large muscle groups and big movements which are not precise. Fine skills involve small muscle groups and precise movements.

Page 85

6 Performance goals involve comparison to yourself (for example, to beat a personal best), whereas outcome goals refer to the actual outcome (for example, to win).

Page 88

7 Input, decision-making, output, feedback.

Page 90

8 Beginners need visual and perhaps some verbal and manual/mechanical guidance.

Elite performers tend to need verbal more than visual guidance.

Page 94

9 Arousal is a physical and mental (physiological and psychological) state of alertness/excitement varying from deep sleep to intense excitement.

Page 95

10 Answers must link the level of arousal required to the chosen skills.

11 Somatic is using the body; for example, deep breathing. Mental is controlled inside your head using thoughts/the mind; for example, mental rehearsal.

Page 97

12 Direct aggression is when there is actual physical contact between performers. The 'aggressor' uses physical contact to directly and deliberately inflict harm upon their opponent.

Indirect aggression does not involve physical contact. The aggressive act is taken out on an object to gain an advantage over an opponent.

Page 99

13 A person with an introvert personality does not need a high level of arousal. They can become over aroused when overstimulated. They are shy/quiet/thoughtful/happy in their own company/tend to play individual sports.

A person with an extrovert personality needs a high level of arousal. They can lack concentration and often seek exciting situations; for example, team sports.

Page 100

14 Motivation is the drive to succeed or the desire (want) to achieve something.

Practice questions

Page 82

1 Skills are learned and when mastered are consistently done in a way that looks easy and with the right technique.

Abilities are inherited. They are known as 'traits', which remain fairly stable during your life.

2 • A shot in football during open play is an open skill. It is affected by the changing environment; for example, you may try to bend it round defenders, hit it with the laces to exert power past a diving goalkeeper. Your choice of what type of shot to use depends on factors in the environment.

 • A volley in volleyball is an open skill. You may alter the way you perform a volley because of changing factors in the environment; for example, teammates who move/change position, the movement and positioning of the opposition, etc.

 • A forward roll in gymnastics is a closed skill. It is not affected by a changing environment or people around you. You try to repeat the same action each time.

 • A high jump is a closed skill. It is not affected by a changing environment or people around you. You try to repeat the same action each time.

 • A goalkeeper trying to save a penalty flick in hockey is an open skill. This is because the action of saving the ball may be different depending upon what the opponent does. You may need to save low or high, left or right, with feet or with stick depending on the penalty taker. Thus it is affected by the environment.

Page 83

3 Discus is a gross skill. It involves powerful use of large muscle groups.

4 Answer should demonstrate knowledge of definitions of a self-paced skill (performer decides when to start or at what pace) and an externally paced skill (pace is controlled by opponents or an external source) (AO1). Answer then applies skill classification; for example, swimming at a pace decided by you is self-paced, whereas swimming at a pace dictated by opponents is externally paced. Then there is a development of the argument to analyse parts of the race; for example, swimmer starts at their own pace (self-paced), sticking to the pace they have practised. As race develops, if opponents are ahead, this may force swimmer to change pace (externally paced) to give them a chance of winning the race.

Page 85

5

	PERFORMANCE GOAL	OUTCOME GOAL
A complete beginner playing badminton against a more experienced player	To hit the shuttle more consistently than the last game	To score a point
An elite level javelin thrower performing at the Olympic Games	To beat their personal best throw	To win gold

Page 88

6 Selective attention involves choosing the most appropriate sense/ information/cue at that time and discarding the others.

7 Input:

- Performer takes in information from the display (senses – sight of ball, hearing ball being hit, etc.).
- They choose which sense is the most important to them at that time; for example, sight of the ball coming towards them.

Decision-making:

- If they have hit the ball in the last 30 seconds they may recall how to hit from the working memory (short-term memory).
- If not, they will recall an appropriate response to hit the ball from the long-term memory.

8 Answer should demonstrate knowledge of the stages of a basic information processing model (input, decision-making, output, feedback) (AO1). The stages should be applied to a sporting skill; for example, input includes sight of the futsal (AO2). There should be reasoned conclusions about the relative importance of each stage; for example, feedback is important as it will guide and inform how a similar decision is made in the future – if they receive positive feedback, they are more likely to make the same decision the next time they face a similar situation, etc.

Page 90

9 Manual involves physical touch whereas mechanical involves the use of equipment or an aid.

10 Visual guidance could be a coach's demonstration or video/DVD (or equivalent).

Verbal guidance could come from a coach's feedback, a parent or peer.

Manual/mechanical guidance could involve a coach guiding the player's arm through the movement, for example, of a shot.

11 Answer should describe what visual and verbal guidance is (AO1). There should then be a description of how visual guidance and verbal guidance could be given in a sport of your choice (AO2). There should be reasoned judgements about the use of visual and verbal guidance; for example, the beginner will need visual guidance so that they can build up a mental picture of what is required before attempting the skill themselves.

Page 93

12 Visual guidance.

13 It can demotivate them/cause them to stop/not persevere.

14 Knowledge of results – they are unable to understand the technique in the performance completely but can interpret the outcome; for example, you hit the ball.

N.B. It is also acceptable to state knowledge of performance – hitting the ball is obvious feedback and they may need some simple KP to start to improve their technique.

15 Answer should demonstrate knowledge of what intrinsic and extrinsic feedback are (AO1) and then apply intrinsic and extrinsic feedback to learning to ski; for example, you will be aware of how it feels when you fall over (AO2). It should include reasoned conclusions about their relative importance; for example, although intrinsic feedback is being received, it is hard for the beginner to understand and therefore they will now know what a good skiing technique should feel like.

Page 94

16 As arousal increases, so does performance.

Up to the optimal level/point.

If arousal increases further, performance will decrease.

Page 97

17 Self-talk OR mental rehearsal.

18 Deep breathing is a physical (somatic) technique which involves the performer exaggerating their breaths in and out.

19 Answer should demonstrate knowledge of mental rehearsal, deep breathing and self-talk, linking mental rehearsal and self-talk to cognitive (mental) techniques and linking deep breathing to somatic (physical) techniques (AO1). These techniques should then be described with reference to a chosen specific activity; for example, golfers could mentally rehearse the shot to be played prior to taking it. Deep breathing can be used to control arousal prior to driving the golf ball. Self-talk can be carried out mentally prior to taking a putt (AO2). It should also include developed arguments about the use of these techniques; for example, mental rehearsal can easily be done in a sport where time is available, such as while waiting to take a shot in golf. The reduction and control of arousal may allow a suitable swing to be used, resulting in a good shot being played. Deep breathing is quick and easy to do and can control arousal in a relatively short time. Self-talk is discreet and can be done without the evaluation of others and can therefore be used regularly.

Page 98

20 Direct – physical contact has been used to deliberately hurt the opponent.

Page 99

21 Usually shy.

Page 100

22 Motivation is the drive to succeed or the desire (want) to achieve something. Intrinsic motivation is the drive that comes from within the performer themselves.

23 Extrinsic motivation is the drive experienced by a performer when striving to achieve a reward (tangible or intangible).

24 Answer should demonstrate knowledge of intrinsic and extrinsic motivation (AO1). This knowledge should be applied to the context of the question; for example, the trophy is an extrinsic motivator, which may generate pride (intrinsic motivator) (AO2). There should be reasoned conclusions about the value of the trophy as an extrinsic motivator; for example, many believe that the pride achieved is a greater motivator than the trophy itself but the performer may be motivated by money, rewards or trophies more than the feeling of pride or satisfaction (AO3).

Activities

Activity 1, page 81

A forward roll is a basic skill. It requires little or no decisions to be made to ensure it is successful. It is often taught to beginners.

A double somersault is a complex skill. It requires decisions to be made such as how much tuck to have or when to open out so that the performer can land safely.

Activity 2, page 83

- A javelin throw is self-paced. The performer chooses when to start the run up and how fast to run.
- A sprint start is externally paced. The sprinter decides to start because of the gun (external source).
- A conversion (kick) in rugby is self-paced. The rugby player starts his/her run up to take the kick when they want to.

Activity 3, page 85

S – Specific (to the demands of the sport/muscles used/movements involved).

M – Measurable (it must be possible to measure whether they have been met).

A – Accepted (it must be accepted/agreed by the performer and the performer's coach – if they have one).

R – Realistic (it must actually be possible to complete the goal; that is, they are physically capable).

T – Time-bound (it must be set over a fixed period of time).

Activity 4, page 86

Answers must apply the stages of input, decision-making, output and feedback, making reference to the demands of the chosen skill.

Activity 6, page 93

BEGINNER	WHO REQUIRES THE FOLLOWING AND WHY?	ELITE PERFORMER
Definitely need visual guidance to understand what a skill looks like	Visual guidance	Are unlikely to need visual guidance other than to highlight minor faults, e.g. use of slow motion
Also need verbal guidance but it should not be too long or complex	Verbal guidance	Will need verbal guidance. It is likely to be longer and more complex than that given to a beginner. It allows fine-tuning of technique
Are also likely to need manual/mechanical guidance to support or guide them through the correct technique	Manual/mechanical guidance	Elite performers are unlikely to need manual/mechanical guidance unless there is an unexpected flaw in technique
May be demotivated by negative feedback	Positive or negative feedback	More accepting of negative feedback
Cannot interpret complex feedback on performance	Knowledge of results or performance	Elite performers can interpret complex feedback on performance
Cannot provide themselves with feedback	Extrinsic or intrinsic feedback	Can provide themselves with feedback

Activity 7, page 96

SPORTING SITUATION	AROUSAL LEVEL	DO THEY NEED TO CONTROL/ ADJUST THEIR AROUSAL LEVEL?	IF YES, SUGGEST AN APPROPRIATE TECHNIQUE
Archery	Medium	Yes – it should be low for a fine skill	Any from: deep breathing (physical) mental rehearsal/ visualisation/ imagery (mental) positive self-talk (mental)
Weight-lifter	High	No – it should be high	Not applicable
Snooker player	High	Yes – it should be low for a fine skill	Any from: deep breathing (physical) mental rehearsal/ visualisation imagery (mental) positive self-talk (mental)

Activity 8, page 98

ACTIVITY	DIRECT OR INDIRECT?
A tennis player smashes a return.	Indirect – no contact
A sailor cuts across an opponent's sailing line.	Indirect – no contact
A netball player deliberately sticks her elbows out to catch an opponent's face.	Direct – physical contact
A hockey player tackles an opponent, swiping their legs with their stick.	Direct – physical contact

Activity 9, page 99

INTROVERT	EXTROVERT
Pistol shooting	Seek excitement
Shy	Rugby player
Snooker player	Sociable
Calm	

Chapter 5a Socio-cultural influences

Check your understanding

Page 104

1 Participation levels of different groups of people.

2 Fixed, simplified ideas about a group/person.

3 Afro-Caribbean; Pakistani; Indian; Bangladeshi; Black African; Somali; many others.

4 Low disposable income; expectation of domestic work; fewer opportunities; low media coverage, etc.

Page 105

5 Role models; media coverage; low cost to participate; others.

6 • Young people – participation will be high because of compulsory PE in schools.
   • Young people post-school – there is a high dropout rate; young people tend to play team games.
   • Older people will have lower levels of participation; participation tends to be in individual activities.

Page 107

7 Disabled individuals performing with non-disabled individuals.

8 Unjust or prejudicial treatment of different categories of people.

9 Sensory, motor and mental impairments.

10 Reduced discrimination, less stereotyping, fewer barriers.

Page 109

11 Opinions about people and things.

12 Television (terrestrial cable and satellite), radio, newspapers, magazines, internet.

13 Change start times/seasons/rules; reduces attendances/participation; only major sports; sensationalise.

Page 112

14 Lack of facilities; lack of disposable income; lack of role models; negative attitudes.

15 Family commitments; lack of familiarity with activity; sexism; lack of leisure time.

16 Increased media coverage; increased ease of access/more opportunities; education/health reasons; role models, etc.

Practice questions

Page 103

1 Yes:
- Women have more leisure time/less tied to home/housework.
- Women have greater disposable income/greater mobility/accessibility to transport.
- Women encouraged to participate on the grounds of health/fitness/weight loss.
- Promoted by the media/fashionable activity/role model.
- Improvement in childcare facilities/creches/allows for more opportunities.
- Positive discrimination by local leisure centres to encourage women's participation/women-only sessions.

No:
- Lack of equal opportunities/male-dominated sports.
- Rules/regulations/preventing women/girls playing with/against men.
- Sexual harassment/verbal abuse discourages participation.
- Sexual stereotyping channelling girls/women into female-appropriate sports.
- Lower tournament earnings; for example, Wimbledon/lack of media coverage.

Page 105

2 Stereotype/lower expectations by society.
- Self-perception/low self-esteem/inferior/less confident.
- Lack of specialised coaches/trained staff.
- Lack of specialist/adapted/suitable or equivalent facilities/access ramps.
- Discrimination.
- Lack of competition/clubs.
- Lack of mobility/transport/personal income.
- Lack of information/poor media coverage/lack of role models.

Page 107

3 Any two from:
- Treating people differently/unfairly through prejudice.
- Based on stereotyping.
- Illegal in UK.

4 Stereotyping – shared image/simplistic generalisations/judgement of a group of people.

Inclusiveness – including all kinds of people/everyone within an activity or group.

Page 112

5 Any four from:
- Stereotyping/lower expectations by society/discrimination.
- Self-perception/low self-esteem/feel inferior/less confident.
- Lack of specialised coaches/trained staff.
- Lack of specialist/adapted/suitable or equivalent facilities/access ramps.
- Lack of mobility/transport/personal income.
- Lack of information/poor media coverage/lack of role models.

6 Answer should describe factors affecting participation (AO1), and how these factors affect participation (AO2), then evaluating, with reasons, which are the most and the least important factors in your opinion (AO3).

Activities

Activity 1, page 107

Any six from: wheelchair athletics, wheelchair rugby, wheelchair tennis, wheelchair basketball, wheelchair fencing, seated volleyball, seated shooting, seated archery, visually impaired football, goalball, cycling.

Activity 2, page 110

EVENT	WOMEN	MEN
Football World Cup	2015 Third Place	2014 Group stages
Rugby World Cup	2014 Winners	2015 Group stages
Cricket World Cup	2013 Quarter Finals	2015 Group stages

Activity 3, page 112
- Family commitments.
- Lack of leisure time.
- Lack of familiarity with activity.
- Lack of sufficient knowledge through education.
- Socio-economic factors.
- Lack of disposable income.

Chapter 5b Commercialisation of physical activity and sport

Check your understanding

Page 115

1 Using sport as a way of selling and buying goods.

2 Sport/spectators; sponsors/business; media.

3 Providing goods/money in exchange for publicity.

4 Publicity; association; support; tax deductible.

Page 118

5 TV, newspapers, magazines, radio, internet, social media.

6 Provide detailed information/statistics.

7 Broadsheet; tabloid.

Page 120

8 Provide clothing; equipment; footwear; transport; facilities; food/drink.

9 Invasion of privacy; time taken up; loss of sponsorship; negativity linked to product.

10 Affect timings; affect what/who is shown; interfere with viewing experience/adverts; repeated breaks/time-outs; change rules/format.

11 Benefits – increased income; fame; travel. Disadvantages – increased criticism; loss of privacy.

Page 121

12 More matches; more informed; better standards; better facilities.

13 Cost; isolation from performers; lack of interaction.

14 Huge audience; exciting activity; winning; lots of publicity; sponsor's name on TV; increased sales, etc.

Page 123

15 Benefit – accurate decisions. Disadvantage – time wasted waiting.

16 Improved nutrition; fitness; training; recovery; safety; equipment, etc.

17 Time wasted; unfair due to cost/not for everybody.

Page 125

18 Better/accurate decisions; accurate measurements; better equipment/ performances/facilities/clothing/footwear; more informed spectators.

19 Time-consuming; stops flow of game; decisions still matter of opinion.

20 Better advertising; better spectacle; more matches/opportunities, etc.

Practice questions

Page 114

1
- Media uses sport to gain viewers/readers.
- Media used by business for advertising.
- Business pays for media advertising space/time.
- Business pays sport to act as advertising medium.
- Sport must be in media to attract sponsorship.

2 Benefits to sport:
- Sport gets money for allowing events to be televised.
- Business pays sports for advertising at grounds/events/sponsorship.
- Sport becomes popularised/more fans.

Disadvantages to sport:
- Media sensationalises sport/reports dysfunctional aspects.
- Media affects organisation/timing of sport.
- Media can change nature of sport/breaks/length/method.
- Only popular sports are televised.
- Business – players spend too much time working/on TV appearances.
- Business – more pressure to win due to sponsorship pressure.

3 Answer should describe the ways in which sport is commercialised (AO1), and then the advantages and disadvantages of sport being commercialised (AO2). It should analyse, with reasons, whether the commercialisation has been good or bad (AO3).

Page 115

4 Answer should describe the different forms of media coverage of sport (AO1) and how media coverage is used by, and affects, sport (AO2). It should then evaluate, with reasons, the benefits and possible disadvantages of the media coverage to sport (AO3).

Page 118

5 ● New competitions/formats introduced.
● Playing times/seasons altered.
● Ticket allocations given to sponsors, not fans.
● More popular sports gain more coverage at expense of minority sports.
● Fewer viewers for some sports due to pay-per-view/subscription channels.
● Lower attendance at events that are televised.

Page 120

6 Answer should cover at least four of the following points, and include both positive and negative aspects:
● More fame/higher profile makes officials support fair play in sport as it reflects positively on them if they are seen to stick fairly to the rules.
● Increase in salary/paid more money and can become a full-time profession or career pathway.
● Increased funding in sport means more and better technology that allows officials to make better and more accurate decisions.
● Better funding can lead to greater support of the network of officials and so more and better training.
● More coverage of the sport increases pressure on officials to make the right decisions.
● Criticism, a bad performance or a wrong decision is more public so it could mean they lose their job or suffer a damaged reputation.
● Officials can become dependent on technology or not confident in making decisions without it.

Page 121

7 ● Increased money/sponsorship.
● Performers become well known/role models.
● Increased participation/more spectators.
● Money for better facilities/equipment/training/coaches.
● Performers able to train full time.
● Increase in number of events/competitions.

Page 124

8 ● Ensure correct decisions are made.
● Use of Hawk-Eye/TMO.
● Officials communicate with each other.
● Timing/measurement accurate.

Activities

Activity 7, page 119.

£90 million.

Chapter 5c Ethical issues

Check your understanding

Page 127

1   Unwritten rules about behaviour during sport.

2   Shake hands after match; not arguing with referee; not appealing for a throw; returning ball to opposition for free kicks, etc.

3   Bending but not breaking rules to gain advantage.

4   Unwritten agreement to play by the rules to the best of your ability and to let opponent do the same.

Page 128

5   To mask pain; delay fatigue; increase alertness.

6   Power/strength athletes.

7   Low blood pressure; loss of concentration; coma.

Page 130

8   Increased red blood cells/better oxygen transport.

9   Reduce/flush out water content.

10 Endurance performer/marathon runner/cyclist.

11 Drug that reduces effects of adrenaline.

Page 131

12 Increased fame; income; status; everybody is on level playing field.

13 Cheating; bans; fines; loss of reputation; health risk.

14 Loss of reputation; credibility; income/sponsorship.

Page 132

15 Increased income – better players/facilities; creates atmosphere.

16 Most results are wins for home team/loses for away team.

17 Violent, destructive behaviour by football fans.

Page 134

18 Increased pressure; hooliganism; safety costs.

19 Reduced participation; rivalries; media hype; alcohol; gang culture; frustration; display of masculinity.

20 Early kick-offs; all-seater stadiums; segregation of fans; improved security; alcohol restrictions; banning troublemakers; campaigns/role models.

Practice questions

Page 127

1   Bad sportsmanship; it's a form of cheating; trying to get a free kick; against the rules.

2 Any two from:
- Penalties within/after the event – bookings/free kicks/sin bin.
- Fair play awards/allocation of place in major event based on disciplinary record.
- Clubs fined/points deducted.
- Matches played behind closed doors/spectators banned from watching.
- Fair play charters/code of conduct/campaigns.
- Drug testing.

Page 129

3 Increase numbers of red blood cells; better oxygen transport; endurance performers.

4 Increase muscle mass; speed up recovery; train more frequently/intensely.

Page 131

5 Advantages – increased fame; income; status; everybody is on level playing field.

Disadvantages – cheating; bans; fines; loss of reputation; health risk.

Page 134

6 a) Early kick-offs; all-seater stadiums; segregation of fans; improved security; alcohol restrictions; banning troublemakers; campaigns/role models.

b) Rivalries; media hype; alcohol; gang culture; frustration; display of masculinity.

7 Answer should demonstrate knowledge of various strategies to combat hooliganism, such as segregation of fans, CCTV, alcohol bans (AO1). It should show how these strategies affected the fans (AO2) and then evaluate whether you think the strategies have worked, identifying what, in your opinion, is the most effective strategy, giving reasons for this answer.

Activities

Activity 3, page 130

EFFECTS ON ATHLETE	TYPE OF PED	SPORT THAT MIGHT BENEFIT
Enhance alertness	Stimulant	Sprinting
Reduce heart rate	Betablockers	Archery
More red blood cells/better oxygen transport	EPO	Cycling
Mask drug use	Diuretics	Any drug-taker
Increased muscle strength/power/recovery time	Anabolic agents	Weight-lifting
Mask pain	Narcotic analgesic	Football

Activity 4, page 130

Advantages – better performance, success, fame, income, level playing field.

Disadvantages – cheating, bans, fines, loss of reputation, health risks.

Activity 5, page 132

Rivalry, alcohol, culture (or gangs), ritual, frustration. An example of a suitable phrase could be **R**eferees **A**lways **C**ause **R**epeated **F**ouls.

Chapter 6 Health and fitness

Check your understanding

Page 136

1 Health: A state of complete physical, mental and social wellbeing and not merely the absence of disease or infirmity.

Fitness: The ability to meet/cope with the demands of the environment.

Wellbeing: A mix of physical, social and mental wellbeing that gives people a sense of being comfortable, healthy and/or happy.

Page 138

2 Wearing a team strip provides not only clothing but also a sense of belonging; a team strip suggests friendship and support as well as some value in society and social activity.

Page 141

3 Some potential consequences of choosing to have a sedentary lifestyle are: gaining weight/becoming obese, heart disease, hypertension, diabetes, poor sleep or insomnia. Also can experience poor self-esteem or self-confidence, feeling tired or lethargic, and could have a lack of friends, poor communication skills.

Page 147

5 Ectomorph – tall, thin, low fat content.

Endomorph – pear shaped, high fat content.

Mesomorph – thin waist, high muscle content, wedge shaped.

Page 148

6 Male 2500 kcal, female 2000 kcal.

Page 150

7 Seven classes of food: Carbohydrate, fat, protein, fibre, vitamins, minerals, water.

Balanced diet: Eating the right amount (for energy expended)/the right amount of calories, according to how much you exercise. Eating different food types to provide suitable nutrients, vitamins and minerals.

Page 153

8 55–60 per cent carbohydrate, 25–30 per cent fat and 15–20 per cent protein.

9 Vitamins and minerals are for maintaining the efficient working of the body systems and general health.

10 Dehydration: Excessive loss of body water interrupting the function of the body.

Hydration: Having enough water (water balance) to enable normal functioning of the body.

Rehydration: Consuming water to restore hydration.

Practice questions

Page 139

1 Any two from:
- Social health and wellbeing: a state of complete physical, mental and social wellbeing and not merely the absence of disease or infirmity.
- Mental health and wellbeing: the ability to meet or cope with the demands of the environment.
- Physical health and wellbeing: a 'feel-good' chemical released during exercise.

2 Health: a state of complete physical, mental and social wellbeing and not merely the absence of disease or infirmity.

Fitness: the ability to meet or cope with the demands of the environment.

3 All body systems working well.

Page 141

4 Sedentary lifestyle is choosing to take part in little or no exercise.

5 Any three from:
- gaining weight/becoming obese (physical health and wellbeing)
- suffering from heart disease (physical health and wellbeing)
- suffering from hypertension (physical health and wellbeing)
- suffering from diabetes (physical health and wellbeing)
- suffering from poor sleep/insomnia (physical health and wellbeing)
- suffering from poor self-esteem/confidence (mental health and wellbeing)
- feeling tired and lethargic (physical/mental health and wellbeing)
- having a lack of friends/poor communication skills (social health and wellbeing).

Page 143

6 Obesity is a term used to describe people with a large fat content – caused by an imbalance of calories consumed to energy expenditure. BMI of over 30 or 20 per cent or more above ideal weight for height.

Any one from:
- Can lead to depression.
- Can cause a loss of confidence.
- Can make the individual feel like they can't contribute to society (wellbeing).

7 Any one from:
- Limit stamina/cardio-vascular endurance – thus making it difficult to perform any activities of a long duration.
- Limit flexibility – making it difficult for performers to use a full range of movement at joints when attempting to perform skills.
- Limit agility – making it difficult to change direction quickly.
- Limit speed/power – making it hard to react quickly enough or produce force.

8 Answer should demonstrate a knowledge and understanding of the term sedentary lifestyle (AO1). It should describe the effect of being sedentary on someone who decides to take part in a team game activity; for example, they may be obese, may have health problems, may lack confidence, etc. (AO2). It should finish with a reasoned conclusion; for example, as they may have put on weight, they may be slow on the pitch or lack the fitness to keep up with play, until they increase in fitness over time.

Page 147

9 An ectomorph is tall and thin with a low fat content. They would suit an activity requiring height; for example, high jump (or equivalent).

10 Mesomorph.

11 ● Little fat/weight to carry round a long way.
  ● Long limbs to take longer strides.

Page 150

12 Too much: the recommended daily intake is 2500 kcal for an adult male.

13 Average daily intake for a female adult is 2000 kcal. Energy is derived from food and drink intake. Training requires more energy, therefore more intake is required.

Page 153

14 No – too much fat. Justification – recommended amount is 25–30 per cent. Accept that it is OK, as long as it is linked to a factor; for example, very tall, training a lot.

15 Any three from:
  ● The blood thickens (increased viscosity), which slows blood flow down.
  ● The heart rate increases which means that the heart has to work harder. This can cause an irregular heart rate (rhythm).
  ● The body temperature is likely to increase meaning that the body may overheat.
  ● Reaction time increases – in other words, it gets slower and general reactions are poorer. This of course means that decisions made may be negatively affected.
  ● An individual may suffer muscle fatigue and/or muscle cramps.

16 Carbohydrate is the main energy source for the body. Fat is also an energy source *at low intensity*. Protein is for growth and repair of tissues.

17 Answer should demonstrate a knowledge of what carbohydrates, fats and protein are (AO1) and an explanation that carbohydrates provide energy at all intensities, fats at a low intensity and protein helps the team performer's muscles to recover (AO2). There should be a reasoned conclusion about the diet; for example, the different intensities during a game require fats and carbohydrates, but games may be close together so protein for the recovery is as important, etc. (AO3).

18 Answer should demonstrate knowledge of the term hydration (AO1) and an explanation of why hydration is needed by both a discus thrower and a long-distance road cyclist (AO2). It should contain reasoned conclusions; for example, dehydration may affect the discus thrower's decision on when to turn in the circle, but a road cyclist is more likely to suffer dehydration so may need to take water on during the long race (AO3).

Activities

Activity 1, page 139

TERM	DEFINITION
Health	A state of complete physical, mental and social wellbeing and not merely the absence of disease or infirmity
Fitness	The ability to meet/cope with the demands of the environment
Social health and wellbeing	Basic human needs are being met (food, shelter and clothing). The individual has friendship and support, some value in society, is socially active and has little stress in social circumstances
Mental health and wellbeing	A state of wellbeing in which every individual realises his or her own potential, can cope with the normal stresses of life, can work productively and fruitfully, and is able to make a contribution to her or his community
Physical health and wellbeing	All body systems working well, free from illness and injury. Ability to carry out everyday tasks
Wellbeing	Involves physical, mental and social wellbeing. It is a dynamic process of the three parts that give people a sense of being comfortable, healthy and/or happy
Serotonin	A 'feel-good' chemical released during exercise

Activity 4, page 147

ACTIVITY	BODY TYPE REQUIRED
Hammer throw	Mostly endomorph / Some elements of mesomorph (muscle bulk)
Pole vault	Mostly ectomorph for height / Some elements of mesomorph for shoulder power
400 m sprint	Mostly mesomorph
Marathon	Mostly ectomorph – low fat content

Activity 7, page 153

TERM	DEFINITION
Dehydration	Excessive loss of body water interrupting the function of the body
Hydration	Having enough water (water balance) to enable normal functioning of the body
Rehydration	Consuming water to restore hydration

Chapter 7 Use of data

Check your understanding

Page 155

1 Quantitative data involves quantities, numbers and facts. It can be collected through questionnaires or surveys.

Qualitative data involves subjective opinions gathered through interviews or observations.

Page 157

2 a) The dependent variable is 'heart rate'.

b) 'Types of audience' should be on the *x*-axis.

c) You should use a bar chart because there is no relationship between the different types of audience.

Practice questions

Page 155

1 Qualitative data: Data which is subjective, involving opinions relating to the quality of a performance rather than the quantity.

Quantitative data: Data which can be quantified as a number; for example, time in seconds, or goals scored. There is no opinion expressed (qualitative). It is a fact.

Page 158

2 a)

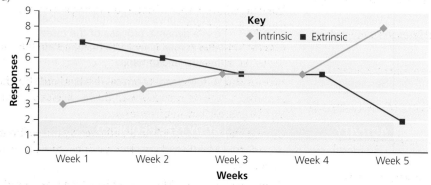

b)

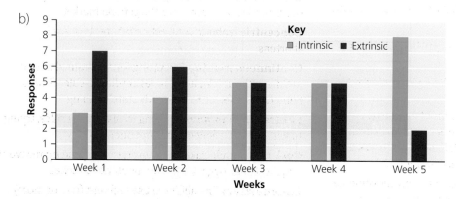

Glossary

A basic model of information processing This shows the simple processes that a performer carries out in order to decide what skill to use.

Abdominal muscles The muscles which help force air out of the lungs and so speed up expiration.

Abduction Movement where limbs are moved away from the body.

Abilities Inherited from your parents, abilities are stable traits that determine an individual's potential to learn or acquire skills.

Adapted sports Competitive sports for individuals with disabilities. While they often parallel existing sports played by athletes without a disability, there may be some modifications in the equipment and rules to meet the needs of the participants.

Adduction Movement where limbs are moved back towards the body.

Adrenaline Naturally occurring hormone that prepares the body for 'fight or flight'.

Aerobic exercise Exercise which uses oxygen.

Agility The ability to move and change direction quickly (at speed) whilst maintaining control.

Agonist The prime mover – muscle that causes movement.

Alveoli Many tiny air sacs in the lungs which allow for rapid gaseous exchange.

Anabolic agents Drugs that help athletes to train harder and build muscle.

Anaerobic exercise Exercise in the absence of enough/ without oxygen.

Analyse Break things down into smaller parts or identify the relevant parts.

Antagonist Muscle that relaxes to allow the agonist to contract.

Artery Blood vessel carrying blood away from the heart.

Atria Upper chambers of the heart that collect blood from veins.

Attitude An opinion about something that tends to make people respond in a certain way.

Balance Maintaining the centre of mass over the base of support.

Balanced diet Eating the right amount (for energy expended)/the right amount of calories/eating according to how much you exercise/eating different food types to provide suitable nutrients, vitamins and minerals.

Ball and socket joint Joint that allows many movements – flexion and extension, abduction and adduction, and rotation.

Bar chart The use of rectangular bars which show the data quantities.

Barrier to participation An obstacle that prevents a group within society from participating in sport or physical activity and therefore reduces overall levels of participation.

Beta blockers Drugs taken to calm the performer down by reducing the effects of adrenaline.

Biceps Muscle causing flexion at the elbow.

Blood doping Artificially increasing the number of red cells in the blood.

Bradycardia Lowered resting heart rate due to long-term exercise.

Bronchi Carry air from the trachea into the lungs.

Bronchioles Carry air from the bronchi to the alveoli.

Bursae Fluid-filled bags that help reduce friction in a joint.

Capillaries Very thin blood vessels that allow gas exchange to happen.

Capsule Tough fibrous tissue – surrounds synovial joints; usually supported by ligaments.

Carbohydrate Food source that acts as the body's preferred energy source.

Cardiac cycle Sequence of events that occur when the heart beats.

Cardio-vascular endurance The ability of the heart and lungs to supply oxygen to the working muscles.

Cartilage Covers ends of bones providing a smooth, friction-free surface.

Circuit training A series of exercises performed one after the other with a rest in between.

Circumduction Movement when a limb is held straight and is moved as if to draw circles with the hand/foot at arms's/ leg's length; e.g. bowling in cricket.

Closed skill A skill which is not affected by the environment or performers within it. It tends to be done the same way each time.

Commercialisation The process by which a new product or service is introduced into the general market.

Concentric Isotonic contraction where the muscle shortens.

Continuous training Exercising for a sustained period of time without rest. It improves cardio-vascular fitness. Sometimes referred to as 'steady state' training.

Contract to compete Agreeing to play by the rules, trying to win but also allowing your opponent to play.

Cool-down Undertaken after exercise to speed up recovery – e.g. walking, jogging, followed by static stretches.

Co-ordination The ability to use different (two or more) parts of the body together, smoothly and efficiently.

Cramp Involuntary contraction of a muscle.

Cruciate ligaments Attach tibia to femur in the knee joint.

Cultural group A group of people who share a common race, religion, language or other characteristic.

Deep breathing A physical/somatic technique which involves the performer exaggerating their breaths in and out.

Dehydration A condition that occurs when the body loses more water than it takes in, interrupting the functioning of the body.

Deltoid Muscle causing flexion at the shoulder.

Dependent variable In a graph or chart, the factor that changes in response to the independent variable.

Diastole Term used to describe the relaxation phase of the cardiac cycle.

Disability A physical or mental impairment that has a substantial and long-term negative effect on a person's ability to do normal daily activities, such as sport.

Discrimination The unjust or prejudicial treatment of different groups of people, especially on the grounds of race, disability, age or sex.

Dislocation When the bones of a joint separate from their normal position.

Disposable income Income available to be spent or saved as one wishes.

Diuretics Drugs that remove fluid from the body.

DOMS (delayed onset muscle soreness) The pain/stiffness felt in the days following strenuous exercise.

Dorsiflexion Movement at ankle where the toes are pulled up towards the knee.

Eccentric Isotonic contraction where the muscle lengthens – used to control downward movements.

Ectomorph A somatotype characterised by being tall and thin with narrow shoulders and hips.

Education The process of learning, especially in a school or college, and the knowledge that you get from this.

Effort The force applied to move the resistance or weight; in the body, the effort is provided by muscles exerting a force.

Embolism When a blood clot blocks a blood vessel.

Endomorph A somatotype characterised by a pear-shaped body with high fat content, wide hips and narrow shoulders.

Engagement patterns Trends/tendencies in involvement.

EPOC Increased rate of oxygen intake following strenuous activity.

Ergogenic aid A technique or substance used for the purpose of enhancing performance.

Ethnic group A community made up of people who share a common cultural background.

Etiquette The unwritten rules concerning player behaviour.

Evaluate Use the information provided to decide upon the worth of or reasons for something.

Expiration The expulsion of air from the lungs.

Expiratory reserve volume The additional air that can be forcibly exhaled after the expiration of a normal tidal volume.

Extension Movement where the angle between bones increases.

Externally paced skill The skill is started because of an external factor. The speed, rate or pace of the skill is controlled by external factors, e.g. an opponent.

Extrinsic feedback Feedback from an external source.

Extrinsic motivation The drive experienced by a performer when striving to achieve a reward (tangible or intangible).

Extrovert Personality type characterised by being sociable, active, talkative and outgoing – usually associated with team sports players.

Family commitments Having to invest a certain amount of time to fulfil obligations that assist parents, siblings, partners and other family members.

Fat Food source that provides energy at low intensities.

First class lever Found at the elbow joint, where the triceps cause extension of the lower arm.

Fitness The ability to meet/cope with the demands of the environment.

Flexibility The range of movement possible at a joint.

Flexion Movement where the angle between bones reduces.

Frontal plane and sagittal axis Plane and axis for side-to-side movements – direction for abduction and adduction.

Fulcrum The part of a lever system that pivots; joints are the fulcrums in the body's lever systems.

Gamesmanship The use of dubious methods, that are not strictly illegal, to gain an advantage.

Gastrocnemius Muscle causing plantar flexion at the ankle.

Gluteals Main agonists at the hip during hip extension.

Golden triangle The financial relationship between sport, sponsorship and media.

Guidance Methods to help a learner understand movement patterns.

Haemoglobin The red pigment found in red blood cells.

Hamstrings Group of muscles causing flexion at the knee.

Hawk-Eye An optical ball-tracking device used as an aid to officiating in tennis and cricket.

Health A state of complete physical, mental and social wellbeing and not merely the absence of disease or infirmity.

HIIT (high-intensity interval training) An exercise strategy alternating periods of short intense anaerobic exercise with less intense recovery periods.

Hinge joint Joint that allows flexion and extension.

Hip flexors Main agonists at the hip during hip flexion.

Home-field advantage The psychological advantage that the home team has over the visiting team as a result of playing in familiar facilities and in front of supportive fans.

Hooliganism Rowdy, violent or destructive behaviour.

Hydration Having enough water (water balance) to enable normal functioning of the body.

Hyperbaric chambers High pressure chambers that force oxygen into an injury to speed up recovery.

Hypertrophy Increase in size of muscles/heart due to long-term exercise.

Ice baths Immersion in cold water to speed up recovery from exercise.

Inclusive Including everybody.

Independent variable In a graph or chart, the factor (variable) that you purposely change or control in order to see what effect it has.

Information processing This is making decisions. It involves gathering data from the display (senses) and prioritising the most important stimuli to make a suitable decision, e.g. choosing a suitable skill.

Inspiration The intake of air into the lungs.

Inspiratory reserve volume The additional air that can be forcibly inhaled after the inspiration of a normal tidal volume.

Integration Involving the full participation of all people in community life, but usually referring to people with a disability.

International Olympic Committee The independent authority of the worldwide modern Olympic movement. It organises the Olympic Games.

Internet A global system of interconnected computer networks. It carries a huge range of information and services, such as documents that link to other resources, World Wide Web (WWW), email, communication systems and file sharing.

Interval training Training method that incorporates periods of work followed by periods of rest, e.g. work, rest, work, rest.

Intrinsic feedback Feedback from within, e.g. kinaesthetic feel.

Intrinsic motivation The drive that comes from within the performer.

Introvert Personality type characterised by being quiet, passive, reserved and shy – usually associated with individual sports performance.

Isometric Muscle action where the muscle stays the same length – used in balances.

Isotonic Muscle action where the muscle changes length – causes movement.

Joint Place where two or more bones meet.

Knowledge of performance (KP) Feedback about the quality of performance, e.g. technique.

Knowledge of results (KR) Feedback about the outcome.

Lactic acid Waste product from anaerobic exercise.

Latissimus dorsi Muscle causing extension at the shoulder.

Leisure time The time we have when we are not working, taking care of ourselves or completing our family and home duties. It has increased as a result of shorter working careers and increased life expectancy.

Ligaments Join bone to bone.

Line chart The use of plotted points (markers) to show data, which are joined together by a line.

Long bones The bones of the legs and arms. Long bones support the weight of the body and help with gross movements.

Lungs Pair of large, spongy organs optimised for gas exchange between our blood and the air.

Manual guidance Physically moving the performer, e.g. the coach supporting the movement through physical touch.

Marketability Ability to be sold.

Massage The rubbing and kneading of muscles and joints with the hands.

Match analysis Computer software that provides detailed statistical data about individual and/or team performances.

Mechanical advantage The benefit to a lever system of having either a short effort arm (giving rapid movements over a large range of movement) or a short resistance arm (giving the advantage of being able to move a heavy weight).

Mechanical guidance Using mechanical aids to assist a performer, e.g. using a float in swimming or a harness in trampolining.

Media The main ways that people communicate (television, radio and newspapers) collectively.

Media coverage The content included in the media (television, radio, internet, print, etc.).

Meniscus Cartilage acting as a shock absorber between the tibia and femur in the knee joint.

Mental (emotional) health and wellbeing Defined by the World Health Organization as: 'a state of wellbeing in which every individual realizes his or her own potential, can cope with the normal stresses of life, can work productively and fruitfully, and is able to make a contribution to her or his community'.

Mental rehearsal A mental technique involving the performer picturing themselves performing the skill perfectly before attempting it. This mental/cognitive relaxation technique involves control of mental thoughts and imagining positive outcomes.

Mesomorph A somatotype characterised by muscular appearance with wide shoulders and narrow hips.

Minerals Inorganic substances that assist the body with many of its functions.

Motivation The drive to succeed or the desire (want) to achieve something.

Movement Muscles contract to pull the bones of the skeleton.

Muscular endurance Ability of a muscle or muscle group to undergo repeated contractions, avoiding fatigue.

Narcotic analgesics Painkillers that mask pain caused by injury or fatigue, which can make the injury worse.

National Governing Body Organisation with responsibility for managing its specific sport.

Nausea Feeling of sickness during/after exercise.

Obesity A term used to describe people with a large fat content – caused by an imbalance of calories consumed to energy expenditure. BMI of over 30 or 20 per cent or more above ideal weight for height.

One repetition (or rep) Completing one lift of a weight (up and down).

One set The completion of a number of reps.

Open skill A skill which is performed in a certain way to deal with a changing or unstable environment, e.g. to outwit an opponent.

Outcome goals Focus on the end result, e.g. winning.

Oxygen debt Temporary oxygen shortage in the body due to strenuous exercise.

Oxygen (hypoxic) tents Tents that contain high oxygen concentrations to speed up recovery after injury.

Oxyhaemoglobin Formed when oxygen combines with haemoglobin.

Pectoral and sternocleidomastoid muscles The muscles which help increase the size of the chest cavity, allowing more air to enter during inspiration.

Pectorals Muscles causing flexion at the shoulder.

PED Performance-enhancing drug.

Peer group A group of people of approximately the same age, status and interests.

Peptide hormones (EPO) Naturally occurring chemicals. EPO increases numbers of red blood cells and therefore improves oxygen delivery to muscles.

Performance goals Personal standards to be achieved. The performer compares their performance against what they have already done or suggests what they are going to do. There is no comparison with other performers.

Philanthropic Trying to benefit others; generous.

Physical health and wellbeing All body systems working well, free from illness and injury. Ability to carry out everyday tasks.

Pie chart Displays the proportions of data as sections of a circle.

Plantar flexion Movement at ankle where the toes are pointed towards the ground.

Post-school drop-out The reduction in participation levels in young adults after they leave full-time education.

Power The product of strength and speed, i.e. strength × speed.

Prejudice Preconceived opinion that is not based on reason or actual experience.

Progressive overload Working harder than normal whilst gradually and sensibly increasing the intensity of training.

Prosthetics Artificial aid; often replacing a limb.

Protection Some bones surround and protect vital organs from damage.

Protein Food source which is predominantly for growth and repair of body tissues.

Quadriceps Group of muscles causing extension at the knee.

Qualitative data A measure of descriptions and opinions. More subjective than an objective appraisal, relating to quality of performance rather than quantity.

Quantitative data A measurement which has been quantified as a number, e.g. time in seconds, or goals scored. There is no opinion expressed (qualitative). It is a fact. It is often the case that quantitative scores in fitness tests can be compared to national averages/ratings.

Radio An easily accessible form of media that provides detailed information about sport. Radio programmes can include commentaries from sports events and in-depth interviews, with performers or sports experts giving information and opinions.

Range of movement A measure of the flexibility of a joint in terms of the different movements allowed.

Reaction time The time taken to initiate a response to a stimulus.

Red blood cells Carry oxygen to muscles.

Rehydration Consuming water to restore hydration. Replacing lost water, minerals and carbohydrates during and after exercise.

Residual volume The volume of air that remains in the lungs after a maximal expiration.

Resistance The load to be moved by a lever system; usually this involves weight when the body's lever systems are involved.

Role model A person looked up to by others as an example to be copied.

Rotation Turning a limb along its long axis.

Rotator cuff Group of muscles causing rotation at the shoulder.

Sagittal plane and transverse axis Plane and axis for forwards and backwards movements – direction for extension and flexion.

Second class lever Found at the ankle, where the gastrocnemius causes plantar flexion.

Sedentary lifestyle A person's choice to engage in little, or irregular, physical activity.

Self-paced skill The skill is started when the performer decides to start it. The speed, rate or pace of the skill is controlled by the performer.

Self-talk A mental/cognitive technique whereby the performer talks to him/herself in their head to reassure themselves.

Sexism The belief that one sex is naturally superior to the other. It involves and leads to prejudice, stereotyping and discrimination.

Skill A learned action/behaviour with the intention of bringing about predetermined results with maximum certainty and minimum outlay of time and energy.

Social groups People who interact with one another, share similar characteristics and have a sense of unity/togetherness.

Social health and wellbeing Basic human needs are being met (food, shelter and clothing). The individual has friendship and support, some value in society, is socially active and has little stress in social circumstances.

Social media Websites and applications that allow users to create and share content.

Socio-economic group A group's place within society; depends on a number of factors, including occupation, education, income, wealth and where they live.

Somatotype A classification of body type – ectomorph, endomorph or mesomorph.

Spectators People who watch sport; can be at the event or watching/listening/reading – 'armchair spectating'.

Speed The maximum rate at which an individual is able to perform a movement or cover a distance in a period of time, i.e. distance ÷ time.

Sponsorship Where a company pays money to a team or individual in return for advertising their goods.

Sportsmanship Appropriate, polite and fair behaviour while participating in a sporting event.

Static stretching Stretching to the limit and holding the stretch isometrically.

Stereotype Widely held but fixed and oversimplified idea of a particular type of person or group.

Stimulants Make athletes more alert and mask effects of fatigue.

Strength The ability to overcome a resistance.

Support Bones keep us upright and hold muscles and organs in place.

Synovial fluid Produced by the synovial membrane to lubricate the joint.

Synovial joint Type of joint commonly found in the limbs; contains a **synovial membrane** that produces synovial fluid.

Systole Term used to describe the contraction phase of the cardiac cycle.

Technology A method that is developed to try to improve performance.

Television Modern TV includes local and national terrestrial, Freeview, subscription or pay-per-view, interactive, on-demand, Red Button services, satellite and cable.

Television Match Official (TMO) Used in rugby union and rugby league to make decisions using replays of incidents.

Tendons Attach muscles to bones.

The press News media, traditionally with reference to printed newspapers and magazines, but can now also include news reports via the internet.

Third class lever The majority of the body's joints act as third class levers, e.g. the biceps acting at the elbow to cause flexion.

Tibialis anterior Muscle causing dorsiflexion at the ankle.

Tidal volume The volume of air breathed in (or out) during a normal breath at rest.

Trachea (or windpipe) Carries air from the mouth and nose to the lungs.

Transverse plane and longitudinal axis Plane and axis for rotating movements – direction for rotations and spins.

Triceps Muscle causing extension at the elbow.

Vasoconstriction Reducing the diameter of small arteries to reduce blood flow to tissues.

Vasodilation Increasing the diameter of small arteries to increase blood flow to tissues.

Vein Blood vessel carrying blood towards the heart.

Ventricles Lower chambers of the heart which pump blood out of the heart to the arteries.

Verbal guidance Guidance that is provided by another person speaking to you.

Vertebrae Bones that form the spine or backbone.

Viscosity How 'thick' a liquid is.

Visual guidance Guidance that you can see, e.g. a demonstration.

Vitamins Organic substances that are required for many essential processes in the body.

Wellbeing A mix of physical, social and mental factors that gives people a sense of being comfortable, healthy and/or happy.

White blood cells Fight infections.

x-axis Shows the independent variable.

y-axis Shows the dependent variable (the thing you are measuring, e.g. heart rate).

Index

For definitions of terms see the
Glossary pages 205–10. For individual
sport examples of topics see the
'**sports examples**' index entry.